Heartsearch

Heartsearch

TOWARD HEALING LUPUS

by

Donna Hamil Talman

North Atlantic Books
Berkeley, California

Heartsearch: Toward Healing Lupus

Copyright 1991 by Donna Hamil Talman

ISBN 1-55643-072-8

Published by
North Atlantic Books
2800 Woolsey Street
Berkeley, California 94705

Cover art by Ruth Terrill
Cover and book design by Paula Morrison
Printed in the United States of America

Heartsearch: Toward Healing Lupus is sponsored by the Society for the Study of Native Arts and Sciences, a nonprofit educational corporation, whose goals are to develop an ecological and crosscultural perspective linking various scientific, social, and artistic fields; to nurture a holistic view of arts, sciences, humanities, and healing; and to publish and distribute literature on the relationship of mind, body, and nature.

Library of Congress Cataloging-in-Publication Data
Talman, Donna Hamil, 1941-
    Heartsearch : toward healing lupus / Donna Hamil Talman.
      p. cm.
    ISBN 1-55643-072-8 : $12.95
    1. Talman, Donna Hamil, 1941—Health. 2. Systemic lupus erythmatosus—Patients—Massachusetts—Biography. 3. Systemic lupus erythmatosus—Alternative treatment. I. Title.
RC924.5.L85T34 1991
362.1'9677—dc20
        90-21860
        CIP

To my Mother and Father with love.

Acknowledgments

Many people helped extensively in creating this book. The power and beauty of that cooperative effort lives as my strongest memory of the project.

Nephrologist Bill Briggs and internist Coleman Levin verified medical facts. My therapists, Alexander Lowen, Ildri Ginn, and Sue Vogel read the manuscript and improved my comprehension of themes and theories. Myron Sharaf has been a mentor who contributed his fine mind, eloquent language, and warm heart. Rebecca Nourse and Karen Vadas were steadfastly available for emotional support and idea-sharing. Lois Warburton typed and critiqued more pages of barely legible scrawls than she would have for anyone but a very good friend. Marsha Zafiriou sustained me through the last phases.

Stan Grof, Pat Mazza, Jacques Vonèche, Barbara Zwiebel, Jeanne Anderson, Ed Svasta, Marlene Narrow, Sue Swander, Mark Cutler, Mara Gordon, Lee Geltman, Lee Monro, Cindy Curlee, Deborah Knox, Judy Nourse, Marilyn and Jim Benjamin, my sister Karen Browne, and my parents all read parts or all of the manuscript and offered feedback.

Rockie Blunt, Laura Fillmore and Jean Edmunds helped with the early writing, and Sue Brick patiently typed. Richard Grossinger of North Atlantic Books believed in *Heartsearch* enough to publish it. Alison Bond, my agent, guarded its integrity in early stages and Lindy Hough, as editor, made it more accessible.

My clients deserve a special thanks. In allowing me to participate in their growth, they have helped heal me. Often when I was unclear about an idea or was having difficulty finding the right words, the next individual or group I worked with brought some clarity.

My son Adam put up with not only a sick Mom, but also a mother writing about him. More than anyone else, my husband David contributed his intelligence, love and tireless behind-the-scenes legwork to make this book possible.

Preface

Developing a serious or prolonged illness is a lightening rod for a series of soul-searching questions about oneself. This is true no matter what form the illness takes, but is particularly important for those attempting to understand and cope with autoimmune diseases, since the causes and prognoses are often clouded with ambiguity. *Heartsearch* gives us a very personal and emotionally stirring description of Donna Hamil Talman's experience with systemic lupus erythematosus, a disease of somewhat mysterious origins which tends to have a prolonged course and may be associated with serious and sometimes fatal complications. We share the raw edges of the author's physical and emotional pain and the inner peace which gradually emerges in response to her participation in a variety of therapeutic milieus within modern medicine and alternative healing modalities.

The shock of becoming so ill triggered a process of progressively deeper self-examination. In the course of that search, layer after layer of human experience unfolds, rich with insights into the emotional and spiritual spheres of life. Mobilizing and utilizing multiple resources for emotional support seems essential to confronting illness and to promoting healing. Donna Hamil Talman creatively pulled together a network of family, friends, and therapists and confronted the equally complex issue of how to internalize external support.

Those of us involved in the care of patients are painfully reminded of the personal traumas of physical illness and the need to constantly strive toward better communication, thereby minimizing the risks of misunderstanding and the potential aggravation of suffering. Every health-care provider in training would benefit from reading, discussing, and comprehending the many health-care issues presented. Compassion and humility, essential to optimal therapeutic interactions, are enhanced by such exposure.

The limitations, as well as the benefits, of allopathic medical practice are discussed. Donna Hamil Talman emphasizes the importance of considering the potential value of all healing modalities, especially those which stimulate and amplify both the healing energy within us and energy from a dimension of life undetectable by our usual senses. Through intense emotional work, self-discipline, and life-style change, she found ways to integrate into her life that combination of healing practices most suitable to her. As a result, she began to tap inner and universal sources of energy and developed her own prescription for health. The depth and breadth of the author's examination of illness and healing is remarkable. In sharing her story and the lessons learned, *Heartsearch* represents a gift of love and grace to all of us.

William A. Briggs, MD
March 1990

Introduction

Rarely does a professional have the opportunity to plunge her-self into the stuff of her craft, to become a living example of an abiding intellectual concern. Long before I began training as a psy-chotherapist and before psychoneuroimmunology came to the fore, I had been fascinated by the interrelationship of body and mind and had come to believe they are different expressions of the same energy. I graduated from the casual interest of an armchair explor-er when, in 1975, I contracted the autoimmune illness, lupus ery-thematosus.

At its heart, this is a book about transformation, about healing, a movement toward greater wisdom, humility, and compassion. Anything that shakes up an accustomed order of life—from divorce to marriage, financial ruin to winning the lottery—has the potential for triggering such change. Disease just happened to be my catalyst.

I used what treatments modern medicine had to offer, but was immediately determined to understand the illness beyond what the doctors told me. More drawn to life beneath the surface, I wres-tled with the deeper, difficult questions: To what extent had I helped create my illness? Just how did my emotions affect my body, and my body, my emotions? Eventually, action took precedence over knowl-edge, as I asked, "In what ways and to what extent can I heal my-self?" As I began to use alternative therapies and grasp more about holism, I realized inner homework was as important as technique. Who am I? What's right for me? What's right for me now? were the important considerations. Without that deeper level of under-standing and integration, the best methods were merely Bandaids, external, superficial remedies.

Instead of a rap to beat, lupus slowly came to be a spiritual lesson, a *koan*. Whatever else lupus did, it catapulted me beyond my realm of understanding. I was forced to find a new way to make sense of my existence and to explore myself in greater depth than I ever imagined was possible.

Seminal to this process was my writing. Early on, I kept a journal and, after a dramatic turning point in 1980, I was drawn to look at the entire course of the illness, to give the experience form and order. Writing became a means of gaining detachment and perspective and, thus, an important healing method in itself. My personal voice as a woman coping with the dramatic effects of lupus on my daily life, my marriage, and my family is interwoven with my professional voice interpreting the experience and identifying the principles I discovered in striving to integrate my body and mind into my heart. The eventual result was this book.

I hope *Heartsearch* conveys the complexity of illness and recovery and reflects a depth of perspective that comes from having examined these issues for more than a decade. I came to believe that there isn't any right or wrong way to face illness, but that the process of making choices, of committing oneself to those choices, and of acknowledging the part of healing that is beyond our control is empowering.

For many of us, getting well necessitates a far greater degree of commitment than we have ever before been called upon to make. *Heartsearch* should help readers tackle the mountain of hard work required after even the best of decisions and to see that surrender has a magical power which, in fact, enhances the possibility of healing. Fear can be transformed into courage, anger into love, and despair into hope.

Donna Hamil Talman

Contents

1

The Initial Shock

My sense of well-being was extraordinary as I lay in front of the fireplace with David, my husband, and our four-year-old, Adam, at 3:00 p.m. A light snow fell outside. I saw a lacy square of white flakes out the window across the room. Cozy times near the fire were common, but my emotional and physical state this particular Sunday afternoon in January 1975 was unique. Time slowed down. My thoughts, like a movie projector freezing on a still frame, had stopped. Instead of planning what to fix for dinner or daydreaming while I gazed at the fire, I focused easily on it. My eyes absorbed its colors of red, blue, and orange slowly weaving different patterns. The crackling noises sounded melodic. Every pore of me slowly absorbed its sounds as they mingled with those of Beethoven on the stereo. I couldn't tell where the sounds ended and I began. I was fully present. This was a rare experience for me.

I lost this state briefly as I recalled events of a day earlier. Making love then had seemed sweeter than usual, and the physical sensations of orgasm continued into the night. In fact, they were still with me now. This had never happened before. My mouth still felt wonderfully soft and receptive, and my lips quivered deliciously as if the loss of self that occurred in communion with a single human being now extended to all humanity, even to inanimate objects. Absurd as it seems, the mauve-colored coral and the lithograph resting on the mantel, even the white walls, seemed radiantly alive. I tingled all over. A warm, powerful current of energy continued to stream from my pelvis up to my throat. The current radiated from that central shaft outward in all directions to the tips of my limbs. My body felt at once supremely relaxed and supremely alive. In addition to feeling at one with my surroundings, I felt joyous, deeply compassionate, and boundlessly energized. In my entire life, I never remember feeling so unutterably vibrant.

After half an hour or so, still lost in colors, sounds, and sensations, my hand moved to my forehead a few times. It seemed a little warm. I took off a sweater and moved a little farther from the flames. My curiosity turned into vague annoyance in another half hour as I got up to fix dinner, for I still felt warm. I began to wonder if I had a temperature.

After dinner, I finally used the thermometer; it read 102 degrees. By 10:00 p.m., the thermometer read 103°. By midnight, I was taking my temperature every fifteen minutes. By 2:00 a.m., it had climbed to 105°. I woke David, asleep beside me, to tell him what was happening and that I was afraid. As he began to drift back to sleep after putting an arm around me, I began to shake him and shriek hysterically, "Don't let me go to sleep. If I go to sleep, I'm afraid I'll die."

Such drama was not characteristic of me. More typical was a rational analysis of the situation or, at the extreme, worrying aloud about whether I should call a doctor.

When I was twelve and happily working cattle with my father on our ranch in Colorado, a part-Shetland horse that had been mine for years suddenly lay down in the ditch we had been standing in and rolled over on me. This was totally unexpected. I trusted this creature not to hurt me. The saddle and saddle horn saved me from being crushed, and I was not injured at all, but for a brief moment I was terrified. There had been other equally terrifying moments in my life, mostly brief moments. None could really be called a close encounter with death. Shortly after I married at twenty-five, I had a severe kidney infection requiring hospitalization for three weeks. The infection was painful and quite serious, the doctors told me afterward. Except for an eye injury in adolescence, it was my only serious illness. I'd taken good health for granted. Even in any of these rare, frightened moments, I never doubted I would live.

For the first time in my life, during that long night, I thought I was dying. I could make no sense of what was happening inside me. David, meanwhile, despite my noise, went back to sleep. Any other time his action might have reassured me that I was exaggerating the situation, that I obviously did not look close to death to him. Tonight I did not feel reassured. I hated him for his insensitivity, but I was too terrified to dwell on this.

Maybe if I keep moving, I'll stay alive, I thought. I felt too weak to do so, yet somehow staggered down the carpeted stairs onto the wood floor in the piano room. As I moved onto the quarry tile floor in the kitchen, my hot, bare feet began to cool. I craved milk. That was strange, for I hadn't drunk a glass of milk in years. I grabbed for a glass with one hand and the refrigerator door with the other. As I poured a glassful, my hand seemed steadier than I thought it would be. After gulping it down, I poured another. When I finished that glass, I felt hungry, which reassured me fleetingly of my urge to live. My hand (for it didn't seem that the movement was generated by a thought) was drawn to a box of Ritz crackers in the cupboard because Adam liked them. I opened the box, took a few out, began to bite into one, and slowly, carefully, chewed it. In some strange way, I was sure that Ritz crackers had been the first solid food I ate as a baby. The surety with which I felt this was striking. I had an image, as I stood in front of the kitchen cupboard chewing crackers and sipping milk, of myself on Mother's soft lap. I no longer wobbled much since, as a plump enough seven-month-old, I'd nearly mastered the art of sitting up. I finished a bottle. Coming toward me from across the room were my daddy's familiar, warm eyes and his big hand, stretching out to give me something. I dropped my bottle, reached, and captured the thing on the first grab. I push it toward my mouth, like everything else. It crumbled, but I got a piece in. It tasted good. Milk and Ritz crackers. The edible symbols of love and caring from my parents, as comforting to me now as a frightened adult as they must have been in childhood.

Like older people who become childlike again in their later years and repeat the scripts of their youth, I thought I was, in the

space of the few hours before my death, going through a com-
pressed version of that stage.

Still alive at 7:00 a.m., I decided I must have a generous case of
the flu. David, his prematurely gray hair brushed neatly as usual,
encouraged me to call our family doctor, his prep-school and college
classmate and tennis pal. I hesitated, because I always hesitated
about calling doctors, preferring to see if time will lead to healing.
The extent of my fear was reflected in my dialing the phone a little
later.

"I don't know what's wrong with me, George. My only symptom is that I've had a fever of 104° and 105° most of the night."

He suggested that I come to the office.

"I don't think I can drive myself there." My own words surprised me.

He said he couldn't come by until the end of the day, but, for
some reason, he appeared at our back door within an hour. He
pulled out his stethoscope and asked me a few questions. The only
thing I remember about the encounter is the word "gray." I don't
know if I said I felt gray or he said I looked gray, but his next comment was, "I'm driving down the street to City Hospital. Why don't
you come with me?"

The previous week had been registration week at
Quinsigamond Community College in Worcester, where we lived.
Since September, I had been replacing an acquaintance who was
on sabbatical for the year. It was my perfect job. After finishing my
master's degree in 1968 and completing additional years of group-
and then family-therapy training, I had always found satisfying
work in my field. At this moment, however, I couldn't have created
a happier job description than my current one: half-time counseling
as one of the staff of counselors available to students and half-time
teaching an experiential course emphasizing self-awareness and
group dynamics in the psychology department. Community-col-
lege students often had no previous exposure to psychotherapy,
and, since the counseling service was voluntary and my course not
a required one, those students who used my skills in either setting
were often hungry for self-knowledge. Responding was the most
pleasurable kind of work. I loved every second of this job and felt
lucky I had been asked to take it. I needed to be on campus only

between 8:30 a.m. and 2:30 p.m., when Adam was in day care, and I had little take-home work.

* * *

Classes were to begin Monday, January 20, 1975. Instead, I entered the hospital. My world went no further than the sheets that touched my skin. I felt desperately isolated.

Three days later, my temperature remained at 104°. I did not move, even to turn over. Parched, I was too weak to lift a glass to drink water. I got out of bed only twice in the next three weeks. I felt like a lobster that has just shed its shell: raw, exposed, and fragile. My mind raced in vivid and continuous imagery. Scary scenes, as if I lived in a haunted house.

I kept rerunning scenes from Alan Lelchuk's *Miriam at Thirty-Four*, which I had been reading. Miriam, newly separated, took her first solitary walk in years at night in Cambridge and was raped. The police who interviewed her glared at her and said stonily, "Do you have a lawyer, lady?" "Call your doctor." The coldness of the authorities horrified me as much as the rape itself.

Lines from the novel came to me as I lay in the hospital bed, thinking I was dying. "Dr. Stanley Brown had filed in Third District Court of Middlesex County, Cambridge, for custody of their two children." I wondered if that was the courthouse a few blocks from where I had once lived. I could see the judge slamming the gavel, and the children walking away from their mother. I didn't know if these book scenes bombarded me merely because I had finished the book the day before I went to the hospital or because I suddenly felt as ravaged and as powerless as Miriam.

My temperature decreased, but there was a sharp pain in my chest when I breathed. In a few days, my chest hurt when hardly breathing at all. I became conscious of every breath, limiting movement in order to lessen pain.

Sometime during the first week for about forty-eight hours, I experienced a period of inner calm. Fear, reminding me of the times when, as a child, I mistakenly touched an electrified barbed-wire fence on our ranch, vanished. My thoughts, words on metal ticker tape which shot through my head and crashed head on, stopped. My world still ended at the bedside, but the sheets suddenly, magically, felt comforting. Soothing waves seemed to emanate from my heart. Although stabbing chest pains and general achiness were still with me, I felt them less. Muscles, blood vessels, my very cells seemed to soften, melt, and expand. My chewed fingertips, the cue to my inner state, healed completely. Besides feeling peaceful, I also felt warmly compassionate, just as I had on the day illness struck.

Both dramatic events seemed significant. I couldn't explain this pocket of tranquility any more than I could explain why my temperature had skyrocketed a few days earlier after feeling so vibrant. How could I become so desperately ill after such sensual, physical, emotional peace? How could I now, despite weakness and pain, fall into a pocket of such peace?

After that, buffeted by the next riptide of energy, I flipped back into a bodily anarchy and stayed there.

Each day groups of six or seven white-suited men came in, the leader announcing he was Dr. X, a rheumatologist, or Dr. Y, a urologist, or an infectious disease specialist, an internist, or a gynecologist. They examined me and asked questions. The most frequent visitors were infectious disease teams. They always asked "Have you been to a tropical island recently?"

My eyes opened to narrow slits to grasp the scene and then closed for the duration of their visits. Normal voices sounded like shouting; a gentle poke felt like a stab. Many of the doctors left my johnny untied and me uncovered after their examination. My eyes squeezed shut, my teeth clenched. I raged silently at their insensitivity and my helplessness.

One or another antibiotic was tried, but the frequency of the visits and the continuing barrage of questions reaffirmed that there was no real diagnosis yet. It seemed more serious and complicated than the flu.

On the fourth day my temperature remained high. My chest pain accelerated. When all four infectious disease doctors came into my room together to begin another round of poking and questions, I felt panicky again. After they left, I dragged myself to a pay phone. Ashen-faced and limp as a rag doll, I sensed that I needed every ounce of available energy to heal. Even fingering the phone dial would divert energy. I called my psychotherapist whom I had last seen the day before I got sick.

His wife answered, "He's not at home. He's on an emergency."

Since he had returned from a Caribbean island the day before I saw him, I asked, "Have you and your family been feeling well?"

"Fine," she answered.

Relieved, I asked her to have him call me and staggered back to my room. My chest felt like a rubber band stretched to its limit.

The pain in my chest, they shortly discovered, was inflammation in the lining of the heart and lungs: pericarditis and pleurisy. Now they waited to see if puncturing the tissue to drain the fluid could be avoided. I was moved into intensive-care. The visual boundary of my world continued to end at the bedsheet. I never opened my eyes to see what the unit looked like, but I pictured an above-ground cemetery from a recent newspaper photograph. When I had first seen this picture of walls filled with tombs, I had mused, perversely, about what it would be like to open the ends and see hundreds of feet staring me in the face.

These people weren't quite dead yet but were noisily pursuing their death rituals. A woman shouted, "Mommy, Mommy, come to me," in a four-year-old voice. Another man yelled in a grown-up voice, "Mabel, you're a bitch. You never did care." The man in the bed next to mine yelled regularly, all day and all night, at what seemed to be exactly five-minute intervals, one of three lines: "Get these damn tubes out of me," "Get me out of here," or "I have to pee, nurse. I have to pee." He continued whatever line he chose until a nurse came. Then she would yell at him, since he was apparently hard of hearing, "Stop that. Don't pull those tubes out. We'll have to spank you if you don't," or angrily, after having given him a bedpan which was returned empty, "You don't have to pee."

I was appreciative when a nurse asked, "What would you like to make you more comfortable?" No one had asked that before. Except for freshly squeezed orange juice, I couldn't think of anything. When I didn't respond, she asked if I'd like my legs shaved, as if shaved legs is something a dying woman thinks about. My acquiescence may have expressed a flicker of hope, however inappropriate, that if I acted as if everything were normal, it would be. My skin felt as if it were being scraped away, but, since my sense of touch was heightened, I just gritted my teeth and imagined I was exaggerating until I heard her say, "Whoops. We don't even have any bandaids." I opened my eyes long enough to see blood trickling down my legs in several places.

I don't think I ever slept while in that unit. There was only one positive aspect to the experience: I had to conclude I was more alive than the others. Later I discovered that the intensive-care unit was a semicircle of beds with wooden walls between each bed, so that a nurse sitting at the supervision desk saw a sea of feet.

* * *

After I was back in a regular room, my body was still a wild riptide of currents and pain. But my mind must have worked better than I remember, since those three hospital weeks marked a turning point in regard to my personal relationships. I watched cards, flowers, and gifts come in and people come to visit. Detached, I came to some decisions about real friendships based on those feelings.

One woman to whom I felt quite attached never even acknowledged my existence in the hospital or later. She had a capacity for quick and easy intimacy and eventually told me she didn't contact me because she did not wish to "pick up any negative energy." With a jolt, I understood that this kind of relationship was meaningless; to the extent caring was shown, I could have been dead. Although durability without depth in friendship was boring, I had just learned that depth without durability was equally meaningless. I decided to get rid of such a friend.

Second, I suddenly knew that I wanted to deepen a few of my friendships. This awareness came to me when I realized that most of the superficial communication during my hospital stay meant little. Counting the cards, flowers, and visitors, I could feel reassured of my lovability. I was reminded of my high school days when I ran for almost everything and was usually elected. In high-school and in college, I had wanted to have the longest, most impressive activities list in the yearbook. Gradually, however, being popular had become less important. Now in my early thirties, I cared less about masses of people acknowledging my importance than about having a few people to whom I felt richly and deeply connected.

I had grown up trusting men more easily than women, sharing most of my secrets with my boyfriends. I'd been involved in the women's movement since the sixties and was still very committed to my weekly consciousness-raising group. Yet, I felt close to few women, regardless of how close they felt to me. When I shared myself with women, I awaited their ultimate betrayal. Lying in bed, I resolved to risk more to let those I cared about get to know me better.

The third decision was to make more friends of my own. David had been born and raised locally. Many of the people who sent flowers and cards and visited were David-connected, as were most of the doctors. Many of these came as a result of his position and stature as a lawyer in the community, not mine. Frequently, it seemed as though I was only "the wife of…" and "the family of…" but rarely "Donna…."

When I graduated from the University of Colorado close to home, the university placement office said my political science degree would be useful only if I got a master's degree, or, since I was a woman, a doctorate. Otherwise, they advised secretarial training. I didn't want to get married immediately, so I opted for an excruciatingly boring year of secretarial training at the Katharine Gibbs Secretarial School, which trained executive secretaries. The following year and a half, I lived in Boston and supported myself with the best-paying secretarial job I could find. Then I spent a year as the secretary to the headmaster at a private, secondary American school in Lugano, Switzerland, on the palm-tree-lined lake with snow-covered Alps in the background. Often I was assigned to convey administrative messages to the Italian-speaking staff at the school. I became enamored of Italian. Before returning to America, I spent six months in Perugia, one of the hill towns between Florence and Rome, at a language school.

I considered myself to be adventurous and independent. Until this moment, I had been unaware of how much marriage had changed that. Never in the seven years since I had married and moved to David's hometown had I felt my lack of independent identity so powerfully. In addition to the impotence that everyone feels when sick, I felt the impotence of being a woman in a male-dominated medical world. My own resources seemed few. I felt determined to try and change this, just as soon as this strange illness receded.

* * *

I missed Adam. I had been a breast-feeding, take-my-child-with-me mother. We had spent very few nights apart since his birth in 1970. There was no dark golden mop of unkempt curls to run my hand through. No bright, mischievous eyes to look into. No fleeting glimpses of a graceful body in constant motion. I couldn't see a thing in this dreary hospital room, but I could remember every detail of that lively little boy's form.

I kept recalling two incidents involving Adam which occurred during a vacation in Jamaica when he was three. The nanny sitting for him in our room ran into the dining room in great agitation. Adam had slipped away from her in the hotel corridor, darted into an empty room, and slammed the door behind him. She hurried to the housekeeper for a passkey and then discovered that Adam had flipped the safety lock, too. He refused to answer her calls. While the housekeeper dashed for another key, the sitter raced to find us. Finally we all opened the door, only to find Adam in the bathroom behind another locked door. When we reached him, he was perched contentedly on the toilet. His only explanation: "It was nap time. I didn't want to take a nap."

Near the hotel entrance the next day, and for the first time ever, I lost Adam. Traffic rushed by beyond the front door, and Jamaicans drive wildly. The other doors opened onto a series of patios with a maze of interconnected pools and wall-to-wall people. Beyond that was open beach, more people, thousands of places into which a child could vanish forever. I lunged toward any spot that seemed familiar or that I thought would intrigue a child. Staff and strangers rallied to help, but seconds still seemed like hours. Eventually he came into view. A crowd had gathered to watch him confidently kneeling on all fours at the tip of the diving board and gently swaying it up and down, as if to understand its finer physics. Adam seemed totally absorbed in his experiment, but I think he was aware of his audience.

When we checked out at the end of the week, one of the waiters who had made Adam's acquaintance came up to David and exclaimed, "Mon, I *like* your son. He *know* how to *live.*"

Adam's liveliness seemed especially precious now, juxtaposed against my lifelessness.

Now, lying in my hospital bed, I longed to see Adam; yet when David brought him, I felt nothing. Usually a hugger, I had no impulse to reach out. For Adam, parents were, among other things, climbing toys. He must have sensed I was untouchable. David said Adam paused long enough to glance at me, then quickly found the buttons that adjust the bed and was asking, "What are these for?" as his fingers jabbed in their direction. After that, I didn't encourage David to bring Adam often. The gloomy hospital seemed a horrible and sterile place for a child. I had no resources to give him—no toys, no ability to make him feel it was a fun and interesting place. It wasn't. I worried about him surprisingly little: I still assumed life would return to normal as soon as I left the hospital.

* * *

Two-and-a-half weeks after I was hospitalized there still was no diagnosis. Fewer medical teams entered my room asking questions. A woman intern I had known previously in a women's group took pity on me, risking criticism from her superiors, and told me what the doctors had suspected for over a week. She was enraged at their lack of communication, and I might have been, too, had I not been so weak. They talked with David about their speculations; David didn't pass them on to me immediately. Later David said, his voice sounding tighter, that he was reluctant to cause what might prove needless anxiety. This was probably true, but, although he is kind and considerate, he is also deeply, if quietly, paternalistic. I was only beginning to know that for me more information means less fear.

The intern said they thought I had something called SLE, or systemic lupus erythematosus. They were waiting for confirmation from blood tests being developed in Boston. Her sympathies were aroused because her mother had lupus.

The tests were finally returned: it was lupus. Clinical words and phrases like "chronic," "collagen disease," "connective-tissue disease," and "inflammatory—somewhat related to arthritis" reverberated in my ears, and a definition : "Lupus erythematosus translated from Latin means 'wolf,' so named because the skin lesions of the illness look like bites of a wolf."

I was confused. The relationship to arthritis I could fathom because my muscles and joints hurt, but there was nothing wrong with my skin.

"People have a whole variety of symptoms," the doctors said. "Some people never have any skin involvement. The whole body is composed of connective tissue, so illness can affect any part." The doctors seemed tremendously excited at labeling me, yet impatient with my questions—almost as if diagnosis was their only goal.

When I asked about prognosis and cure, their answers were vague and skimpy. "Many more women than men have lupus. Some get very sick. Few die these days. Some people have one episode such as yours and never have any recurrence. Some have continued mild discomfort; most have ups and downs over time." When I asked, "What about me? What category do I fall in?" I received a variety of "We don't knows." Lupus seemed a mysterious illness.

It was only later that I learned lupus is a disease of unknown cause in which there are striking changes in the immune system. As part of their job in protecting the individual from infections, certain cells of the immune system make antibodies, protein molecules that can react with foreign substances and lead to their elimination. In lupus, the body makes large quantities of antibodies that react instead against the person's own normal tissue. Common symptoms are a butterfly-shaped rash over the bridge of the nose, weakness and lack of energy, diminished appetite and weight loss, anemia, muscular aches, joint pains and swelling, frequent infections, and chronic or recurrent low-grade fever. Hair loss can occur, and the digestive tract may be involved, leading to nausea, vomiting, and abdominal pain. The membranes around the heart, lungs, and abdominal organs may become inflamed. Lupus may become life-threatening when it affects the vital organs, particularly the kidneys or central nervous system.

I also learned later that the current treatment by the medical establishment is medication, most of which dependably relieves pain and reduces inflammation, but none of which is curative. In mild cases, aspirin is used. In more serious cases, as mine proved to be, antimalarial, immunosuppressive, and the cortisone family of steroid drugs, such as prednisone, are used. Cortisone is a synthetic form of hormones normally produced by the adrenal glands.

In bed, staring at the hospital ceiling on that particular February afternoon, however, I felt only shock. I wasn't ready to digest such facts. Instead I was tormented by the universal questions people ask at such times. "What did I do to deserve this?" I thought."I'm thirty-three, in my prime. I've never felt more attractive, more vital. Why me? Why now?" Like most people, I felt I was being punished, but for what?

Desperate to make sense of this experience, I asked David to bring in *Das Energi*, a small, poetic, philosophical book by Paul Williams. The friend who had recently passed it on to me said Williams was a contemporary song writer. Little did I know that "energy" would become the main subject of my life in the ensuing decade. I asked for the book then only because I remembered a page that seemed relevant. Although I could barely hold the book, page seventy-eight was quickly dog-eared.

> Sooner or later a person begins to notice that everything that happens to him is perfect, relates directly to who he is, had to happen, was meant to happen, plays a little role in fulfilling his destiny.
>
> When he encounters difficulty, it no longer occurs to him to complain—he has learned to expect nothing, has learned that loss and frustration are a part of life, and come at their proper time—instead he asks himself, why is this happening? ... by which he means, what can I learn from this, how will it strengthen me, make me more aware? He lets himself be strengthened, lets himself grow, just as he lets himself relax and enjoy (and grow) when life is gentle to him.
>
> Strengthened by this simple notion, simple awareness, that life is perfect, that all things come at the proper moment and that he is always the perfect person for the situation he finds himself in, a person begins to feel more and more in tune with his inner nature, begins to find it easier and easier to do what he knows is right. All chance events appear to him to be intended; all intentional actions

he clearly perceives as part of the workings of Chance. Anxiety seldom troubles him; he knows his death will come at its proper moment. . . .

Reading this some days, I thought it nonsense. But I was desperate. More often, I returned to it, received temporary solace, and closed the book, repeating, "What can I learn from this?"
Other lines in the book were less comforting:

> "It's all up to you."
> "You are completely responsible for your life."
> "You are the creator."

Unquestionably, I felt responsible for dealing with lupus now that I knew I had it. Yet if I could have some part in the cure, I might also be part of the cause. Intellectually, I knew that taking the responsibility was not the same as taking the blame, but I had difficulty separating the two. My "response-ability" to getting sick seemed ample, but responsibility for causing the illness was something else. I felt panic and bewilderment at the idea that I could have created the illness.

* * *

A few days before leaving the hospital, I began to include the walls of the room in my world and tried, with the doctors' encouragement, to walk. I had to think to put one foot in front of the other. Looking at my body when putting on my bathrobe, I was aghast. My slender curves had become jagged edges. I must have still stood five feet, four inches, but I felt as shrunken and shrivelled as an eighty-five-year-old. On my first venture down the twenty-five-foot hallway, I almost fainted.

2

Hospital to Home

All I remember about going home is red Valentine's decorations in the hospital corridors as my wheelchair was pushed to the entrance door. I was too weak to open the car door. In the car, I closed my eyes, occasionally taking a peek. The colors, shapes, and sounds of the outside world were still too overpowering.

Three days later, I taught an evening class. The college had hired someone to replace me temporarily. Word had it that I was on my deathbed, so they told the replacement I would probably be out at least the rest of the semester. Being written off as dead ignited the most ferociously willful part of me—my will to live. Although I couldn't articulate it at the time, my deepest conviction was that if I acted well, I would be well.

That day, David looked shorter than usual. His outsized shoulders drooped. His extra-long arms seemed to hang to his knees. His hair was longer because he hadn't found time for a haircut; his shirt, unironed. Behind his glasses, his eyes looked puffy.

He wouldn't drive me to the college, claiming I was crazy to be teaching while sick.

Determinedly, I arranged for Brenda to drive. She'd been a delightful student, one who read everything on my reading list and asked for more. She was sweet-natured and devoted to me, and soon came to live with us. She drove me to the doorstep, holding my arm as I tottered toward my classroom and dropped onto a hard-backed chair. I saw no reason to shorten the class time, although if I had responded to my body rather than my will, I would have toppled off the chair onto the wooden floor within five minutes.

I hardly moved from bed for the next week. My next big adventure was to stumble a hundred yards to my neighbor Barbara's house. We'd met her and her warm-hearted husband when they lived in the same garden-apartment complex we did after we married. Our children were the same age. For Barbara, children came first. While carrying on a conversation with me, her antenna was always alert to her children's needs. When she paused to attend to a child, she was so smooth it hardly seemed an interruption. Our friendship had two years to take root before I became ill. We'd become more informal and spontaneous, each feeling comfortable asking for last-minute help. I remembered my resolve in that hospital bed: let women you care about get to know you better. Barbara was one of them. I had no idea that she would soon become Adam's second mother.

The walk to Barbara's was all downhill, but I felt as if I had climbed up a mountain. Before tackling the return trip home with Adam, I needed to rest an hour.

Over the next few weeks, I gradually returned to my job. I was unaware of how fifty milligrams of prednisone daily affected me. For the first three weeks after I left the hospital, I ate like a horse. I regained some of the weight I had lost. My cheeks had an unusually healthy-looking flush. I began thinking I was far healthier than I was.

In retrospect, it seems ridiculous that I pushed myself to return to work so quickly or at all, but I couldn't bear the thought of my students' developing affection for anyone else, and after a few stretches of employment I had not enjoyed, I really appreciated this job. I had no assurance that another perfect job—or *any* job, for that matter—would come my way again. Financial independence meant autonomy to me, my own life and identity separate from the family or my marriage. I valued my career. After getting my master's degree at Clark when I married and moved to Worcester, I'd been steadily accumulating more professional training and experience, all part-time and mostly evenings because that fit with my concept of mothering. I also worked with parents of teenagers who came before the Worcester Juvenile Court. Under the supervision of a behavior-modification psychologist, I'd designed and administered a training program for professional and lay leaders of small discussion groups for these parents. Before that I'd worked two afternoons a week at a local nursing school as a counselor for students. The job at Quinsigamond was my first full-time job in recent years.

I had no idea how sick I was and what the future of my health would be. Never before in my life had I been laid up for more than a few weeks with illness. Never before had I had the need to consider whether I had strength enough to walk across a room. Any other illness went away quickly; I always got stronger. Why not this time?

But this illness didn't go away quickly. As it turned out, I made some gross misjudgments in the process of adjusting to this new reality.

Like many couples in 1975, David and I were in the midst of negotiating role changes. Before lupus, childcare had been primarily my responsibility, but David certainly took care of, changed diapers, and fed his son. As a baby, Adam often fell asleep lying on his father's chest. Grocery shopping, meal preparation, dishes, and trash were my jobs, as were general indoor household upkeep, hiring plumbers, painters, and the weekly housecleaner, and doing the laundry and mending. Relationship responsibilities, my family and his, were mine, as was initiating most social invitations.

Now each weekday soon evolved into a set routine. I somehow managed to get clothing on and food into me and Adam. Then I dropped him off at his day-care center a few blocks from our house. I drove ten minutes to the college, parked in the handicapped section, walked fifty-seven steps to my office door, sat down in my swivel chair, and did not leave except to go to the third floor by elevator to teach my classes or to go to the bathroom. Lunch was sometimes nothing, sometimes a few scoops of homogenized peanut butter from the jar on my bookshelf and a piece of fruit, or even occasionally cracker snacks from the junk-food machine next to the bathroom. Making my former sack lunches or walking to the cafeteria was impossible.

I finished teaching at 3:00 p.m. and drove back to the day-care center, collected Adam, and flopped on the living-room couch until Brenda announced that dinner was served. I hit the couch again after dinner, hoping that Adam would go to sleep at 8:30 so I could. That gold living-room couch was becoming an appendage to my body. I felt less "sick" lying there than in bed. The stairs to our bedroom seemed endless, like the quarter-mile dirt road to our mailbox when I was a small child.

My friends told me people were saying, "She deals with her illness so admirably... amazing how she's able to hold a job and be a wife and mother with *that* illness." To an outside observer, the comings and goings in our household seemed about the same as before the illness. I tried hard to maintain the facade that my life had not changed. I was influenced by the conventional wisdom in my childhood: women got sick by not having enough interests or being too self-absorbed.

Inside the house, as inside my body and mind, chaos reigned. Often I was almost desperate by the time we went to work. Grouchy from waking with pains that shifted daily, angry at the fact of the illness, and not having resolved certain angers at David before I got sick, my voice held an undercurrent of anger in every interaction with him. Typically, I would yell, "Why don't you drive Adam today? You could get his clothes on, you know. You could feed him. Or at least fix his breakfast."

That was followed by guilt so strong it almost doubled me over. Before I became ill, David had been genuinely making an effort to assist with household chores. That is not to say he always rushed to help now. He no longer dared to say publicly that he viewed my career as superfluous, primarily a nuisance that put us in a higher tax bracket. But the undercurrent in his voice usually conveyed, "If you have the strength for your career, you had better have the strength for childcare and household chores." I was much clearer about my own values before lupus.

Of course, if David had responded with, "Okay, I'd be glad to help dress Adam," that might set me off with, "No. I want to do it." Before lupus, I wasn't an overburdened mother. The time spent in simple life tasks with Adam had been enjoyable.

Already I could see how difficult illness was for spouses.

David's needs had proved to be as few as the lovable St. Bernard that had frequented my college sorority house. His style of protection was similar and equally generous. To survive, that huge pet needed only regular food and occasional stroking, for which he seemed inordinately grateful. In exchange, he offered unfailing loyalty and steadfast protection. The dog's protective skills were never tested, but I hoped he would have proved *less* unflappable and more emotionally demonstrative than David. His sleeping in the midst of my panic the night before I was hospitalized was not the first time dynamite was needed to rouse him. Generally, though, I admired his simplicity, particularly when combined with his quiet intelligence. He graduated from Harvard College and Law School, and as a civil-trial lawyer, he is known to be a skillful, tough negotiator. At home, however, he had been long on gratitude and humor and had no bad moods that a hearty jog or a game of tennis wouldn't cure. His midlife crisis, I teased him, had lasted an entire *two days*. One could hardly imagine a spouse who would be less upset by the trauma of illness.

But a sick wife was not what he'd bargained for, not at all. The marriage ceremony said "...in sickness and in health," but neither of us gave it much thought, since we hadn't experienced or witnessed serious illness. We met on a double blind date arranged by a college classmate of mine; David selected me merely because I was the taller of the two women in the package. Apparently, he was as intrigued by a spirited Colorado *shiksa* as I was by a refined New England Jew. That I seemed willing to pull my own oar and was athletic impressed him. On our second date, a ski trip to Vermont, we shared the driving. Since I had driven regularly to school after I turned 16, I didn't think driving was any special evidence of willingness to do my share, but David did. It also pleased and amused him that I could keep up with the guys on the ski slopes and tennis courts. His amusement seemed sweetly patronizing, and I explained it by his being nine years older than I, to be expected from someone who called dating "courting." Depending on my mood, I found that charmingly eccentric or hopelessly antiquated. Given my current predicament, it was ironic that when we married I had worried our age difference might mean that *he* would not be able to keep up with *me*. Fate would decree, however, that for the indefinite future, I wouldn't be able to keep up with him.

By 3:00 p.m. on even the most tranquil days throughout 1975, I was a wasted zombie, saving my last ounce of energy for Adam. Much as I adored my career, mothering was far more important to me. I always hoped for loving scenes with Adam: having downed apple juice and one or another kind of cracker, as ubiquitous in his early years as milk and Ritz crackers had been in mine, he tugs at my hand, "Mommy, read me the Leo book." *Leo the Late Bloomer*, a story about an underachieving tiger cub, was one of his favorites.

Grabbing my hand, he would trot toward the living room couch. As I dropped down into its inviting gold-velvet folds, he jumped up beside me. Eagerly he would open the big orange book. Soon a little headful of loose curls would burrow toward my middle and snuggle into the curve of my waist.

Since he could recite the story verbatim, he ignored the story line. Soon he would chirp, "Look at the butterfly, Mommy," and "I like the *pink* flowers best," pointing at them. Simply glancing at the curves of his round little hand, which I judged to be perfect, like the rest of his body, was a balm to my wounded self. His upturned face and lively eyes soothed me even more.

I would begin to relax, ready to cuddle for an hour more.

Sometimes this fantasy became reality, but often it did not. Today, Adam squirmed after five minutes and speedily turned into a wiggleworm. I had only one sentence of creative cajoling in me, not fifteen minutes.

"Mommy, I want to go outside now. Let's go out and play catch."

I felt like shouting, "Sit still a minute. Can't you just *sit still!*" My own need for nurturance and tranquility had become so overwhelming that his normal change of interest seemed like a personal attack. I managed to say, "I don't feel up to it right now, Adam. Don't you want to hear the end of the story? I'll keep reading."

"No, I already know it. You know that."

"Well, pick another book which has a story that's new to you."

"No. I don't want any more stories. I want to go outside."

"Well, I'll try it. Why don't you go get the ball you want, and we'll go to the front yard."

"I don't know where the big ball is. You get it."

"Why don't you look downstairs in the playroom. I think you had it there yesterday."

"You look, Mommy. And I want crackers and juice. Before we go out."

I couldn't think clearly anymore and yelled, "Adam, first find the ball. You can do that. You can do *something* for yourself!"

"You walk to the car when you take me to day care, and you go to the office. Why can't *you* get the ball?" Before I could answer, he added, "Anyway, now I just want some apple juice and crackers."

I could barely restrain myself from throwing him against the wall. Realizing that I over-reacted and being unable to change that made me feel even more desperate. My mind was on lupus. What would happen to me? Who had it? Were there other women around suffering with it?

Adam's experience with Brenda was different. She had a stocky, square frame, rounded out with soft edges. Adam loved stuffed animals. She must have seemed as huggable as the biggest and best in his growing collection. Shoulder-length, dark, wavy hair, always shiny, framed her round face. She had an upturned nose over which was sprinkled a few tiny freckles. Her smile and dark eyes conveyed innocence and a hearty desire to please. Her clothes were basic: jeans and a shirt. Comfort came first, as it did for Adam. When she was on all fours playing horsey or building with Legos, she seemed fully engaged. At such times, I'd glance down and think I had two children. When Brenda read to him, Adam was just as wriggly as he was with me. But Brenda didn't seem to mind. She waited patiently for his comings and goings, happily available to be sat on, climbed on, or cuddled with. It was some comfort to observe that even Brenda's energy was limited. After sharing Adam's care with me, preparing supper, and doing dishes, plus a full day at college, she was worn out.

Weekends were the worst for me, since it was much easier to deal with adult students in time-limited slots than with a robust child all day. To Adam's requests for attention, Brenda's for simple things like what to fix for dinner, and David's for almost anything, I gritted my teeth and tried to spill out something. Mostly I wanted to scream, "Leave me alone." I seemed to have energy for no one but myself.

That spring I began to withdraw, making a conscious decision to let warm Brenda, stable David, positive Barbara, and whoever was on duty at the day-care center take more space in Adam's life. I came home at 3:00 p.m. to the couch and let Brenda or David pick Adam up at 4:30 or 5:00. What if I died? Adam would feel the loss less if he had been building strong emotional ties to other grownups. Since I was generally acting as if lupus were the flu, I flinched, startled, whenever I caught myself muttering, "What if I die? What *if* I die?"

* * *

Dr. Bird was the hospital rheumatologist brought in on my case. He seemed well informed about lupus and experienced with it. About my age, muscular and dark, he looked healthy. At the very least, I wanted a physician who *appeared* healthy. His lively wit somehow reminded me of Adam.

He continued to feed me information about lupus, but he spoke so rapidly.

"Lupus," he told me, "can begin with any number and combination of symptoms. During the course of the illness, each symptom can be transient or prolonged and often occurs independently of other symptoms." This squared with what I'd been reading. He continued. "The disease varies considerably from person to person and even over time in the same person, with spontaneous improvement or even remission (total disappearance of symptoms) occurring between active periods. Periods of improvement can last for weeks, months, or perhaps years before the next flareup."

At first I had read to check up on Dr. Bird. Increasingly, I read simply to keep the facts straight.

The first booklet I found was *Lupus Erythematosus*, published by the Lupus Foundation of America. My sister-in-law soon sent another, *Primer on Lupus Erythematosus*, by two physicians. The woman intern in the hospital who told me the doctors suspected lupus had recommended a book by Henrietta Aladjem, *In Search of the Sun*, which describes her personal course with the disease.

The Massachusetts Lupus Society had only recently been organized, and meetings were in Boston. That was too far away. Support groups didn't exist. I spoke with others who had lupus. Everyone I talked to had been sick for years and sounded worse off physically and emotionally than I. That discouraged me enough to stop reaching out. I thought, perhaps I should stay away from sick people if I want to get well.

Combining books and doctor, I learned more about the prednisone. First, it should be taken in doses sufficient to control the symptoms thoroughly. Second, if taken for long periods, it could cause side effects—glaucoma, diabetes, peptic ulcers, osteoporosis, congestive heart failure, and cataracts, to name a few of the forty or so listed in the *Physician's Desk Reference*. Third, it caused the adrenal glands to shrink in size because they no longer had to supply cortisone. The dosage had to be reduced very gradually because the adrenal glands often took several months to start normal production of hormones again. Dr. Bird emphasized that point: "Cortisone in lupus patients is somewhat like insulin in diabetics. Sudden withdrawal of the synthetic hormone can precipitate a serious crisis. Some people notice the return of their symptoms and new disease activity after missing only one dose."

These facts made me aware of the finesse required in administering prednisone. The trick was to take enough, yet not a milligram more than was necessary, since the higher the dose, the longer I would need to stay on medication, which, in turn, would increase the chances of side effects. My rheumatologist seemed to have excellent clinical intuition. That, plus his experience with the disease, would help him guide me in taking prednisone wisely.

Nevertheless, after I'd been taking it a while and the dosage was reduced to forty milligrams daily, my pink cheeks faded, and my face became moon-shaped. My appetite waned. I ate mostly from habit or duty. It also gave me a hopped-up, unpleasant high, such as some people experience from caffeine. Twenty-four hours a day, no matter what I was thinking, feeling, or doing, my heart pumped, and my body was wet with sweat. When I was lying on the couch, the racing sensation seemed even more exaggerated, as if I were wired for 110 voltage and had 220-volt current pumping through me. It felt as though my adrenals were trying unsuccessfully to produce extra hormones to support the stress, and prednisone rushed in to fill the gap. Prednisone was artificial energy. It created the illusion that I could support the overcharge. By the time

I went to bed, I felt like an overtired child, too tense to sleep, who could only scream itself to oblivion.

* * *

As the weeks passed, I found myself resisting even the couch for resting. This balking was more than a reflection of my if-you-act-well philosophy. My mother, an indoor bookworm, had often read on our brown couch in the den. At times I viewed her couch time as creative, a way to find pleasurable space for herself during busy days. Other times it was an unpleasant memory, as if it had lasted hours each day and was filled with relentless inquiries and commands: "Isn't it about time to begin supper? I think those potatoes need to be used up before they spoil. Why don't you make a sauce for the broccoli? You didn't finish your practicing (piano) this morning. You'd better do it now." And, a little later, "What are you doing now? Well, hadn't you better get busy with...? Would you bring me a glass of orange juice, please?" Friction is typical between mothers and their teenage daughters. Who knows what actually happened? Whatever the truth, my mother's couch hours evoked two images of her: one as weak and helpless and the other as critical, a wicked stepmother-queen, commanding her slaves from her throne. I'd become Cinderella and transformed my mother into the mean stepmother.

I vowed to be different. A muscular outdoorswoman like my two younger sisters, as I grew up I had become a doer. Now I filled my days with activities. Besides household responsibilities and my psychological pursuits, I loved making pottery and clay sculpture. In recent years, I'd attended weekly classes (occasionally with Adam in a basket when he was a baby) and had created a studio in my basement. When the Quinsigamond job arose, potting had to go. That had been hard. Year-round, two or three times weekly, I played tennis, singles or doubles, sometimes with David and other couples. Following my parents' model of community service, I'd been a member of the Friends of the Worcester Public Schools, a lay group begun by a local business executive to support and advise the local school administration. For a time, I shared leadership of the Worcester Women's Alliance. Before Adam's birth, David and I often headed for Boston for dinner and movies, plays, or concerts.

After we needed sitters, we found these activities in Worcester. Besides Saturday night entertaining or dinners out with other couples, we biked, hiked, swam, sailed when invited, and skied downhill and cross-country.

To re-energize myself, I'd do *more* or a different activity, not rest. Exercise jettisoned depression as well as exhaustion; a whirlwind of housecleaning ousted anger, frustration, and tiredness. The recipe worked well. I scheduled little empty time and, in fact, relished the self-sufficiency that my mother's couch commands had helped create.

Now, however, each time I went near the couch, my stomach clenched. Muscles all over my body twitched and jerked. For every tired muscle that longed to receive the support beneath me, another screamed, "Get up. Move. Keep busy. Don't be so lazy. Do something constructive." The conflict sometimes kept me upright, staggering aimlessly from room to room.

I talked with David about it. "Do you remember when I told you how out of control my mind was in the first days in the hospital? When I was fantasizing about being raped and being in a cemetery?"

"Vaguely."

"Well, I don't seem to be getting better. The second I touch the couch, my thoughts drift. It's like some mysterious magnet pulls them to images and conversations I don't choose. I don't even know what the images or conversations are. The instant I become conscious I've drifted, the thought fades. Just like that. They're lost forever," I said, snapping my fingers.

"That must be frustrating."

"When I 'come to,' my whole body is tense. I'm tight as a drum. Paralyzed. I feel something more specific than tension. But I can't say if it's anger or fear or sadness."

"Well, you're the therapist. This is your area, not mine. I don't know what to do about that." His voice escalated. I imagined he wanted to change the subject. "I'd have to have time alone to have daydreams. My work day is too busy for that."

Clenching my fists, I said, "I've got to relax. How can I heal if I can't even relax?"

"Why don't you watch television or read? Television is my

great soporific."

"I do read. You know that. But my eyes are too tired now for television or reading."

This conversation went further than most. I needed more psychologically oriented people with whom to discuss these topics.

Although I didn't know it, I was in a stage I had often observed in my clients in which repressed feelings begin to surface. Such feelings pop up at strange times and places, perhaps provoked by a snatch of song or the intonation of a voice, but they only make one feel strangely out of control since there is no awareness of the historical sources of the feelings.

My head was telling me to turn off these uncapturable scenes. I'd read Herbert Benson's *The Relaxation Response* and had tasted meditation in my training and group personal-growth experiences. Benson said a quiet environment, an object to dwell on (a word or sound repetition, gazing at a symbol, or concentrating on a particular feeling), a passive attitude, and a comfortable position were prerequisites. I lay pillowless on the couch and attempted to focus on the word "peace." That didn't work. After the second "peace," my mind was elsewhere. And after the third. And fourth. Each time I tried to bring my mind back, my body tensed more. I tried following my in-and-out breaths, since that was another technique I'd been exposed to. I could not and only got exhausted from trying. My mind seemed like a gigantic snowball that gathered speed and volume as it careened down a steep incline — as uncontrollable as my body.

I tried other ways to untie my body and mind from the resulting knot. I gravitated to a simple physical exercise because it fit my prone position and because it worked: legs up in the air, perpendicular, heels up and knees straight, focusing on breathing. The position forced a fuller inhalation and exhalation.

When in one of my "knots," I hardly breathed at all, suspending my breath at the end of a slight inhale. In this legs-up position, at the very least, I was drawn to focus on the pain in my chronically tight hamstring muscles. If I stayed with it long enough, I felt my head turmoil dissipating and energy, like liquid, flowing from my head to a more even distribution in the rest of my body. I actually felt my legs, which I could not in the earlier tense, contracted state. My breathing became deeper and fuller, the flow of oxygen moving all through my chest cavity and into my lower abdomen. I always felt better afterwards, but it was tedious. Like having an aching tooth pulled, the process didn't feel good, although relief from pain afterwards did.

* * *

Psychotherapists often used to begin their training with a grounding in Freudian theory. Until recently, I'd resisted Freud. He was too pessimistic about human potential; he denied that life was important after age six and that there were other dimensions of life besides sexuality; he was sexist. Psychoanalysis was outrageously expensive, and the role of the analyst too authoritarian. I was drawn to the idea of the unconscious and, at the same time, offended by it. That this flamboyantly wild, primitive, and uncontrollable component in us could have such power appalled me. I ignored it in hopes that mature rationality could somehow purge it. My choice of a cool, reasonable David as a husband no doubt reflected that hope. I had no idea then how much lupus would highlight my inner conflict between rationality and unconscious desires. This theme was to be as important as any during the coming years.

Of the modalities to which I had been exposed, the one I had found most useful and to which I felt most philosophically attuned was Gestalt. Its foundations were Freudian, but Fritz Perls, its originator, emphasized pathology less and the uniqueness of each person and of each situation more. The therapist was less an authority and more a midwife who helps uncover self-support. Since who we are is also expressed in our movements, postures, and voice, the therapist attended to these, too. The first time I read Perls' *The Gestalt Approach* and *Eyewitness to Therapy*, I had underlined the section about body-mind unity:

> What is a psychosomatic manifestation? If we maintain the old mind-body split to which the highly limited concept of the unconscious is so closely related, we can describe it either as a somatic disturbance related to a psychic event or as a psychic disturbance caused by a somatic event. But with our unitary point of view we do not have to fall into this trap of causality. We describe a psy-

27

chosomatic event as one in which the gross physical disturbances are more impressive than the ones that occur on a mental or emotional level.

Although I considered this concept the essence of Perls' theory, I didn't really understand it when I became ill. This principle that my illness was psychosomatic became the foundation for all my action in dealing with lupus. That did *not* mean physical symptoms were directly caused by my mind, were "fake," or were not organic. It simply meant that *since body and mind cannot exist apart from one another, my illness had both physical and mental components.*

The other theoretical framework that interested me was Reichian. It began where Perls left off, helping me concretize the body-mind interaction. Wilhelm Reich said that humans are bundles of sexual (meaning "life") energy. He proposed a larger network of feelings, structures, and capacities for pleasure and pain which were reflected in all aspects of the organism's life. The function of psychotherapy was somatic—to soften the neuromuscular blocks in the individual's body that developed from suppression of energy. I rejoiced: finally a modality that included direct work with the body. In reading Myron Sharaf's biography of Reich, *Fury on Earth*, I was reminded of how much Reich's ideas meant to me. I became fascinated with almost everything Reich said: the sense that "unarmoured" man could lead a more vital life; the idea of a more joyous, richer sensuality; his belief that social structure had to change before individuals could achieve these goals; even his notion of a universal energy identical to the energy that moved in sexual excitation. I was, however, a closet Reichian, intoxicated by his ideas but too conventional to admit it, since many people dismissed Reich as a crazy sexologist. Even I shared the impression that toward the end of his life, he was "nuttier than a fruitcake," as a psychiatrist who reviewed one of his books described him.

Even though I knew Reich meant much more than the sexual act when he talked of orgasm, one thing that drew me to his theory had to do with sexual orgasm. People I knew had experienced peak moments by climbing mountains, meditating, and jogging. I'd even kidded a music-lover friend about having "orgasms" when key changes occurred in good concerts. But for me, no high had ever been greater than in sex. No orgasm had been nearly as dramatic or long-lasting as on the day before I became ill, but the combination of passion and compassion I'd experienced on other occasions was almost as good. In years past, I longed for it, even though I didn't know what "it" was exactly. And, after I'd had such a loving exchange, I found it to be all I'd hoped for. I always wanted more. There was something irresistibly compelling and incredibly powerful about my heart and pelvis in loving communion.

In addition to reading Wilhelm Reich's books, I had learned about his ideas from reading Alexander Lowen, a psychiatrist who had drawn upon Reich's theories to form a therapeutic system he called bioenergetics. How could I not be drawn back to Reich and bioenergetics now, given the strange phenomena I was experiencing? I had certainly never become ill after sex before, but I wondered if I had ever become ill following a positive, exciting experience. I recalled one occasion from my childhood.

Our family was friendly with the Curlees, who also had three children, two of whom were girls near my age. I liked them immensely. Their mother Dorothy was fond of me and I considered her my surrogate mother. They were as close to me as my own relatives who lived near us.

For a few years, one of our rituals with the Curlees was to attend the National Western Stock Show in Denver. The drive, staying in the Shirley Savoy Hotel, dressing up, eating out, the rodeo itself, all excited me. This particular year, around my eleventh or twelfth birthday, the Curlees invited me to spend the night at their house before we left. I was beside myself with anticipation.

During the night, my leg began to ache. I tried to ignore it, but eventually had to wake the girls, and they, in turn, their mother. I can still smell the Ben-Gay. I used most of a tube in hopes of banishing the pain. We drove to Denver as scheduled, but I felt miserable and spent the entire time in bed with a feverish flu.

One such incident probably happens to most children, and the flu is miniscule in comparison to lupus, but the circumstances were strikingly similar to those surrounding the onset of my lupus. The symptoms began at the height of good feeling (not after a disappointment, as might be expected), as if my system couldn't tolerate any more excitement or expansion. But, illness after *positive* stress?

Did we have to remain emotionally inert in order to stay well? That seemed absurd. And yet someone I knew developed breast cancer six months after her second marriage, which she describes as the happiest time of her life. Later I read literature which verifies precisely that: illness is just as likely to follow excessive positive stress as it is negative. It would be years before I *truly* understood that it was not necessarily the stress itself that was a trigger, but rather my body and mind's inability to accommodate to the stress. For example, while making love and during the following day, I had been in an exceptionally expanded state. My bodily system apparently could not sustain that expansion. So I had contracted. Grossly oversimplified, the disease reflected the contraction and some kind of imbalance that led to it.

It was all easier to understand when I viewed myself as a total energy system. I took in food and air and, after a series of complex chemical procedures, eventually transformed them into free energy. This energy could then be used in any of the processes of life: thoughts, feelings, or movements. Since all activity requires energy, my life was, at base, a continuous process of energy charge and discharge. The schema went like this: charge—tension—discharge—relief.

My weakness was so debilitating, I could hardly fathom how I could be sufficiently charged to feel tension, but apparently whatever positive energy I had, hardened into tension. Both my head and my body verified that this tension wanted to be discharged. But it took energy to discharge it, and I didn't have enough for that. Relaxation, paradoxically, required even more energy.

"How can prednisone be healing?" I wrote in a journal I began to keep, hoping it would help me better understand what was happening. "I imagine the best solution would be to find ways to slow my energy movement and to eliminate the tension." I had no idea what a big task that would be.

* * *

Throughout the spring, my journal was becoming my constant companion. I had some blind faith that introspection was not bad, that self-reflection could help. Knowing myself seemed important in understanding my illness, and writing was one way to know that self.

Here at the beginning, however, I simply recorded symptoms, hoping I could identify patterns of some kind. Although weakness and fatigue were my most abiding symptoms, others were evident. One day I wrote, "Cannot bend left elbow to comb hair in back of head," and two days later, "Right knee swollen and painful." In other words, in three days, the arm joint was fine and the knee symptom was new. Four days after that I wrote, "Chest pain" and "Cannot bend right arm." Chest pain, since it could indicate a return of the heart and lung symptoms for which I'd been hospitalized, was more worrisome. At first, Dr. Bird asked to see me whenever I had chest pain. After several trips, when no malfunction was found, however, I waited a few days to see if the pain disappeared before I called. By the time I was in the office, the chest pain was often gone, and a whole new set of symptoms had appeared. I knew that capriciousness of symptoms was typical of lupus, but I felt like a hypochondriac. My body was still wildly out of control. What symptoms would crop up next?

3

Asking the Questions

Late March brought vacation week at the college. I had been out of the hospital for a month. Vacation meant extra couch time to read, even though I could take in only small bits and had difficulty remembering what I read. I could grasp one idea clearly but could rarely integrate several at once.

I read anything I could find that addressed the questions which had begun to obsess me. Was disease random and devoid of meaning? Why did I get sick now? Why in this way? What was the relationship between my body and my mind? How did my psychic state affect my physical state and vice versa? My brain needed proof —scientific, objective proof. A period emphasizing rational awareness of my illness began.

Surely, I thought, there must be some talented writer who had been sick or had a sick loved one and wrote of that experience, autobiographically or in fiction. I would trust a writer's description of someone more than that of a psychologist who used labels like "helplessness prone personality." I preferred to be shown rather than told. John Gunther's book about his son's brain cancer, *Death Be Not Proud*, described his son's countenance as almost always cheerful. Gunther wrote, "Johnny was the only person I have ever met who, truly, never thought of himself first, or for that matter, at all; his considerateness was so extreme as to be a fault." A sweet, undemanding nature would be very pleasant for family and friends, but I wondered if such a personality could put up much of a fight against cancer. It seemed too brutal even to consider how a young child's personality might have predisposed him to such a serious illness.

Jessamyn West, in *The Woman Said Yes: Encounters with Life and Death* about her sister's cancer, wrote, "She was living the life the body she had been given had destined her for." That explanation seemed unhappily fatalistic.

I reread *The Sun Is My Enemy* by Henrietta Aladjem in one sitting. But my heart dropped, and I knew she would offer me no data on the subject so close to me when I read a dialogue in the last part of the book in which she discussed her recent remission with a psychiatrist. He said, "You don't seem to feel the need to be ill any longer," to which she replied, "No, I don't want to feel ill anymore. I never did. Why should anyone want to be sick?" Having been ill with lupus for twenty years, how could she not have at least momentarily considered the possibility?

When I read *My Second Twenty Years*, I thought I had finally found a kindred spirit, someone who had thoroughly examined the chance-versus-individual-responsibility arguments. Richard Brickner writes:

> Even if one happens to be the offspring of two psychiatrists, as I am, one is not necessarily convinced that accidents must be self-willed. The son of two psychiatrists, in fact, may resist the idea all the more; so may the psychiatrists. True, I was driving the car; I drove off the road, causing it to flip over. Still, when I return from time to time to the scene of my youth, I whisper into the wings to Freud, "You are wrong, there are accidents, pure and accidental." My accident happened with a suddenness beyond my control, out of the blue.

Later in the book he concludes:

> Ever since the accident I have been absorbed— impressed, entertained, stricken—by fate's outwitting of hope or hopelessness, by the brutality of coincidence or the pointedly inappropriate.

He had lived twenty years in a wheelchair. I felt respectful, for I was listening to an experienced person, one who had reason to contemplate the subject thoroughly.

As I launched into a debate with myself about the degree of my own responsibility for lupus, my conclusions sounded so final. They weren't, of course. I was at the outset of a long, involved process. I would constantly oscillate between the possibility of having caused lupus and believing it was random chance that I got it.

My therapist teachers had often been of the "we choose what happens to us" school. As I re-examined the choice-versus-chance question, I concluded that most of us think we have less power and control over our existences than we do. Yet something about the "we choose" philosophy seemed insufficient, peculiarly American, and at base, a denial of mortality, a way to avoid facing fear of death. Taken to its logical extreme, it meant that if I could choose what happened to me, could I not choose immortality?

The most constructive attitude when faced with a trauma like lupus is, "How can I get well?" Clearly, some illnesses and some accidents are the results of personal carelessness or ambivalent action. I wasn't so sure I had chosen my illness. *Causing. Choosing.* They both seemed such potent, and potentially punitive, words.

The exact medical cause of lupus is not yet known. One theory holds that it may be genetically predisposed, not inherited as a specific disease but as a tendency. Another says it may be caused by a virus, perhaps a latent one, caught, for example, during one of the common childhood illnesses like chicken pox and reactivated by current stress. Certain drugs can induce both laboratory and clinical symptoms of lupus. Whether the drug uncovers a person who has a lupus tendency or causes some change in body tissues which leads to lupus is not understood, but the symptoms and laboratory findings usually disappear when the drug is stopped, often within a few months. One of the older theories, still unproved in 1975, suggested that lupus and other rheumatic diseases are autoimmune, or self-allergic, diseases in which people become allergic to their own tissue. Tissue proteins are damaged so that normal defense mechanisms see them as foreign or "not self" and attack them. Or, the immune system, normally programmed to recognize tissues as "self" and not react destructively, develops malfunctions which cause it to attack body tissue inappropriately.

All these explanations seemed likely possibilities to me. Quite quickly, I was happy to attribute primary causality to genes and/or viruses and, therefore, to conclude that my psychological state or personal carelessness was not the primary cause of lupus.

All sources agreed that viruses and bacteria weren't killing off many people these days, that today's major diseases were stress-related. I sat bolt upright when I read in *Man Adapting*, one of several of René Dubos' books that addressed such issues:

> There is absolutely no question that one can over-shoot the stimulation of the endocrine system and that this has physiological consequences that last throughout the whole lifetime of the organism.

That we are exquisitely balanced organisms that get thrown out of balance in a variety of ways and, when off-balance, are more susceptible to viruses, bacteria, allergens, and carcinogenic chemicals made perfect sense to me. Disease generally requires a susceptible host. Lupus fit in perfectly as a stress-related illness.

Since they were the only factors I could hope to control, I began to explore *secondary* causes, the possible stresses related to my illness' onset. Perhaps I was responsible to the extent that I had chosen some of those stresses.

Normal body tissues, I read in a lupus brochure, could be altered by a variety of situations that put unusual stress on a person, such as a severe cold or the flu, worry and emotional upset, excessive fatigue, infections, and exposure to various chemicals. Any of these might lower a person's resistance. Review of the case histories of a large number of people with lupus had revealed that, in many, lupus started after a severe sunburn, streptococcal infection, major or even minor illness, or some other systemic stress.

What, I wondered, were my stresses? Why might a latent virus or genetic predisposition surface now? I wasn't the young wife and mother whose body broke down at its weakest point from the cumulative effects of staying up too many nights with a sick child, worrying about family finances, skipping meals, drinking coffee, and smoking cigarettes. I did not smoke or drink coffee. The only sickness my child had ever had was the common cold. I did not have to worry about balancing the budget, and, by my standards then (and by the average person's), I ate well—regular and balanced meals, including as much fish and chicken as meat, fresh fruits and vegetables (in the winter, more frozen), and few processed foods. I got sufficient rest and exercised regularly.

It seemed important to review events preceding January 19 minutely and see if I had created a condition ready for the onset of disease by January. I had a cap on a tooth replaced the day before the fever began. It was a simple procedure, done without medication. When they were unable to diagnose my illness, the doctors had suggested David call the dentist. He discovered that the dentist was sick in bed, too. Had I entered the hospital with a virus caught from him? Possibly.

During the summer of 1974, preceding that January, I had had the deepest tan ever and had spent many hours getting and keeping those bikini lines, something I had never done as religiously before. My snow-white skin made me seem only lightly bronzed next to most tan people, and some have theorized that light-skinned people are more vulnerable to lupus. That August, at the height of the tan, I had a strange, red facial rash and had felt weak and dizzy. The rash could have been the classical "butterfly" shape distinctive of lupus, over the bridge of the nose and cheeks, and I could have been carrying the disease then without recognizing it. The rash disappeared after several days, so I forgot about it.

Before I became ill in January, I had been taking Motrin, a mild anti-inflammatory medication, which has been implicated in drug-induced lupus. A month earlier, I had gone to an orthopedic specialist, after putting it off for three months, about an intermittent elbow pain. The doctor said it might be fibrositis, something in the arthritic category that my *Merck* manual said was not serious. Maybe it was an early signal of lupus, but again, I certainly didn't know that.

The pain first occurred after my own psychotherapy session. I had begun individual therapy a year and a half earlier. I wanted to address the issues that had arisen in my first venture into therapy with David a couple of years earlier. I also thought therapy was a necessary rite of passage to becoming a psychotherapist. Yet I still felt ambivalent about it. I'd been raised to believe that asking for help was a sign of weakness and that therapy was for crazy people. Solving problems without professional help and keeping family secrets meant you were "normal" in my family. My therapist, John, was trained in both Gestalt and bioenergetics. I had wanted a woman but hadn't come up with any locally.

Not much had been happening of late, perhaps because I didn't trust John. We hadn't spoken about this.

I remember parts of the therapy hour preceding the elbow pain as if they were happening now: I walked into John's small, informal office and sat in one of two director's chairs. I felt tense, frustrated. I can't remember what we talked about early on, but at some point, he asked me to hit the mattress with a tennis racquet, first yelling, "No," then "Yes," then "Die." "Why not?" I thought, shrugging my shoulders. There seemed nothing better to do. Maybe this would make something happen.

I stood in front of the fabric-covered mattresses, stacked two high, and picked up the racquet.

He directed me. "Put your feet a little farther apart, toes straight ahead. Hold the racquet with both hands, like this." He took the racquet and demonstrated. "Lift it straight over your head, so the racquet head will hit flat on the mattress, and so you won't hurt your back."

My first few smacks felt stiff. My voice grew louder as I shouted, "No." I felt self-conscious.

I was about to stop when he said, "Go ahead," in an encouraging tone.

Soon I began to get the rhythm and the flow of it. Each stroke became an undulating wave originating in my toes and moving with a slow, steady whoosh up through my torso and out through my arms and the racquet. I knew how to hit. I did it with ease. I saw an image of myself and my schoolmates on the softball field beside the schoolyard. I was ten. The pitcher had thrown the ball and it was coming in my direction. I tightened up. My arms pulled back to wind up. I focused intently on the ball. The racquet became the bat. As I pulled it down over my head, it smashed! A homer! And another! And another!

I began to hear the sound of my voice as I shouted, "No." The sound welled up from my toes, pulsing through me, and bellowed into the world. With each blow, my voice deepened and swelled. But I didn't feel angry when yelling it. Should I have? What came into my mind was, "You can't make me. I won't. I don't want to. Leave me alone."

"Why don't you try switching to 'Yes?'"

After several strokes, I noticed I wasn't hitting as hard and that my voice was slightly flatter and higher. Each "Yes" was less convincing. I was surprised at the change. I paused to tell him.

"We'll talk later," he said quickly. "If you stop now, you may lose your momentum. Keep going."

I turned to the couch and continued. Nothing changed. I had no images. My voice stayed flat.

When he encouraged me to switch the word to "Die," the change inside me was even more dramatic. The instant the first "Die" left my mouth, the energy drained from me. My voice went dead. I felt uninvolved. I became as self-conscious as at the beginning of the exercise. I was watching myself. I turned to him, "I want to stop. This has turned into a phony, stupid game. I feel as self-conscious as when I started hitting. 'Die' is an empty word. Empty. I want to stop."

I put the racquet down. "I feel disoriented and dizzy," I said.

"Bend over at the waist. Let your hands hang toward the floor."

As I did that, he added, "That's it, let your head hang loose. Bend your knees a little. Weight on the balls of your feet. Breathe. This'll help you feel your feet under you again."

After I sat down, John said, "Let's talk about what went on in you."

I talked about the baseball-field images, concluding with, "I like that feeling of power and ease with my body. That moment when I 'lose myself' in whatever I'm doing. It sometimes happens in a client's story, or molding a piece of clay. During sex, or in reading to Adam. There really is *joy* in it. A kind of celebration."

"And," he added, "also a sense of loss when the moment goes, as it always does?"

"Yes. But the memory remains. And the desire to feel that way again."

I felt a bit sad. Uncomfortable with that, I hurried on. "'No' felt better to me than 'Yes.'"

"Well, 'No,' 'Yes,' and 'Die' reflect important life themes. Usually we learn to say 'No' in life before we can say 'Yes' to it. Maybe you're in the 'No' phase. To me, genuine assertiveness is comparable to 'Yes.' Here is what I want, and I am able to ask for it. I have much less reason to be angry if I know what I want and am able to ask. Sometimes before people can do that, they often go through a stage in which they are angry about what they didn't get because they weren't able to ask. You've cried in this office, but we haven't seen much anger." He looked at his watch. "We've gone overtime again. We'll have to discuss this more next week."

The next morning I woke up with the sore elbow.

What did a hurt elbow and the Yes-No-Die exercise have to do with becoming ill? Did I stir up feelings and excitation that, in a Reichian sense, my system wanted to release but couldn't? Maybe I couldn't get into the feelings because they were at an emotional level I wasn't ready to entrust to this therapist.

Partly I seized upon the elbow ache because it was the only physical symptom I had just before the illness and because the elbow pain I had after lupus felt the same. It could have been the first identifiable symptom.

Somewhere I had read that if one could find the first moment, the very earliest one, when a disease manifested itself and examine that event in depth, the symptoms would disappear because they would no longer serve a purpose.

Later I would understand that the importance of examining any precipitating event was primarily because it led one to the underlying precedents, patterns which have likely been years developing. This was important. I would have to search for the subtle beginnings of lupus, the conditions that started small and grew over time.

I agreed with John that "No," "Yes," and "Die" reflected important life themes, that one must be able to say "No" in life before one can say "Yes" to it. Apparently, I was still in the "No" phase. "No" reflects anger, too. I was on the verge of more anger than I thought I could ever contain. In my inability to relate to "Die," I was as phobic as anyone else, totally out of touch with my own fear of death. "Die" could be examined from other viewpoints, too. It is an imperative. Figuratively speaking, my parents had to die before I could let go of them or let go of the inhibiting habits of theirs I'd adopted. "Die" could also be said to a husband, not because you wanted him to die, but to cast off dependence and domination. Spiritually, one must "die" to one way of thinking before accepting another.

Repeatedly I wondered if I actually did have the flu when I first entered the hospital, and was that the precipitating stress? Was it the sun? The medication? The physical exertion of that therapy hour? Or some unconscious emotional connection with the words in that therapy hour?

Perhaps all these could be sufficient to precipitate lupus. But I suspected they were not my whole truth. Even if these temporary stresses could fell me so powerfully, I thought I would be bouncing back faster if there weren't more factors involved.

* * *

I was shocked that I had become ill immediately after feeling so vibrant, so expansive and filled with good will. Was it coincidental that after feeling so intensely *loving*, the lining of my *heart* became inflamed? I also puzzled over the forty-eight-hour period of intense peace in the hospital. I had experienced that same special peace twice since the hospitalization, both on days when I felt particularly weak. Each peaceful episode was bracketed by fatigue, as if I had suddenly flipped from one level of awareness to another.

Once when I finished teaching early, I decided to pick up Adam. Why, I'm not sure, since I was weaker than usual. Very weak. Undoubtedly, I drove toward the day-care center from some combination of want and should. Walking up the steps I thought of an activity I thought I could survive: a trip to Elm Park.

Adam was excited at the prospect of going to the park. We drove the three blocks. I searched for, and soon fell upon, an empty bench, as tense, distracted, and hopped up as ever.

Adam began his usual forays into the environment. He circled away from me as one thing or another caught his attention and, intermittently, swooped back to touch base. "Mommy, come look at this tree. I think I see a squirrel's nest. Mommy, do you think those bumps are buds? Come look." I stumbled towards him, thinking that walking would do me good. It didn't. I couldn't see anything, much less appreciate it. All I could think of was getting back to the bench. I lunged toward it gratefully.

"Mommy, look at the swings with the chinning bars. Let's go over there." I mustered, barely audibly, "I'll wait here. I'm very tired today. You go and then come back and tell me about it."

"No," he persisted, poking his hand out. "You come." Tired was not in his vocabulary. I was all guilt, gritted teeth, and chewed fingertips.

The bench I was on faced a duck-filled pond and a small, wooden footbridge, recently refurbished by the city to resemble its century-old original. Adam climbed onto the bottom of the bridge and hung onto the end of the railing with one hand to balance himself as he leaned out over the water. He seldom had accidents, and the water was shallow, but I tightened anyway, thinking I should move closer.

Then, in the kind of flash that brought about the change other times, my inner camera lens opened. My fairy godmother waved her wand or gave me LSD, or so it seemed, since I had no other explanation. My inner turmoil vanished. My mind cleared. My adrenals stopped pumping.

No new energy poured forth to respond to Adam's enthusiasm, but my perception changed radically. When Adam said, "We forgot to buy bread. The ducks want some," not only did I see the ducks, all female, for the first time, but the grey and brown shades of their feathers were as infinite, as distinct, and as beautiful as the shades in a Monet painting. Adam pointed again, "Look at all those goldfishes. Next time I'm bringing my pole." I saw them, too, darting tangles of orange light. The sun reflecting on pockets of water in the breeze was like shards of splintering crystal. The intricate ironwork on the bridge railing resembled fine, old lace, and the symmetry of the planks on the bridge was exquisite. All were a fitting frame for my darling little red-jacketed son.

Within an hour, alas, my camera lens shut. I was back to driven exhaustion.

The transformation seemed magical. Was it tensing in response to the impending danger of Adam's falling into the water that pushed me across a subtle, invisible boundary? Had I finally given in to exhaustion? "Surrendered?"

Later I wrote in my journal:

Today I had another of those peaceful episodes. What a different way to live. Simple events of the moment become more meaningful. I no longer feel I have to give or produce to feel satisfied. Just last week a client said, "My father never told me he loved me until the day before he died." Someone else said, "My mother never forgave me until she was deathly ill." People sometimes become radiant, deeply compassionate, and forgiving on their deathbeds, as if they took crash courses in surrender. How does this relate to health and illness? Could lupus be a spiritual malady?

* * *

By the end of that week of April vacation, three months after the onset, I was full of new and nagging questions. After I returned to work in April, my couch time was primarily used to read and sort them out.

How stress worked seemed the next question to explore. I started reading Hans Selye. In *The Stress of Life*, he said that the body responded in the same way to all stresses with what he called a General Adaptation Syndrome (GAS).

GAS has three phases: first, an alarm reaction in which an outpouring of adrenal medullary hormones mobilizes the body's energy to meet the stress. If this reaction is successful in overcoming the injury, the body quiets down and returns to its normal condition.

If the stress continues, Phase Two begins in which the body attempts to adapt to the stress. Adrenal corticosteroid hormones, anti-inflammatory in their action, are produced. Energy from the body's reserves must also be mobilized in order to contain a stressor it has not been successful in eliminating.

Phase Two can go on for a long time, but eventually the body weakens and enters Phase Three, the state of exhaustion. The body can no longer contain the stress and breaks down. In this state people are less apt to tolerate a toxic experience than when the stress system is fully functional. I fit that description.

The hypothalamus, part of the system which reacts to stress, is also a control center for the major regulatory functions of the body, including the immune system. I understood this in no depth, but knowing it made it seem less surprising that I had a disease involving the immune system. One might get a cold from a momentary rundown condition while still in Phase One, but the exhaustion of Phase Three set the scene for a more serious and chronic illness such as mine. Corticosteroid hormones are produced by the body in Phase Two of the GAS, and this gave some credence to my fantasy that my body's supply had been depleted. Prednisone was as a replacement.

All this information made me reconsider my emotional state during the two years before my illness. Yes, I had felt increasingly out of balance, a slowly and subtly escalating tension, one that wasn't strong enough to call anxiety but which was close to it. My excess energy was invested in maintaining a facade of calm and emotional stability. The job reference my superior wrote at the college where I worked from the September preceding the illness to mid-1977 was glowing:

> During the seven years I have been Director of Counseling, Donna is, in my opinion, the best counselor-therapist we have had on the staff. She is an exceptionally competent professional in both individual counseling and therapy and group techniques.

Apparently I functioned well on the surface.

Inside was a totally different story. Tension slowly accumulated. Each day became one slow emotional contraction. Fritz Perls defined anxiety as excitement without sufficient oxygen. At the beginning of each class I was then teaching, my typical mild stage fright, which had formerly turned into excitement and relaxation after I got involved in the hour, remained stage fright and tension. I always tried to deepen my breathing to relax myself. The instant I stopped concentrating on breathing, I returned to shallow, erratic gasps. Sleep, which had also come increasingly less easily, diminished the tension somewhat, but the cycle would begin again the next day. Slowly during those two years, I had also lost the ability to cry.

I longed for some respite, for inner peace and quiet. Was illness, the physical breakdown of my body, the only possible way for my own physical and emotional system to find inner quiet?

Could I, given who I was, have taken any other route? Did I, after all, "choose" this illness? Was my body and nervous system a perfect host for it?

* * *

If recent chronic stress was important, I couldn't avoid examining my marriage. The stress for me was not that David and I had difficulties but that they seemed unresolvable. After a period when he relentlessly denied and I relentlessly nagged, we had doggedly addressed our differences.

Shortly after Adam was born, I'd dragged David to therapy. We stuck with it for several months. At the therapist's suggestion, David sometimes went by himself. This therapy was where he came to understand my desire for meaningful work outside our home, and I became more able to acknowledge my gratitude for his economic contribution.

I was surprised when David said, "It was such a shock that you weren't ready to have children when we married. I was thirty-four and ready. I thought marriage meant you were ready for children. I suppose that's unreasonable, but that's what I thought. Then I found out you wanted to work first. We didn't even discuss this before we married, did we? Of course, in those days, you didn't feel compelled to discuss *everything*."

"Perhaps it had something to do with how we got married," I offered. I'd dated David for a year and a half before leaving for Europe. He'd told me if I stayed there beyond that summer, he'd look for someone else. We'd stopped writing until shortly before I returned home, when he wrote to ask how to dispose of a trunkful of clothes I'd stored in his apartment. I wrote to tell him to send them to Colorado. I mentioned I was returning to the U.S., including the date and time my ship would arrive. He showed up at the dock.

Across the table that night at Umberto's, a tiny basement Italian restaurant in Boston which had been one of our favorites, he asked me about my plans.

Aided by the wine, and perhaps by the gigantic oil painting of Umberto's mother on the wall above David's head, I said gaily, "I'm going to get married."

"Whom are you going to marry?" he asked.

"Whoever asks me first."

He asked. I accepted. We eloped four days later. I had gone to Europe partly because David wanted to get married. I didn't know if I was ready for marriage or if David was the one. I came home ready for marriage. I hoped David was the one.

Much about our families was similar, but there were important differences. David's parents were companions, but not intimate verbally. I wanted a relationship more like my own parents. I liked the sensual, romantic quality in their relationship. They had their momentary battles, but there was lots of affection and warmth.

We concluded that I needed to understand why I'd chosen a man unlike my father in this way. David needed to explore his blocks to closeness, since he claimed that a large part of him really did want more. We drifted from therapy when we left for a trip. David was tiring of it, and I was tiring of pushing it.

In the coming months, we had more good will towards each other. We didn't seem closer, however. David continually said he couldn't change, which I didn't understand. You could change anything if you tried hard enough. I thought again about the two or three years before I became ill. I had been constantly trying—trying to change him, trying to change myself in order to change him, trying to change myself to accept him as he was. Nothing worked. I did not "cope effectively." My helplessness ate at me constantly. Prior to the illness, this was a chronic major stressor.

As Adam got older, we fought over different child rearing styles.

"You *never* set any limits with Adam. It's as if I'm the big, bad, mean witch, and you want to protect Adam from me. How do you expect me to feel warmly towards you when you do that?"

"How do you expect *me* to feel towards you when you're always harassing me?"

"You don't change unless I scream. You don't even try unless I practically bleed. At least when I yell, you make some effort for a few days. I don't like yelling any more than you do."

"Well, I can't stand it." This man of few gestures whipped his hand through the air like a sword. "I really *cannot* stand it. Your yelling alienates me more than anything else."

"But you're so passive-aggressive. You act out your anger at me by withdrawing your affection and then protecting Adam. It's almost like you send Adam out to attack me. Don't make him do your dirty work! I'm your wife. I don't think you care a damn about me when you do that!"

"If you think that all I do around here—*and it's plenty*—shows not caring, then you'd better think again!"

We looked at each other, open-mouthed. After a pause, he continued in his firmest voice, "Look. I am who I am." He shook his hands in the air, palms up, emphasizing his words. "Instead of trying to change me, you've got to accept me *as I am*. I love you. And *I can't change*."

I heard him. I too, wanted to be cared about just as I was. This longing seemed universal.

I thought about this in the days that followed. Did he really care? Was he saying "can't" when he meant "won't?" Perhaps beneath David's contentedness lay a deep streak of resignation; maybe his "can't" was genuine. It was easier to be angry at David than admit my own despair.

I was angry at him and yet dependent on him. David expressed love through caring actions, the day-to-day practical help I needed.

My parents, on the other hand, lived thousands of miles away, and I saw them infrequently. Childhood experiences—the horseback incident was a perfect example—were further away in time. They all seemed dramatic fairy tales I'd made up, completely divorced from present reality. I knew I needed to further consider my childhood to understand my habitual attitudes, particularly my you-can-change-anything attitude. As yet I had no inkling of how fully my illness would force me to explore that unrealistically God-like attitude.

* * *

Since I taught summer school at the college that first year I had lupus, vacation didn't really begin until August when we went to our house on Cape Cod. The Cape house on Flax Pond was close to David's heart. He'd bought the half-acre of land with his first savings as a young lawyer before I knew him. He'd built a Sunfish on the dining room table of the house he rented with some other bachelors in Worcester and bought the land on this fresh-water pond to camp out on and take quiet sails. Memories of fun-filled childhood summers spent on a similar pond near Worcester influenced him too.

The house, a four-bedroom, cedar-shingled Cape ranch, was built when we were dating. That summer David spent his vacation camped out in his car, serving as the carpenters' apprentice. I had suggested a cathedral ceiling. He said it was heat-inefficient and too expensive. Like David, the house was sturdy, practical, and durable—asphalt tile floor and one style of maple furniture throughout, purchased wholesale from a friend. Somehow, it seemed a violation of him to change the decor much.

Early on, there were only two or three other houses around, and the adjacent cranberry bogs and footpaths in the woods were trash-free. To Adam's delight, our house had become surrounded by a closely spaced cluster of modest houses.

"I love Flax Pond, Mom. As much as Dad. I wish I could live here all year."

"What do you like so much?"

"Oh, kids all over the place. I can go in anybody's house whenever I want. They hardly have any rules here." And, after a pause, "Nat's here. And Christopher. Peggy, too." Nat was an older boy who included Adam, and Christopher was a younger boy who followed Adam around, the son of the only neighbors we had much in common with and who were becoming friends. Peggy was the sweet, carrot-haired, twelve-year-old neighbor who had, since his birth, cuddled, walked, fed, and dressed Adam as often as she could, and who was now becoming his sitter.

Adam's voice suddenly sounded tense, accusatory. "Kids here have soda anytime. Nat had six bottles yesterday. And their mothers fix *good* food. I could eat hot dogs every day. And chips and candy bars. Rachel had four at once. Probably if I went to school here, there wouldn't be any homework."

For once I didn't get defensive. "Well, there would probably be homework. Maybe it would seem like less."

"And there's swimming and fishing all the time. Yesterday Nat and I caught three turtles, and I caught six frogs by myself. An eel got on his line by mistake. We might get up real early tomorrow to go fishing. Nat says the fish bite best then."

"No wonder you like it here."

I still played tennis when I was able and sat in the sun to tan, since I had read that only one-third of lupus patients are sun-sensitive. Sometimes I felt worse after the sun, but since the volume of my symptoms and their location changed every few days, even sometimes during a day, no real patterns occurred to confirm sun sensitivity. I had no rashes, and my doctor didn't think I was sensitive. I suppose it was confidence in my general health and the idea that if I acted well, I would be well that made me risk the sun. I was determined to maximize this power of positive thinking.

Even though I did not plan for guests and visitors, people dropped by on their way to or from Martha's Vineyard, Nantucket, or elsewhere on the Cape. Often they were David's bachelor friends and their dates. Those couples pitched in less than married couples. I never got to know any of them enough to want to confide in them.

Such social situations made me aware of my worsening emotional state. I still felt like a molting lobster. It was as if I had the discarded shell sitting next to me, and whenever people entered the room, I picked it up and threw it over me for the time being. They would see a fixed, rigid smile or a blank, dead expression. In my childhood, "Smile" was a frequent command, and to keep my mother from knowing what I felt, I made my face expressionless, playing dead.

A Reichian therapist would have described those expressions as masks. To accompany my masks I would force myself through attentive motions, sitting in ways that seemed attentive, asking questions related to what people said, and, if I could muster nothing else, repeating what they said, a cheap version of a counseling technique I had learned. It may seem strange that I would bother with such machinations after claiming to want to be left alone, but life-long habits are hard to overcome, and although I could not give, I wanted to get. Who would reach out to me if I told them to leave me alone? Intuition told me I needed nurturance—a lot of it. Of course, at this point, the kind of nurturance I wanted would never come from superficial conversations, but I didn't think about that.

Often when I was with other people, my mind was as uncontrollable as on the couch. Why couldn't I capture my thoughts? If I had been able to verbalize them, I imagine I would have been carrying on an entirely different conversation than that of the person with me, just like the crazies in the park.

Somewhere during this month, I also managed to squeeze in ten days of Gestalt training in Maine. I entered a program which would total 350 hours because I wanted to refine the therapist skills I already had, and since experiential training involved semi-therapy, I hoped I could further explore my "knots on the couch." These people were interested in the body/mind questions that absorbed me. I'd stop trying to engage David in conversations that weren't his bent. Training was also a legitimate way to be away from home without family responsibilities and, therefore, to rest, as much as rest was possible. At least my mind would be constructively focused.

I was lowering the prednisone doses by two-and-a-half milligrams weekly, as fast as Dr. Bird thought possible.

I entrusted myself to Dr. Bird, whom I now called Chris, quite wholeheartedly. He interpreted the severity of my symptoms. Although I felt somewhat stronger and less fatigued, I always seemed to have the same volume of rotating symptoms. Whenever prednisone was decreased, the symptoms temporarily escalated until my own adrenals adjusted. It was virtually impossible to distinguish between that kind of escalation and an increase in symptoms which indicated renewed disease activity. Chris often found it impossible, too, even though my bloodwork slowly and steadily improved. I had not come close to lowering the medication at the maximum rate possible, but it had been decreased from thirty milligrams in March to ten by July.

My instinct to continue to work—to stay in touch with normal life—seemed healthy enough. Work and training offered a sense of affirmation for, and connection to, life. I knew people who had become so depressed from illness that they lost their wish to participate in normal life: I felt pleased, even slightly smug, that I had retained that desire.

But this choice wasn't without conflict, and, I would conclude years later, inner conflict slowed healing. David had supported my career grudgingly, but his and my parents, of the women-should-stay-at-home generation, were completely against it. They would deny that, but whenever I didn't say, "Fine," in response to their asking after my health, they said, virtually without fail, "Maybe you're doing too much." If I followed that with, "I can't tell the college that I'll work when I feel up to it," their response was uniformly, "Then quit." I quickly learned to avoid the entire discussion. David's parents lived nearby, and they always helped me in the best way anyone could: they loved Adam heartily and invited us to dinner often. David's mother fed me lots of chicken soup. Nana and Pop's warm, consistent relationship with Adam during this time was a major reason I thought he might grow up relatively unscarred. Since I valued their support, as well as that of my more distant parents, working without it was hard.

I was edgy about societal norms now, too. In 1975, a woman's return to work after illness was not the first sign of health as it was for a man. If a man temporarily put less emphasis on home and fathering during his return to health, few would complain. A woman, on the other hand, was still expected to put home first if she could not be simultaneously competent wife, mother, and career person, although few people would really admit that order of priorities. I had carried all three roles gracefully when well, with little conflict with David. Whenever conflict had occurred, I had energy to deal with it. Now, with energy such a precious commodity, each inner skirmish, each tiny oscillation, was major. I resented these easy assumptions of others about what I "should" do and was aware that feeling resentful consumed healing energy also.

In retrospect, maintaining my job was still a defensible choice. Taking on the training was less so. But it met my expectations as an opportunity to deal with blocked emotions, to rest, and to discuss body/mind topics with interested people.

My family's way to resolve upsets was often not to focus on them. Instead, one should keep busy, and if that didn't work, do something for someone else. As a group, my relatives were strong, good people, maybe a little boring, but hardly martyrs. They seemed quite fulfilled and were generally robustly healthy. Observing them, I concluded that keeping busy and doing for others was good advice.

* * *

I returned to the office in September. Nine months with lupus felt like nine years. My weekday routine followed exactly the same pattern as when I first returned to work in March: from home to day-care center to office, then back home to the couch. The routine didn't vary for the rest of 1975. Listening to clients in my office, I became aware of an additional reason for continuing work: to consider ultimate issues. Client hours were the single occasion when I could genuinely listen to someone else. It was a relief to listen to others' feelings and emotions. Momentarily escaping my own turmoil and losing myself in theirs, I always hoped their inner experience might have relevance for me. Every hour spent exploring someone else's existence felt like an hour spent exploring my own.

My weekend routine, which had previously meant more time with Adam and David and more couch time, changed. During the academic year, the Gestalt training involved one weekend a month. Anxiety and guilt from being away from the family escalated substantially as Friday drew closer.

There was no change at all in the way I spent couch time. Reading took on even more importance because it was the only way I could keep my mind away from those dreaded emotional knots. Reading Anne Sexton's *The Death Notebooks* was a powerful pull at this time, although I did not want to know precisely why. When I tried to read professional literature, I quickly got a base-of-the-skull headache, or my right arm and entire right side became numb. Those symptoms did not crop up when I read things related to my inner existence or my illness, unless I read for too long at one time. I'd read a few paragraphs, close my eyes, and think.

I asked Chris' opinion about the relationship between stress and illness. He said, "I doubt there's much connection." I reworded the question and got the same response. This was prior to the time when people seemed to think stress caused practically any illness, long before lay people knew what psychoneuroimmunology meant.

Some Worcester residents believed you had to go to Boston for the best hospitals and doctors. To get the best of both worlds, I found a lupus specialist, Dr. Simon, an academic rheumatologist, in Boston. I planned to consult him occasionally. He was a short, friendly man about my age who'd come highly recommended. On our first visit, I'd found him to be both bright and humane. I liked him.

My second visit was scheduled while I was filled with questions from Hans Selye's work about stress and its effects on the body. The appointment was going well. He supported Chris' treatment plan and made a few suggestions about additional clinical measures Chris could use. He said he'd write him. Near the end of the time, I found an opportune moment to slip in my question.

I broached the subject carefully: "I've been fascinated by Hans Selye's ideas about stress and illness... you know, the General Adaption Syndrome?"

"There has never been an ounce of proof for Selye's work," he cut in knife-clear, his voice suddenly louder and sharp.

I felt stunned, totally thrown. I wanted to throw up my hands for protection and back up six feet. I certainly didn't have the nerve to reword my question and run it past him again. He was prestigiously educated, experienced. He was world-famous as a lupus specialist, a researcher himself. Who was I, with no medical training and an ordinary mind, completely new to this territory, to question him?

His response discouraged me deeply. I sought compatriots in the medical establishment, since I wanted to act on ideas that had some credence in the scientific world. It was almost the end of the year before I recovered from the specialist's blow. A decade later, he said he only meant there had been no specific research about lupus and stress.

Nothing seemed to be working in my favor to resolve the tense feelings. My stress was of the "imaginary" kind, the feelings that resulted remained locked in, and the whole process relentlessly pushed my adrenals to action.

Yet Selye had been perfectly clear: the only cure for adrenal exhaustion was rest. Genuine relaxation, not merely lying on a couch. That meant somehow getting rid of those bodily knots and the accompanying blocked emotions. Only then would lying on a couch be restful.

One relevant solution might be to shut off my mind, or at least to change it to other channels. I tried again to meditate, but the more I tried to focus or empty my mind (as I defined meditation then), the greater my resistance. I felt desperate.

Next, I advised myself to be with nature, to walk or take a

drive in the country whenever I had the energy. Good advice but useless. David was always game, but the power of the repressed feelings was so compelling that I could not focus on a wooded scene, however beautiful, for more than seconds at a time—and that by force of will.

Since I had always exercised, I did not think more about exercise as a tool. Chris and the lupus specialist said, "Do it when you feel up to it," and "When your joints are inflamed, don't move. Rest." They encouraged my work with statements such as "It's wonderful that you can," and "Lead as normal a life as possible." The Lupus Foundation booklet said, "...activity should be encouraged, as well as normal employment when possible...there is no reason why an individual gifted with athletic ability in one or many sports should not continue to enjoy them, as long as they protect themselves from the sun, if necessary, and from exhaustion.... An unnecessary lack of activity simply leads to increased weakness, boredom, and self-pity, all of which are detrimental to both the patient with SLE and her or his family."

As the first year ended, I was feeling increasingly trapped, unsure of which way to turn. I was a lupus initiate, embarked on a journey through a totally new territory, but without maps or compasses to know how to navigate.

4

Knotted Tight

By New Year's 1976 lupus had been my companion for almost
a year. I was still weak and had one symptom or another every day,
but since August I had taken no more than five milligrams of prednisone daily. That dose was considered side-effect-free.

There had been a few setbacks. In the fall, my eyelids had
become red and swollen, and as winter set in, my fingertips and
toes became sensitive to cold. If I touched an ice cube with my
fingers, they turned blue and stayed that way for an hour. Chris
diagnosed the latter as Raynaud's phenomenon and reassured me
that it was common in lupus and not serious. In December, I had
difficulty breathing. The pleuritis might be returning. Fortunately,
that passed.

I thought it was only a matter of time, six months or so, before
I would feel stronger and stop hurting altogether. Whatever the
source of the "repressed emotions" episodes on the couch, I hoped
that as my body healed during the next six months, the troublesome emotions would disappear.

I tried not to make much of the fact that my emotional facade
had become even more fragile: the lobster now often couldn't find
her old shell. Casual social encounters were becoming impossible.
Whenever I met an acquaintance or a neighbor in the grocery store,

I shook—a cold, electric current running up my spine and radiating shock waves to the outlying limbs. There was no chitchat in me. Hypersensitive and super-self-conscious, I could pick up the subtlest emotional states in others, and without my shell, I began to think people could see me as I felt: exposed bones and organs, skinless, so fragile that I felt my flame might be snuffed by someone else's breath.

When people asked how I felt, if I told them the truth, I had to deal with their reactions. For some, illness, like sex, was something you didn't talk about. For others, it showed weakness, and their responses exaggerated the self-blame I already felt. A few were clearly frightened they would catch lupus if they stood close to me. It was easiest to say, "Fine," no matter how I felt. Often their response was, "You look so good."

Even though I knew some people didn't look, some didn't see, some denied what they saw, and sometimes I really did look good, this reaction left me confused. Being told I looked healthy when I felt so bad made me think, "Maybe I'm crazy. Maybe I made this whole thing up," or "If I look healthy, I don't need to try to get well." I withdrew further, finding whatever comfort possible with fewer than a handful of people.

Rebecca, a new friend, was one of them. She, also, wrestled to combine career and motherhood, and her son attended the same wonderful day-care center as Adam. We lunched together every few weeks. Throughout the year, any number of luncheons were similar, but I recall one in particular shortly after New Year's at our favorite restaurant. That day, as on most other days, her general presence left a stronger impression than the details of her physical form. Only as she came within a few feet of me did I remember she was so short she almost fit under my arm. Once we were seated, I realized I was afraid I wouldn't be able to stop talking once I started. I decided to divide the time we'd allowed in half and would encourage Rebecca to talk first. I glanced at my watch. It was 12:10.

I pushed out a mechanical, "How are you?"

Rebecca was very down to earth. That day she was not so fine, and she recited concretely and clearly what had been happening, first with her son and then with her husband Bob. She had recently become assistant director of Family Planning in Worcester, her first full-time, paid job since Matthew's birth. She loved the job but was feeling overwhelmed. A huge grant was due in two weeks, and her boss, who was childless, wanted her to work overtime until then. She didn't see how she could and wanted to spend her evenings with her family.

Although she talked personally, she was not, of course, as personal as she would have been in her own therapy hour. I couldn't hear any other level of talk. I really wanted to say, "Shut up. I have no energy for you." Instead I ran through my listening repertoire: attentive mask, nodding head, and, since I missed half of what she said, guesses at relevant questions. I stole a glance at my watch occasionally. The base of my skull throbbed. For all the attention I gave my soup and salad, I shouldn't have bothered ordering them.

Finally my watch read 12:55. My turn. Losing my train of thought again and again, I talked nonstop nonetheless. The instant a word left my mouth, I couldn't remember it. My sentences were garbled or drifted into nothing midway. My best-kept secrets and blackest pain seemed all of me. I knew the pain only after the words spilled out, graceless and crude. The message underlying every word that left my mouth was, "Will you love me if you know I...?"

Rebecca's degree of warmth was invariably the right temperature. Whenever I dared to look, her soft, brown eyes offered a refuge. But I was thinking, how can she stand this? She hardly knew me before I got sick. Why would she want to know me now?

I was even more exhausted than usual when I returned home. And guilty. I was more tired for Adam.

Rebecca remembered luncheons during this time as normal enough. She didn't think I sounded incoherent, but then she was also one of the more patient listeners around. What I described as my blackest pain, she heard as "understandable concerns about mothering, marriage, and a little talk about health. Not much about your health, come to think of it." Apparently, my defenses were stronger than I thought. I did not reveal the real pain inside my shell.

Rebecca seconded the sentiments of Lois, a friend from graduate school days. "Again and again," she wrote years later, "I am struck by how well you hid your suffering, both physical and mental, from even those of us who considered ourselves close to you. As facades go, yours was a pip."

* * *

In its original version, my journal writing was equally as incoherent as my luncheon talk. Disordered phrases sputtered out, one on the other, and required several rounds of surgery to form a coherent sentence, to say nothing of an aesthetic one. Often there were lectures to myself: "Do what you can that is pleasurable. You enjoy cooking: do it. You haven't enough energy to work with clay as you used to. But putting a meal together can satisfy some of your creative urges, give tactile pleasure, and perhaps even help 'ground' you. Reassure yourself, through touch, of your connection with Mother Earth. Remind yourself that you can help sustain your basic existence. This is a way you can genuinely give to your family."

I felt a hint of those feelings as I cooked, as much as I could feel pleasure anywhere, but primarily I was lost to a deeper process as I made a meal. I was aware of it one day as I put a few zucchinis on the cutting board.

I decided what size slice I wanted and attended to the first few strokes. Then I drifted off, assuming the usual automatic process would take over, and a natural, easy rhythm would result.

Several seconds and perhaps fifteen slices later, I came to, startled. I was swinging the knife as if it were a machete and with the force required to chop a log. I was tense and holding my breath, aware that this last part was reminiscent of "coming to" on the couch.

I caught my breath, waited, and began again, concentrating intensely on the knife and making myself breathe slowly. By force of will, I made normal strokes, but the second I became unconscious of my motions and breath, I cut faster, more jerkily, and stronger. "Imagine," I muttered. "My imbalance extends even to cutting vegetables."

Several rounds of this were required to make a mere salad, and I was left exhausted. Innate coordination saved me from accidents, but the scene in my kitchen reminded me of watching a movie when the film is speeded up. It happened every time I cooked: I peeled carrots double-time and slambanged utensils wildly.

Always seeking to identify which emotions I'd buried, I examined my kitchen activity for clues and found one. I had, on rare occasion, caught myself slaying vegetables before lupus and had observed my mother and sisters doing the same thing. Was this how women in my family expressed anger?

* * *

Clues to my buried emotions began to emerge. My mind still wandered. My body still ended up in knots on the couch. But in addition to anxious feelings or masses of indistinguishable ones, I began to have specific feelings. It was becoming clearer that unexpressed anger turned to poison within my body. The advantage of acted out anger was that once expressed outwardly, it was, at least temporarily, gone. Undischarged, it continuously haunted me.

Lying in bed at the end of each day, I remembered, exaggerated, and worried over the negative experiences. Ten hours of work could go well: I would focus on the one that didn't. If one patient left therapy with me prematurely and twenty didn't, I suffered over that one. I did feel the positive experiences along with the other twenty, but good feelings left no imprint. I felt them only for the brief moments in which they occurred.

My emotional bottom line had become a tirade against myself. "It's your fault. You're not good enough. You must have done something wrong." Self-blame ran swift and deep. I tried to recall if I had always been self-blaming, if this part of my personality had only been covered by the shell I had lost.

All this reminded me that the medical autoimmune explanation of lupus was essentially one of self attacking self. Was I translating my emotional life into physical symptoms?

The image of being allergic to myself, of being physiologically self-destructive, was potent and negative. More significantly, the chemistry of the malfunction at the cellular level is monstrously complex; any simplistic explanation seemed ludicrous. Obviously, my fighter cells attacked the DNA in my cells, but that might have nothing to do with me psychologically attacking myself, except that I am intrigued by the metaphor because I tend to blame myself. However my blocked emotions related to the concept of my illness as metaphor, I still needed to resolve the psychological content.

I would have to explore illness as metaphor in other ways in the future. Using metaphor constructively, like taking responsibility for lupus without self-blame, seemed highly rewarding. I was determined to do both.

Day after day, self-blaming feelings tugged at me so powerfully that I felt compelled to keep trying to unravel them. I lay on the couch, frustrated, stuck in my head, piling theory upon theory, analysis upon analysis. I tried my own understanding of Gestalt polarities on my anger. Blocked anger might involve one aspect of myself (in this instance, the victim) and its antithesis (the attacker). The therapeutic task in resolving a polarity is to aid each part to full awareness while, at the same time, making contact between them. In this way integration and a new synthesis resulting from the clearer differentiation and encounter between the opposites, can occur.

I had yet to experience myself a process through which I had led certain clients who had solid enough emotional foundations to sustain it. When they felt self-blaming I might ask them to imagine, as part of themselves, one of the pillows on the couch in my office, thus making the victim and attacker separate. Then I encouraged them to say to the pillow feelings such as, "You're stupid," "It's your fault, and "I hate you." They might also hit the pillow with a foam-padded bat or tennis racquet.

Next I asked them to express the same feelings to whomever else the precipitating incident involved—or anyone besides themselves—as much to experience outer-directed anger as for accuracy. Early on in therapy, this might lead only to some working through of resistances:feeling afraid of anger or holding beliefs which prevent feeling or expressing it. "I can't feel that. I was never taught to hate," were typical responses. If that happened, sometimes we needed to clarify that the thought is not equal to the deed or that hitting the couch is not the same as hitting a person.

I assumed that patterns of self-criticism often stemmed from having felt chronically or powerfully criticized, usually in childhood and therefore usually by parents. As adults, we are so familiar with the criticisms we've heard or imagined, they become a part of us; the actual parent no longer need be present to instigate the feelings.

Just because I understood the process did not mean I could skip any steps. The victim in me had to become, if temporarily and in the safety of a therapist's office, the attacker of others. I was confident that the more I expressed the anger, the less I would feel the victim. Of course, the final goal of expressing anger at my parents wasn't simply to transfer blame from myself to them. It was to transcend blame entirely. Blaming them was totally unfair to them. It would leave me as much an angry, passive victim as blaming myself. I'd heal faster without blame.

I knew that experience precedes understanding, that I couldn't understand the blocked emotions until *after* I'd expressed them. My compulsive need to understand and analyze was partly avoidance; I was afraid to feel. But all my analysis served a positive function as well. It was preparatory. Knowing where I was and where I needed to go eventually gave me the courage to do it.

5

Abortion

January of the second year chest pains returned and increased. I took higher doses of prednisone and by mid-March thought I was again on more solid ground.

Our good Swiss friends invited us to visit during spring vacation. We hadn't had a real family vacation since lupus. I made plane reservations, sure that I could take it easy.

Three weeks before we were to leave, I discovered I was pregnant.

David and I wanted more children, but lupus slowed us down. I'd been using my diaphragm. We were waiting until the time felt right.

This was not the moment. I was taking prednisone and didn't know how that could affect the foetus. Could a baby flourish in a body in such turmoil? I could not be a good mother right now; I could barely give the child I already had emotional sustenance. David didn't want another child. He was sure he would have to take care of it.

Chris said there was some risk to the foetus.

Dr. Simon said, "Some lupus patients feel better during pregnancy. Others have exacerbations. Some have relapses afterwards. Some don't. In another decade, the data should be clearer."

"Can the baby be affected by prednisone?"

"Possibly," he said, looking up at me. "The data is unclear in this area, too."

Chris had also referred me to another lupus specialist. I'd travel anywhere to get help with this decision. The new doctor said prednisone would likely affect the baby. "And you have been taking higher doses recently," he said, tapping his fingers on the desk. "That's unfortunate."

A flare-up of the disease I could handle; the increased risk of a defective child I could not. He couldn't know that a decade later, research indicated predisone doesn't affect the foetus much. Neither could I.

I had a hard time even saying "abortion." Labeling it "therapeutic" did nothing to mitigate the emotional pain. It was the most difficult decision of my thirty-four years. The major reason I could live with the decision to have an abortion was because I believed that in a year or two lupus would be gone, and I could have more children.

Chris, my rheumatologist, recommended a vacuum aspiration, not a D and C. "Cutting the tissues," he said, "increases risk of infection. General anaesthesia is always more of a risk than a local."

The gynecologist I'd found, Dr. Pickering, insisted that the D and C and general anaesthesia was safer and that I should stay in the hospital overnight.

"Isn't there increased risk of infection when tissues are cut?" I asked, feeling a wave of nausea as I said "cut."

"Perhaps. But the vacuum approach is new. Sometimes the tissue isn't fully removed and the remaining particles can cause infection. Prednisone can make tissues softer and, therefore, more perforable. You need to be in a hospital in case surgery is necessary. I certainly hope it won't be, but just in case...."

I began to think that the intensity with which both doctors advocated their positions had more to do with their ego needs than with any medical truth. This was the first time I ever felt distrustful of Chris. I didn't admit, even to myself, how much this affected me.

Time was tight. David and I talked with other doctor friends. They favored the D and C. I was leaning toward vacuum, because

I could sneak out of town where I was unknown to do this terrible thing, because I still thought it safest, and because Chris would be there to help should I need it.

We were scheduled to leave for Switzerland in two weeks. The "procedure" had to be done before we left. That left only the following week.

Then I discovered Chris would be gone that week. That threw me. I felt much safer knowing he would be there. At this point, I didn't give a damn about Switzerland, but David wouldn't go without me, and I didn't want to disappoint him and Adam.

I decided to go with Dr. Pickering, and the D and C. Both methods seemed to risk infection. I felt much more secure in a local hospital. If there were any complications, I would at least have the *same* new hospital and *same* new doctor.

* * *

I went into the hospital on Friday, March 20, planning to work the following week and leave for Geneva that weekend. Admittedly, I was anxious about being able to do all that.

Everything went well. I left the hospital the following day, upright if unstable, grateful to have gotten through unscathed and anticipating the comfort of our warm and familiar bed and comforter at home for the weekend.

I asked Dr. Pickering about returning to work. He said, "Things have gone well. If you feel up to work, go. A decade ago, after childbirth and other surgery, rest was advised. Now we encourage moving as soon as possible. Even for someone with lupus that's good advice."

On Monday morning I did feel slightly weaker than usual, but only slightly. Familiar lines cycled through my brain: "If you think you're well, you are." "Get your mind off yourself." "Do something for someone else." I didn't feel reckless going to the office. But perhaps it was a way to push aside the sorrow and emotional pain of losing a child.

The day went well. I happily lost myself in my clients' lives.

As I drove home, I noticed that my abdomen, chest, and legs ached. I decided to crawl into bed right after dinner, and I did. The drama that followed was so bizarre it seemed unreal.

Around midnight, my temperature began escalating. I ached all over. Then I started shivering. Within an hour, all the blankets in the house lay on top of me. Yet I was still ice cold. I felt bewildered.

Soon I was shaking convulsively. My speech was incomprehensible. When David put a thermometer in my mouth, I inadvertently crushed it. I couldn't even spit properly to get the glass and mercury out of my mouth. Bewilderment turned into panic.

As David reached to dial the doctor, the lights went out. Electricity fails no more than once a year on our street. I felt paranoid. Someone was seeking to hasten my exit. But when David looked out the window, all the houses on our side of the street were dark.

"Gec...gec fashike!" I screamed, as David felt his way out of the room to go downstairs. After what seemed like hours, he stumbled back. No flashlight. One of Adam's current occupations was dismantling them. Even if David had found one, it probably would have been empty of batteries, since taking them out was part of Adam's play exploration. I suggested where David might look for a candle, my voice more shrill with each syllable. "Les uz sink. Lithing room, welow glas tagle. Hurry. Hurry." Freezing, flailing, incoherent, I never dreamed such fear was possible. This felt like a repeat voyage of a trip I did not want to take. I was sure I was dying. Like the first trip, it would be a wild and dramatic death.

After another desperate eternity, David returned with a lit candle and called Dr. Pickering.

"Get to the hospital immediately. I'll meet you there," he said.

My next round of shakes were grateful ones. This doctor would be there for me. Then David called Barbara and Imre to ask them if they would take Adam for the night.

After that, even with the candle, David was stumbling around the room, crashing into walls, seeming not to know what to do next. The sight and sound of me must have affected him. The candle undoubtedly illuminated a frightful apparition with clacking teeth, glazed eyes, and arms stabbing out from a mound of jerking blankets. I kept screaming, intermittently, "Helk me. Helk me. Helk me."

David took the candle and walked out of the room. Alone in the dark again, I really cracked. "What rr you doing?" I screeched.

"Dressing Adam."

Terror became crazed fury. A wild-eyed maniac, I shrieked, again and again and again, at the top of my lungs, "Craicor! Craicor! You gon't care if I gie! You gon't care if I gie." My husband was deserting me. If I were drowning, he'd make sure Adam was safe on the shore.

David called an ambulance. Afterwards, he said he wasn't sure he could handle me, but also that I insisted on it. I only remember thinking, why is he wasting time when there is a car out front? Can't he see I need help *fast*? This, too, I experienced as abandonment, total and complete. And I felt *more* rage.

Our old comforter, warm but extraordinarily heavy even for a king-size, seemed my only friend. I wadded it around me and staggered downstairs. The doorbell rang just as David ferreted his coat out of the closet, since we couldn't get my arms through the sleeves of my own. I insisted on the comforter on top of the coat and glared at David as if to say, "You idiot. Can't you see I'm freezing to death?"

The ambulance attendant at the door said, "Which hospital?" turned his back, and walked back to the van. He opened the door, grunted, pointed a finger at an empty bench inside, and offered no help as I stumbled up the steps.

Four uniformed men were inside; huddled forward, sitting on the benches, they all looked over six feet tall. They were joking loudly among themselves and with David during the ride. Since springs were sparse, and I was shaking so violently, the comforter kept sliding off. No one moved to pick it up. I thought to myself, Where's that idiot husband of mine?

One oaf must have opened the ambulance door when we arrived at the emergency entrance. I asked where the door was. No one offered a wheelchair, stretcher, or an arm. I careened wildly, comforter trailing across the snow, to the proper door, followed in the distance by an ambulance full of gigantic, useless hulks.

"Don't bother with them," I told myself. "You've got more important things to deal with."

The doctor arrived at the hospital simultaneously with the ambulance, took one look, and said to David, "She's obviously toxic and in a state of delirium. Endometriosis—inflammation of the

67

pelvis—not unheard of in a lupus patient, since the immune system can't be trusted to respond normally to trauma in the body. Prednisone slows down—and interferes with the body's defense against infection. I was injected with something, but I was beyond figuring out what.

No beds were available in the proper unit, so I was left in the emergency-ward cubicle. I was still very cold but began to shake less. The nurse could not find a vein for the intravenous. My veins are often elusive, and I'm not squeamish about needles, so I felt patient the first two or three times she came in, each time staying several minutes and making a few unsuccessful punctures.

During the next hour, she returned a few more times, still missing my veins. I needed antibiotics fast. I was beginning to panic again. I presumed that if there were other nurses around, she would ask for their help. I asked her. There were no other nurses. I asked her to get a doctor's help. The intern on duty made an unsuccessful attempt, then gave the needle back to the nurse.

I thought if I kept showing confidence in her, this nurse would eventually succeed. Given the volume of stabs she was administering, even a poke with her eyes closed should eventually connect. I lay there wondering why I was not insisting that she get some help. I thought, "Well, she's trying hard."

"Nice little girl," said the me who is my own therapist. "Still hoping that if you don't express your anger, Mommy and Daddy will love you. Beware, it's never worked."

After her eighth trip into my room and what seemed like the fiftieth puncture, my patience and my veins both felt like they were collapsing. She finally succeeded and told me she was applying to medical school. I imagined her to be a total imposter. She was not even a nurse. She was a psychopath who had forged papers and charmed her way in, intent on killing us all.

Two or three days later, when I was strong enough to think clearly, pain-free and without temperature, I asked Dr. Pickering what was flowing through the intravenous tubes attached to my arms.

"Solu-Cortef," he said, "a form of hydrocortisone for intravenous injection. An ordinary infection in a lupus patient usually activates lupus, so both must be treated. And we're giving you antibiotics, Gentamicin and Penicillin. We'll switch you today to Ampicillin, which can be taken orally, so that you will be able to continue it at home."

Somewhere I recalled reading that lupus patients were often allergic to medications, because the immune system was out of whack. "What if I'm allergic to those because of the lupus?"

"Well, you could be. But what else can we do?" He shrugged his shoulders.

The next day my hands and feet became red, puffy, and itchy; my body prickly and hot. No one was willing to guess about the origin of these symptoms, or if it were an allergic reaction, to guess which of the three antibiotics might be the culprit. Had *three* really been necessary? Ampicillin was the most likely possibility. The symptoms began the day I was switched to it.

The symptoms were annoying but not unbearable. Benadryl, an antihistamine, was recommended to alleviate the itching. If I took that and had a new symptom, it would be difficult to tell if it were lupus, the antibiotic, or the antihistamine. I didn't use it.

Before this, my symptoms had been fairly predictable. I hadn't really thought about secondary complications in lupus, drugs needed for those, possible allergic drug reactions, and more drugs for those.

This hospital room seemed even drearier than usual. The silver sheen of the mirror and its metal edge evoked images of knives, slicing, scraping. Blank beige walls reinforced my feeling of emptiness. The view from my window was of dirty, beat-up, brick-building walls. If greenery or other signs of spring were visible beyond them, I didn't see that. The intensity of the middle-of-the-night drama took its toll. A soaring temperature combined with cold, shaking, and pain, a lightless house, the ambulance ride, inept drivers and nurses—all of that happening at once left me feeling desperately helpless.

My mind returned to the scene with those five useless ambulance men. Why on earth had I not said something to them? Rage, together with my amazement at being able to walk in that condition, made me fearless of their size and number. Even if the intensity of my rage would be more than they deserved, so what? David had gotten much more of my anger than he deserved. Those creeps meant nothing to me. I needed them for nothing after the moment they left. I couldn't decide if my silence was wisely avoiding unnecessary stress or one more way to rationalize my fear of confrontation.

These days, whenever I got angry and didn't express or do something constructive with it, I worried. Not speaking up to the ambulance men or to the incompetent nurse were only the two most recent, glaring examples of what I feared validated the self-destructive metaphor of my illness. I was becoming more convinced than ever that unresolved anger was physiologically destructive.

David and I could eventually forgive each other's behavior that black night. We couldn't share our grief about the abortion. I felt incredibly sad at the loss of a wanted child; David felt relief.

* * *

When I left the hospital I was weaker than before, but not as diminished as after the first hospitalization. I walked unsteadily to the car but could open the car door. I was discouraged, however. It had taken me a whole year to lower my prednisone dosage from forty to five milligrams, and here I was back to taking forty.

We did not go to Geneva, of course, but I was back on my feet the Monday morning after vacation week with the rest of the staff.

I walked through my office door. The unwatered plants looked miserable and weak. The cyclamen's leaves, like tiny wads of wrinkled, brown parchment paper, dangled helplessly over the rim of the red clay pot. Wiping my finger through a layer of dust on the brown desk top, I sat, glassy-eyed, and stared out the picture window. This had been no vacation, no way to renew an exhausted body or get that wolf lupus to retreat. The next few days I saw more clients than ever, so that I wouldn't be able to think about what had happened.

Soon I was back to my weekday routine and back on the couch. Occasionally, I asked for Adam's help, which brought back memories of my own mother's couch requests. To my "Would you please...?" Adam might say, "When I wanted to play catch yesterday, you said you were too tired. So I'm too tired today." That left me speechless. Or he might say, "You picked me up at the Center today, Mommy. You're not sick." Those words knotted my belly even more. I was glad he did not view me as sick. On the other hand, I didn't want to raise a selfish monster. It wouldn't hurt the child, on occasion, simply to *obey*, even if a person wasn't sick. Under the best of circumstances, it is difficult to help children be thoughtful about helping others. How could I help my son become generous?

To avoid inner conflict, I learned not to ask. I tried to forget my exhaustion in a familiar way: losing myself in thought. I reviewed what had happened. Taking responsibility for my body was beginning to weigh on me. I had exhausted myself trying to make the best possible decisions at every step along the way, with terrifying results. I felt like giving up, sliding into cynicism and nihilism, wearing blinders and ear plugs, flipping a coin or letting whichever doctor was on hand make my choices. At least if I gave the responsibility for my body to others, I could blame them when things went wrong.

These couch thoughts were peppered with emotional baggage. I felt sad or anxious or angry, yet wasn't expressing any of those feelings. I'd told Barbara about my messy emotional state, but since I put on such a decent front, she probably didn't take me too seriously. One day I said, "There's a debate I'm reading about whether feelings people have during illnesses *result from* being ill or are *released by* the illness."

"The feelings you have on the couch are the released kind?" she asked, patiently trying to follow this topic in the depth I wanted.

"I think so. Repressed and suppressed feelings are that kind. People with chronic illnesses often feel resigned and depressed. Did resignation and depression help lead me to lupus — or multiple sclerosis or myasthenia gravis or whatever — or does having lupus make me resigned and depressed?"

"Well," she responded, after thinking a moment, "it's natural to be upset at being ill. Emotional regression is pretty common during any sickness. When my twelve-year-old gets a cold, he acts about four. The few times I've had minor illnesses for even a few days, I get depressed. I'm an active person. I can't stand being laid up. It's got to be fifty times worse with an illness like lupus."

"Well, it's certainly simpler to think of lupus as a werewolf and myself as the innocent victim. It's much easier if I can explain my feelings as resulting from something over which I have no control."

"You mean if lupus causes depression, it's easy not to take any responsibility for being depressed."

"Exactly. But then, if depression helps bring on lupus, it's easy to lapse into self-blame," I said, raising my hands in a gesture of futility. "As you know, that's my tendency."

* * *

As summer approached, my worries about being on medication forever proved unjustified. Not only was I able to lower prednisone at the maximum rate possible, but I was able to lower it to below ten milligrams in April. In July, I stopped taking it altogether.

It wasn't time for celebration yet. In July, and then again in August, my eyes turned heliotrope and puffed up until they were almost shut. Adam was suddenly solicitous, offering to help. To him, these were the first times I'd ever *looked* sick. Because my eyes had become red and swollen before (although less severely) and temporary doses of prednisone had removed the symptoms, I didn't worry.

In a few more months these last symptoms would disappear for good. All the symptoms I had now were the least serious ones: generalized aching and weakness, skin rashes, arthritic-type muscle and joint pains, swelling and stiffness. Heart, lungs, digestive system, lymph glands, spleen, liver, menstrual periods, and nervous system could be affected. I had experienced only heart and lung symptoms, and those only at the very outset. The more recent lung scares had proved to be nothing.

I felt even more confident when I considered all the possible side effects of prednisone. I had none. I hadn't even had much of the common Cushingoid state, a moon-shaped face.

Throughout that summer, I swam and played tennis, never as much as I would have liked but often enough to sustain my confidence. Adam sustained it, too. Each time he saw me swimming or playing tennis, he noted, "See, Mommy, you're not sick any more." Unfortunately, his comment also reinforced my tendency to think one good day meant lupus was behind me forever.

David said little but generally accepted my invitations for tennis or extended them himself. In our relationship, tennis had special significance. It had been a major form of the companionship David treasured. He belonged to the Worcester Tennis Club, composed mostly of old-line natives who were seasoned players. Recently David claimed that he played with me there in the early years of our marriage only because I was so pathetic no one else would. By now, however, I could give him a fairly decent game.

One evening when we'd agreed to play, I asked, "When can we do it?"

"I can get away around 4:30, but the Club will be crowded then."

"How about at 6:00? Brenda will be home, and the courts start emptying out then."

"Okay," he said.

We headed for the courts after a snack.

Our game was always the same. David was bigger, stronger, better. It was the cat teasing the mouse, a hint of amusement flashing in his eyes as he watched me scramble for his smartly placed, cagily paced shots. I had never beaten him, but often teased that my relative youth and hours of practice would soon close the gap. •
Actually, winning was secondary to me. I enjoyed stretching to hit every ball that landed in the court, simply because it came naturally. I never tired of feeling the graceful flow of my body. It was as exhilarating as hitting homers at age twelve.

Between games, as we changed sides, David glanced at his watch. "We've played almost an hour," and, after looking down at me, "Your face is beet-red. Should you stop? Sometimes you regret playing too long."

I stopped and took time to attend to my insides. I was wet with perspiration, but so was David. It was very hot and humid. I decided I was okay. "Besides," I said, undoubtedly flashing a quick grin, "you're only ahead five to three. Who knows? I might win another game. Let's play one more."

David looked frustrated. "Well, if you think you've got the stamina ... "

"Just one more," I said. With me, it was always just one more.

David finished me off quickly, six to three, but I still ended up overtired and awake all night with a headache. The only way to play tennis, I decided, was to set an alarm for one hour and promise to stop then, no matter what.

Exercise—in the form of tennis, at least—didn't make me feel relaxed. Now I never relaxed. Sometimes I needed two days to recuperate. I believed exercise which was enjoyable worked best. Yet, was this too strenuous? I could play only a running game. I found it so hard to limit the time. Should I not play at all?

By August vacation, I had been off prednisone for two months, but I was losing confidence that my troublesome emotions would disappear. Some of the horror shows I usually kept returning to had diminished—I remembered, but didn't constantly rerun, scenes of the ambulance men and incompetent nurses—but my body on the couch was more tense than ever. I stewed about that and the emotions which caused it.

The Lupus Foundation booklet may have scared me. It said:

> The neurological and psychiatric manifestations of SLE (systemic lupus erythematosus) may be especially disturbing. Central nervous system symptoms can appear as almost any neurological or psychological abnormality. There may be focal (localized) or generalized seizures; hemi or quadriparesis (weakness of the arms and legs on one or both sides of the body); abnormalities of the sensory nerves, causing tingling sensations; or abnormalities of the motor nerves, causing weakness or a decrease in ability to perform normal movements.
>
> Psychiatric symptoms also mimic other psychiatric diseases, such as manic-depressive, psychosis, schizophrenia, or organic brain syndrome; they can include withdrawal, delusions, auditory or visual hallucinations, paranoia, severe depression with feelings of worthlessness, and impairment of memory, orientation, retention or recall. In addition, wild mood swings may occur.... It may be difficult to determine if the abnormalities are caused by SLE, steroid-induced psychosis, or the "normal" problems the patient has in dealing with a chronic illness.

At my next appointment with Chris, I said, "I feel tense and depressed all the time. Do you think my central nervous system is beginning to be affected by the lupus?"

His eyes opened wide, looking as if I were daft for even asking the question. "You have no idea what a lupus psychosis is like!" He sensed I needed reassurance and added, "You seem quite normal to me. Anyone with this level of illness gets depressed. You seem to deal with it better than most of my patients."

"But feeling so tense every hour of the day can't be healing. I'm angry and sad all the time. Could this be a side effect of prednisone?"

"Yes. It could be."

As I left his office that day, I felt relieved. If prednisone caused this tight body and emotional garbage, the tension and depression would stop when I got off the medication. But then I remembered. I'd already been entirely off the medication once. My emotional state and tense body stayed the same. Prednisone wasn't the main culprit.

With each passing day, I felt more cornered, forced to acknowledge that whatever solutions I had tried in the past weren't good enough; I couldn't muster up old defenses. I felt more shell-less than ever. For brief moments, I thought I wasn't going to get rid of my physical symptoms until I resolved these emotions, as if the stress of them kept the disease alive. I recalled proverbs repeated to clients: "The best way to heal a wound is to suffer it to the full," and "The best way out is through." I wasn't sure either way was necessarily "best," but my other options were running out.

6

Tough Skin

I began to teach a graduate course in Gestalt therapy and loved it. Whenever I became the least bit stronger, I committed the energy somewhere outside myself. By healing the world, I would heal myself. I wondered if doing for others was what I needed at this time , but the opposite path seemed so inordinately selfish, I couldn't consider it.

I also decided to resume psychotherapy with a woman therapist. My sister cautioned, 'Maybe you wouldn't have become ill if you hadn't begun your own psychotherapy. You certainly seemed to have opened Pandora's box."

But my emotions were blocked, and as a therapist myself I knew I needed to deal with them.

Ildri was a Norwegian, fifteen years older than me, a psychodramatist who was now studying bioenergetics. Her office, with a mattress for bodywork and the bioenergetic sawhorse with a rolled up blanket on top, showed she did bodywork—which I was a little shy of. There were also two batakas for hitting the couch and, on a small stand, the ubiquitous clock.

Ildri took the smaller chair. As I sat down in the Eames chair, it wobbled. The plants outside her door had looked ill-tended too. That didn't bode well for the quality of care rendered. At this time,

I didn't see this strong pattern in myself: when I was afraid, instead of feeling the fear, I turned critical. First-session jitters became snap judgments about plants and furniture.

Soon I relaxed a little.

Surprisingly, since it is a traditional cornerstone of therapy, the subject of my parents had rarely come up in my former therapy. Immediately, Ildri and I began to explore my childhood.

I'm sure I began with my standard opening line, "Essentially, my family was child-centered, and my parents were very caring and protective." Then I stumbled, coming out with something like, "The most memorable of my mother's comments concerning my birth, barely 10 months after my parents' marriage, were, 'Our birth control techniques should have been better,' and 'I didn't nurse you because you bit me so hard I bled.'

All Ildri said was "Yes," and again, "Yes," expectantly. Her eyes were warm and concentrated. After this glance, however, she faded into the background. She was there to shine the spotlight on me, to illuminate my personality, my life issues, my thoughts and feelings.

I continued. "My mother describes her childhood as happier and easier than I think it was. She was the oldest of five daughters. Her father was a minister. Her mother became crippled in a car accident at midlife. She must have had a lot of family responsibility growing up, although she vehemently denies that."

"You think she had a much more difficult childhood than she lets on? It sounds like she denies a lot."

"Yes." Tears began to leak out my eyes and then stream down my cheeks. I was amazed that I cried so easily. How could I, who approached women so cautiously, trust a strange one so quickly? I couldn't admit the extent of my overwhelming need. My tears must have reflected my immense relief at the mere potential for help in this trying time.

Ildri was about to speak, but I rushed to change the subject, feeling awkwardly compelled to say something about "oral" and "anal," since this was therapy. "My mother wasn't overly worried about getting food into me or bowel movements out." I paused again, then continued. "I wonder if she appreciated having not one, but three fetching daughters competing for the attention of her handsome, new husband?"

"Maybe your mother was jealous of her daughters," she said. "We can explore that later." She was about to say something else when I interrupted again.

"My father had six brothers and sisters. Closest in age were his sisters, and they mostly raised him. He was always at ease with women. He called each of his daughters 'Sweetheart,' and it was easy for me to be soft on him. He was a successful rancher, and we all rode and did the work any boy would. Although he was a tough task master when we worked cattle, he always seemed to have time to pick up a child, pet a dog, or point out a deer or prairie dog when riding horseback or driving the car." I hesitated. "About when I turned twelve, he became a buffer between me and my mother. A lot of mornings I left for school in tears from a battle with my mother."

Near the end of the hour, Ildri summarized the therapeutic issues as she heard them. I forgot her words but felt she understood me. That was more important than anything else.

As I stood up to go, I glanced at Ildri once more. Her baggy, handwoven blouse and slacks made her seem very bosomy. I visualized losing myself in her blouse's soft folds. Although I was far from acting on the impulse, my arms wanted to reach out longingly, to say, "Mommy, Mommy, I'm so glad you're here." Nurturing of the kind we used to call "mothering" was what I needed. Her attention seemed like breast milk.

*　*　*

In the next session, Ildri asked if I would like to explore my parents using fantasy, and I agreed.

She asked me to close my eyes, directed me to relax, and told me to think of my parents. I visualized the painting by Grant Wood, *American Gothic*, a copy of which I thought hung in my parents' living room. I told Ildri and described the image before me: "I see faded green-gray tones, torsos and heads of a simple and austere country couple, plainly, drably dressed. The man holds a pitchfork. Its prongs stick up between the couple in the background."

My mind drifted. "My parents run a ranch in Colorado, but their look and attire couldn't be less like that of the couple in the painting.

"Their appearance is important to them. My mother dresses classically, fashionably. She wears lots of gold jewelry. My father has become a sharp dresser, too. We tease them about the number of suitcases they travel with." I thought about the painting again. "The woman in the painting has long, straight hair pulled back severely in a bun. She looks wiry, thin, and stern. My mother has thick hair, stylishly curled. She's curvaceous, looks younger than her age, and hardly stern. My father resembles the man more. There is a hard-working, determined quality in both men's faces. They seem strong, a bit stiff.

"Grant Wood's farm couple look as if they lead a quiet, insular life. My parents travel. They're well informed about world affairs. The farm couple looks bushed from a hard day's work in the fields together, ready for bed. Even before retirement, my parents loved socializing with other couples. They relish congenial conversation, good humor, and, if dining out, ballroom dancing. They're quite good."

Ildri encouraged me to stay with the image longer. "Try looking at it up close."

I focused again, zooming in like a camera. I was always drawn to faces in pictures, and this was no exception. I was amazed at what I noticed: "The skin of the couple in the painting looks like leather," and I practically shouted, "Leather! " But no associations came. I felt stuck. Eventually I opened my eyes.

Ildri asked, "What are the qualities of leather?"

"Well, leather is impenetrable and yet flexible, like my leather jacket and the wine skin we use on ski trips." Then my breath caught, my hand was in the air. I visualized the faces again. After several more seconds, it was clear. "Something about my father resembles the man in the painting. Daddy's soft-hearted, but he also has a 'tough hide,' like most people who spend lots of hours outdoors. That hide seals up emotions." I paused. "He and his older brother have been business partners for nearly fifty years, and Dad boasts they've never had an argument. Can you imagine that?"

Excited at unraveling this mystery, I spoke faster. "But my mother's skin is the opposite. Soft as a baby's. She's too vulnerable. I've never seen a woman her age with softer and more wrinkle-

80

free skin. It's hidden under makeup, however." I paused, confused. "Well, I suppose makeup has an impenetrable quality, although in a different way than leather." Another pause. "But emotionally she's impenetrable. To the world outside her home, Mother's stance is, 'Be brave and look pleasant. Always turn the other cheek. Never show hurt.'"

Tears rolled down my cheeks—tears of recognition, tears of love. "Their styles were very different, but their message was the same: *contain your pain.*

I glanced at the clock: the time was almost gone. "There are advantages to that style of dealing with pain," I added.

"Yes. It was more typical of your parents' era. You don't burden others with your upsets. You avoid cycles of putting anger out, getting it back, and not getting anywhere. But there are disadvantages, too."

A few weeks later, I lay on Ildri's couch. She asked me to express my desire for help with my arms. I couldn't reach. Or I wouldn't. If I asked for help, I felt humiliated. When I finally did reach out, slowly enough to allow myself to feel, my arms hurt. The experience occurred many times. Reaching out for help and love was as much a problem as striking out in anger.

One set of shoulder muscles that routinely hurt was the rhomboids, commonly known as the "military muscles" since they facilitate rigidly straight posture. "Stand up straight" was a frequent command in our household. We were not particularly round-shouldered, but a square-shouldered look was valued. It seemed no accident my arms and shoulders would hurt, even without lupus.

I felt stuck. My father had saved me from my mother, so he was above reproach. I said I was angry at my mother but had no bodily sensations to accompany my words. The instant I talked of anger at her, I began to think about why she was the way she was, how we all were products of our own life experience, how she had done the best she could, how I could not be angry at anyone who hurt me unintentionally. I tried to understand and forgive her *before* I felt anything. Genuine forgiveness probably wasn't possible until after acknowledging and resolving negative feelings, but I wanted to skip that step.

"You know," I said, "I know better, but I still view my blocked emotions as 'negative.' I want to banish them as if they're poisons. They roll around inside, infecting me."

"As I see it, the goal is full expression of emotion," Ildri said. "All emotions. That means more than expulsion. It means you can be angry, sad, frightened, or joyful *depending on the situation*. The powerful passions contained in negative emotions can be redirected into more constructive channels. Venting anger in the safe space of the therapy room will make healthy assertion easier elsewhere. Anger can be purifying. Compassion and gratitude detoxify fear, anger and pain."

"Compassion! Gratitude! That's what's at the core!" I concluded excitedly.

As I opened the car door to head for home after that therapy session, thoughts zipped through my head. My emotional state would become more flexible, and so would my body. Viewed as a single cell, with my skin as its membrane, my body could become pliant. Lupus was a connective-tissue disease. The entire body has connective tissue in it, of which muscles are a part. As my muscular and ego defenses lessened, muscle tissues, which had hardened into rigid and sometimes painful patterns, would become more flexible and free of pain.

Gestalt, psychodrama, and bioenergetics—active, expressive modes—offered the fastest way to work through locked emotions. "Talking about" feelings had healing effects: knowing someone else understood me and that I was not alone was important. But passive approaches posed risks for me. If my body wasn't involved, therapy might be only a mental and emotional recycling, none of it experienced on a bodily level. My feelings could be merely controlled or explained away; the methods could become subtle forms of suppression. More important, frenzied as I was, I simply could not sit still to use a meditative approach, and I was already "too much in my head" for the cognitive one.

Adding body work to verbal therapy seemed positive in every way. Ildri and I had already used the bioenergetic stool for lying and standing exercises which emphasized breathing. Some of my clients called it the "torture stool," because stretching unused muscles can be painful. One leans over it, usually backwards, in a variety of positions to expand breathing capacity. Where it hurts is usually where one is energetically blocked. Feelings and memories associated with that location pop up along with the pain.

*   *   *

In the therapy sessions with Ildri throughout the fall, my anger was still strongly blocked. During that hour, I could get close to the feeling, but it was driving home sometimes I felt it fully: a bolt of hot lightning shooting up my spine, my shoulders hurting, and my extremities remaining cold. I still felt no impulse to hit or yell.

Soon the bolts shooting up my spine got even stronger. Anger intensified to rage. Some days I felt like a mass of rage in search of a victim. I felt violent, a closet killer. I reran the story. During the two years before lupus, I was more tense more often. My tears dried up. After lupus was diagnosed and throughout 1975, the tension increased. I could not identify the thoughts that created the tension. I could rarely identify specific feelings. By 1976, when I was sad, I knew it. I was able to cry. Then I'd become paranoid and self-blaming; now I'd also moved to anger and that escalated to rage.

As the tension turned to anger and accelerated to rage, what had earlier been faint contractions of early labor moved to hard labor. The forces seeking release and those resisting release were now equal in power and locked in grueling battle. I became even more silent and frozen on the outside, as if my energy gathered force by whirling toward the vortex in me. The more I held back rage, the tighter were my fists and arms, the tighter and more drawn back my shoulders.

Overwhelmed by the intensity of these feelings, I groped for other explanations. Marilyn French in *The Women's Room* wrote, "Scratch the surface of any woman, and you'll find rage."

My anger began to break through outside therapy, often over minor incidents and with much greater intensity than any individual incident deserved. I had the impulse to slug someone who stepped on my toe while I was standing in line to cash a check. I could have smashed the policeman who gave me a deserved speeding ticket. I restrained myself from saying or doing anything because my arms were ready to grab the man's jugular. The epithets that thundered through my head were words I hadn't realized I knew.

Sometimes I knew my responses were out of proportion to the precipitating incidents, but sometimes I lost touch with reality. At those moments, I couldn't tell if someone had stepped on my toe or run me over with a steam roller.

* * *

As fall slipped into winter in 1976, I was off all medication. That meant one less thing to worry about and even more incentive to attend to my emotional life.

Now that I had some sense of what was happening in my interior, I sought additional ways to facilitate the process, hoping to speed it up. Massage was my first choice. Rubbing a shoulder or jaw created an opportunity to become aware of a chronic emotional/physical pattern. Massage stimulated circulation. Perhaps I could also get some gentle, emotional nourishment, one acceptable adult way to get some nurturing. And massage was passive. I could merely lie and receive.

The local Bancroft School of Massage offered the only training course in Massachusetts certified by the American Massage Therapists Association. I signed up, full of good reasons. My experience with Ildri was already so positive that I was developing an interest in becoming a bioenergetic therapist. I was told that becoming a licensed masseuse would give me legal protection to touch clients as part of that therapy. It was relatively inexpensive, and the center was ten minutes from my house.

Unfortunately, the way I chose to utilize massage required giving. Students in training gave a massage in order to get one from another student, often a different person each week. Giving a massage drained me, and having different, inexperienced hands touch me each week was unpleasant. Even when I was only the "receiver" on a particular evening, the process didn't work well. It took energy to receive touch, especially a stranger's, in the same way it did to take in people's words in conversation. More important, only when I could repay someone could I comfortably accept attention. I felt compelled to say, "Thank you," or "That felt good," with practically every stroke. That effort left me anxious and exhausted. All my life I'd operated on the repayment principle. Since I could always reciprocate with ease, I felt no conflict. Having the *capacity* to repay somehow even diminished the need to act. My lack of choice now caused such turmoil.

The conflict was reflected physiologically through my body. After my head, the typical starting place, was massaged, it felt clear and relaxed. The same was true for my arms, which were massaged next, but by the time my whole body had been massaged, it felt granite tight, as if protesting against the escalating debt.

I should have sought the most skilled person I could find, with whom a trusting relationship could develop, for massage. Why didn't I accept my vulnerability and gravitate to environments where I felt protected, rather than telling myself I shouldn't feel what I felt, trying again and again to "conquer" or deny my weakness?

* * *

In early November, as I was cooking dinner and checking a recipe card, I discovered it was hard to read unless it was only a few inches from my face. My vision had seemed blurry when I glanced at the newspaper an hour earlier. Perhaps I was just tired. I stuck my face in front of a mirror and saw that my eyes weren't red nor my eyelids swollen. I called Chris, hoping he was still at the hospital. I was lucky.

He was on his way out the door but said, "If you come this instant, I'll meet you in the emergency ward."

Adam and I put our coats on, and as I reached for the car keys, I remembered that if I couldn't see, I couldn't drive. The frantic feeling set in again. Chris was waiting, David wasn't at home or at his office, and I assumed, however inaccurately, that a taxi would take too much time. This seemed urgent. If I had gone from normal vision to this state in an hour, who knew what would happen in the next one. I decided to take a chance and drive myself. Adam, delighting in such an adventure, offered to be my guide. Thank goodness it was dark so cars had their lights on. I discovered I saw the lights double, so staying in the proper lane and stopping at traffic lights was no problem. However, if Adam hadn't been with me to watch for pedestrians, I'd have hit any jaywalkers.

Chris met me at the door with an opthalmologist. They examined me and said that my optic nerves were swollen. Their later diagnosis was papilladema, or optic neuritis. Both speculated that it was a manifestation of lupus, even though eye involvement was unusual. Nothing was amiss in the eye itself. Vision distortion occurred because blood vessels leading to the eye were inflamed. Since I no longer took prednisone daily, it was prescribed in the same way I had taken it for any recent lupus problems: fifty milligrams for five days, forty for four, thirty for three, and so on, until I was back to the dose I had been taking before the problem occurred. This enabled me to take high doses without getting my body hooked.

*   *   *

Two weeks later, the day before Thanksgiving, my vision gave out again. Within an hour, everything farther than three inches from my nose had become a dull blur. Having a new health problem around vacation time was beginning to seem a pattern.

When Adam returned from school and heard the news, he looked puzzled. "Remember the time your eyes were puffy, red doughnuts?" he said. "You looked yukky. Your face looked like a puffer fish's. Why could you see then, but last time and now, when your eyes look okay, you can't see? I don't understand."

His blank look suggested that my explanation seemed as inadequate to him as my doctors' did to me. Despite that, he believed my loss of vision was real, probably because hospitals meant sick people and because his big adventure to one as my navigator was so recent. He was mad, though, when he realized I would not be attending Thanksgiving dinner with David's family. "You look better today," he coaxed. "You rested all day yesterday." When I was silent, he attacked. "You went to work this week. You just don't want to go. You don't like Nan and Pops."

I felt strangled. Family gatherings were very important to Adam and to me. I knew I needed to keep talking with him until he understood my situation and his feelings more fully, to tell him it was good that he was able to get angry, that he had reason to be angry. But my fuse was short. Soon I was screeching like another six-year-old.

By the time Adam and David left for the dinner, I rested somewhat more easily remembering that Adam was with his beloved grandparents. David brought my turkey dinner on a tray afterwards. Only by means of color could I visually distinguish the cranberry sauce from the yams. This time it took a higher dose of prednisone for a longer period to get my vision back to normal.

After I was confident the medication would work, I was happy to relax in bed. In fact, these blurred-vision episodes were two more instances when I felt the same sense of happy tranquility that I had felt when at my weakest and hospitalized. Once again my world ended at the boundaries of my body, but unlike any other time of peace, I was *not* extraordinarily weak. That raised the questions anew. Was getting sick the only way I could, given who I was and at this moment in my life, find such tranquility? To phrase it differently, did I *choose* the illness?

Lying there, I thought more about prednisone. Beliefs, I suspected, were important in healing: surely my treatments were more effective if I believed in them. I had accepted prednisone because my doctors, who did not seem to be pill pushers, thought it necessary. But I felt ambivalent about the medication. It had some serious side effects. I could feel my body being taxed in utilizing it. Often I thought there was a direct correlation between prednisone and an improvement of my symptoms, but sometimes I didn't. I wondered if the earlier eye symptoms might not have abated without medication. Both my medical literature and Chris said that was possible. Was I taking medication that didn't help at all?

These last two eye episodes convinced me otherwise. Each time I knew exactly when I had taken enough prednisone to check and reverse the symptoms. In the second episode, I waited several hours before taking prednisone to see if symptoms would reverse without medication. My eyes worsened, although that length of time was probably not a fair test. Nonetheless, I suddenly appreciated the speed and effectiveness of prednisone.

I considered the following notions: that releasing blocked emotions (or sleeping or exercising) was one way to generate energy, and prednisone was another; that because prednisone provided "artificial" energy did not mean it was not healing, even if only in a temporary sense; and that it might be equally important as the slower, less risky approaches—without prednisone in crises, I might not have been around to utilize the slower, alternative methods. It seemed appropriate to continue taking prednisone.

On the Monday after Thanksgiving, I returned to work, back to my familiar weekday routine, and back to the couch. Some of my first reading at the onset of the illness in 1975 had been in psycho-somatic medical journals. Many emphasized personality charac-teristics as predictors of illness or examined the relationship between the location of the disease and personality characteristics. Does "lack of closeness with parents lead to developing tumors? Is hope-lessness a good predictor of cervical cancer? Do breast cancer patients have more sex-role difficulty than other cancer patients? Do peo-ple with ulcers have an "excessive unresolved dependency" on maternal figures?

As I read the articles, I always ended up with more questions than answers. Was the lack of closeness with parents experienced by people with tumors any greater than that of a cross-section of the total population? Virtually all these studies were done after peo-ple became ill. If illness changed one's personality, how could the researchers know what their subjects were like before they became ill? Could the onset of illness temporarily change one's feelings about everything, including childhood experiences? Who defines "sex-role difficulty?" The research always lost me in abstractions.

I found no articles specifically about lupus but uncovered many about rheumatoid arthritis. Arthritis was a related illness also thought to be autoimmune, and my joint and muscle symptoms felt like those described by arthritics. More recent research suggests people with lupus and rheumatoid arthritis have many similar per-sonality traits. Solomon and Moos' 1965 study, a typical one, sug-gested rheumatoid arthritics tended to be shy, self-conscious, and inhibited; martyrs; intolerant of anything less than perfection; ner-vous, moody and tense; unable to express anger; convinced their mothers had rejected them and their fathers had been extremely strict; and—oddly—fond of sports.

Did these characteristics fit my profile? I still remembered myself as skillful enough in translating potential angers or stress into assertion before lupus. And, while I might describe myself as shy, self-conscious, and inhibited, few others would identify those as primary characteristics of the president of her college dormitory and the Associated Women Students' senator on a college campus of 10,000. No one who knew me would call me a martyr or—prior to a year before lupus was diagnosed—tense or nervous, nor would anyone besides David or Adam describe me as moody. My father was not overly strict. The only characteristics in Solomon and Moos' study that fit were perfectionism and that odd one, fondness for sports. David disagreed, saying that all except the "strict father" characteristics fit my private self.

I could not even remember who I was prior to lupus. Before going to sleep that night, I asked David which adjectives he thought described me then.

"Vigorous, vital—physically vigorous and active—warm, emotional—by that I mean lots of feelings, all kinds." After pondering a bit, he added, "Aesthetic, introspective, and liberated, that is, determined to experience everything—see the world, have a career, be a mother, and so on."

I liked and agreed with all his choices except "introspective." I'd plunged into that primarily after the illness.

The adjectives used to describe the Type A personality— aggressive, ambitious, competitive, impatient, and work-oriented with a preoccupation with deadlines and time would fit me, at least my current closet self, more closely than those of arthritics. And I hadn't had a heart attack.

This insight had a two-fold effect. I concluded specific personality traits or general personality configuration by itself meant little. *Specific emotions could be correlated with bodily responses*—"chronically sustained hostile impulses," with chronic elevation of blood pressure or "dependent help-seeking trends" with increased gastric secretion—*but these emotions occurred in very different personalities.*

Did my reaction reflect prejudice or fact? Lumping people together had always offended me. An important reason Gestalt held my interest was its emphasis on the uniqueness of humans. On some levels, people are the same or at least more alike than different. But individual differences seemed important. *Every body/mind is unique.*

The implications of this individuality seemed enormous. It didn't deny common causes in particular illnesses, such as genetic predisposition or latent virus in lupus (or the environmental toxin asbestos in the cancer mesothelioma), or common causes in the same illness (sun, for example, as an exacerbant in lupus). But no one else with lupus had exactly the same causes I had. Many people might identify reaching a similar state of adrenal exhaustion in the genesis of their illnesses, but the reasons for each person's exhaustion would be unique. People vary in their responses to the same causes. Lupus joint and muscle pains might seem more threatening to someone who had watched a grandmother become immobilized from rheumatoid arthritis than to me who had never experienced and rarely witnessed serious illness. An adult who had spent a year in bed with rheumatic fever during childhood might deny the seriousness of an illness such as lupus less than I did.

That implied no universal treatment. No one else responded to prednisone in exactly the way I did. Or to psychotherapy. The kinds of exercise with which I felt compatible would differ from someone else's. Another person would gain from my experience primarily an understanding of a *process* of responding to an illness: which questions to ask, whom to ask what, what range of choices are possible, and what the tradeoffs are for each choice.

* * *

Self-knowledge seemed to be helping, so during 1976 I undertook a major record-keeping project toward that end. I resolved to keep track of every aspect of my existence that might shed light on the genesis and control of lupus—every environmental, psychological, and physiological factor that could be related to its cause and cure. Record-keeping kept my mind "constructively" occupied and gave me some sense of control.

I made charts with the days of the week listed horizontally and categories vertically and completed the charts daily. The permanent categories were "Medications, Symptoms, Sun Exposure, Emotional State, Dreams, Daily Cycle and Sleep, Food and Vitamins, Exercise, Pleasure and Play." Several other categories came and went.

Under "Emotional State" I aimed to determine if I felt more symptoms on days or groups of days when I felt angrier, sadder, or more anxious than usual. If the emotions had been expressed, had it made a difference?

Dreams, Freud said, were the royal road to the unconscious. Did dreams predict exacerbations? Was their content related to the location of my symptoms or to the system or organ involved? Did the unconscious emotions as expressed in dreams bring on particular symptoms in particular locations?

Sometimes I awoke in a very tense, uncomfortable position: my arms straight above my head. During 1976, this habit increased in frequency. I could make no sense of it. Perhaps my dreams could give clues to what I might unconsciously be expressing in that gesture.

I added "Daily Cycle" and "Sleep" after reading Gay Luce's book, *Body Time*, which describes the miraculously complex metabolic body processes that recur every twenty-four hours. One such process is the secretion of cortisone, which occurs sometime at the end of Rapid Eye Movement sleep shortly before waking. I had come across research which suggested that taking my morning dose of prednisone at the hour when the body naturally produced cortisone would be helpful.

During Christmas vacation, I began to review my charts. Not once could I recall a dream on mornings I woke with my arms up. My sleep patterns were so disrupted, I didn't know if cortisone was squirting into my system before I awoke at 4:00 a.m. or before I awoke at 8:00. "Vitamins" was the only category in which I could see a definite cause and effect, and that effect was a bad one. The symptoms were too elusive, too numerous, and the complexity of factors too great. I was gathering vastly insufficient data in uselessly primitive ways. The project needed to be designed with the input of experts from the diverse fields involved and to include extensive laboratory data. It seemed impossible without a computer, and in 1976 home computers were essentially unknown.

Yet I had learned a lot from it. I had been talking holism. I had grasped the idea that lupus has multiple causes, unlike heart disease or infectious illnesses such as smallpox, for which single causes can be isolated. But part of me still clung to the doctrine of specific etiology. This belief, which lies at the heart of modern medicine, suggests that at least theoretically, a specific cause can be found for each medical problem and that this will suggest a specific cure. I kept searching for a specific cause and cure for each of my symptoms. Did tennis or sex or laughter make my shoulder muscles feel better or worse? Did total rest help my eyes? Later I understood: *symptoms were usually brought on by a constellation of factors and,* to further confuse me, *different ones each time.* A grand emotional upheaval, plus a little exposure to the sun, might do it one time; moderate sun exposure, overexhaustion, and minor emotional stress the next; or a combination of lack of sleep and too much tennis a third. Also, *the same symptom could be activated by diverse stresses:* emotional stress could cause joint pains one day, and exhaustion could cause them the next.

I needed to move beyond symptom-chasing. Record-keeping focused on symptoms: how nutrition, dreams, sun, emotions, thoughts and activities affected symptoms. That approach encouraged a "prednisone mentality," that removal of symptoms equaled health. But symptom removal is only one aspect of health. I had become lost in the trees and was missing the forest. Lupus is a *systemic* illness. Somehow I needed to keep that broader perspective.

7

Old Scripts

New Year's 1977: a second year had almost passed.

One morning I woke up knowing I would stop reading, that for the moment, I had taken in all I could from the outside world. Instead, I would become more committed to exploring introspective, intuitive processes. I hoped my unconscious could offer untapped resources and become a source of wisdom.

I began to work with my dreams, revealing patterns of family and culturally-imposed high achievement, and then I enrolled in a design course. The major class assignment was to create a project incorporating examples of different design techniques. Without plan, my project became a design book of variously textured papers, the words of which traced my struggle in search of my inner voice.

The first week I sat, pen in hand, art materials scattered before me, waiting to see what would be born. Nothing came. "Sorry, no truths today," in huge block letters, filled the first page of green origami paper. On the next week's page, "Still no truths" was cut through stiff grey cardboard with my X-acto knife to show orange construction paper beneath. And a week later, "I looked and couldn't find any, so I wrote down a few of other people's." One that captured my attention filled the next page:

It is very paradoxical that, the more you dislike the wall, the stronger and thicker the wall becomes, and the more you make friends with the wall, the more it disappears.

I printed the proverb several times in concentric circles so that as a totality it looked like a circular wall. The "wall" I related to my ego and muscular defenses, my blocks to emotions, my shell. Had I been able to make friends with these, perhaps lupus would have been less likely or less severe. Because I disliked my walls intensely, I imagined they became thicker and stronger and set the scene for a more extensive collapse when they finally tumbled down.

For a while I could only write down others' poems and quotes. But gradually my own voice emerged. One poem was a dialogue with my mother:

Conversation with Mother

She: Be perfect.
Me: Okay, I'll be perfect.

She: You don't have to be perfect.
Me: I'll be perfect anyway.

She: Don't be perfect.
Me: Okay, I won't be perfect.

She: Be perfect.
Me: Okay, I'll be perfect.

Etc., etc., etc.

I felt victorious. Finally, I was connecting with the historical sources of my feelings. I relived the feelings as I wrote the words and ended up extremely exhausted. But this had been a long time coming. However elementary my prose was, I had written little resembling poetry before, certainly little from my heart. This poem was from my heart.

As I looked at the poem again, it felt unfinished. So I kept looking at the page and waiting. Soon my hand reached for the box of child's crayons and selected red, blue, and yellow. On the left side of the page, it drew a figure filled with color. Then it began to draw another figure, only a faint, blue outline. After that, it grabbed the red crayon and traced the same lines more firmly.

I looked at what I'd drawn. I assumed I was drawing a mother and daughter, but these images seemed confusing. Which figure is the mother? Which is the daughter? The larger figure looked like the typical self-portrait of a young girl. The smaller, unsymmetrical figure both frightened and intrigued me. It seemed some combination of a haggard old woman, near death, and an unformed child, close to infancy. The circle in the torso seemed like a heart.

The figures seemed to be images of myself. On the left was me before lupus, a smiling, open-armed crowd pleaser. On the right, me afterwards, more primitive and, even if half-dead, more authentic. No arms, but a heart, appropriate for someone who had trouble reaching out for help or love. If I was just beginning as a person, there was potential for growth. I was dying and being reborn.

Later, when looking at the poem, I was reminded of how I often felt as a child. I usually said and did the right thing at the right time. Somehow I got the message that if I didn't do what was expected, I wouldn't be loved. So I figured out what was expected and did it, without knowing what I wanted to do or who I was.

The feelings of satisfaction that I assumed would come from following the rules were brief or didn't happen at all. And when I erred, I felt enormously guilty. Almost all the childhood notes I slipped under my mother's pillow began, "Dear Mother, I'm sorry that I . . ."

* * *

That month my sister Karen, who had never been seriously ill, was hospitalized. My parents came to visit. On a black page covered by a red one, torn to allow a black, jagged line to show through, was the distillation of that encounter. It was more of our family essence and gave me a greater understanding of my shell.

And

And
   My Father said, warmly,
   Your health concerns me . . .
   Here is some
   Advice.

And
   my Mother said,
   Put on some
   Lipstick.

And
   My sister,
   Before her
   Gut
   Was ripped out, said,
   I'm scared.
   We must
   be brave.

And so we were brave.
And so we were brave.

We did not
Cry.

* * *

In March, I became increasingly obsessed with time. Every hour, at the minimum, I looked at my watch. Had I accomplished enough during that hour? I walked around saying, "There is time. There is time," to counter my anxious feeling that time was running out. Was this the same feeling most of us encounter close to midlife that I was feeling in an exaggerated form due to my illness? I didn't know. But "speeding" pervaded everything around me.

Throughout the day, I tried to move slowly, but the moment I became unconscious of what I was doing, I began to move faster. In the grocery store, I walked faster, grabbing instead of reaching for items. Driving to the office or meeting a friend for lunch, I jabbed at the gas pedal. Thoughts came to offer the same punishment as deeds: just thinking about being late, without any actual speeding up of movements, would speed up my system. I was then left in the familiar tense, tired state that I always felt by 4:00 p.m., but since my energetic hours were so few and therefore so precious, it was a great loss to feel that way by 11:00 in the morning. There was no way to reverse the process. There was no such thing as a second wind.

My anxiety soon became specific. In March, campus gossip had it that since I had the least seniority, my job at the college would be abolished in two months due to cutbacks in state funding. Talking about it with my boss, a wonderfully supportive man, I remember feeling faint—the walls got wavy. I felt that I had been told I was dying. Perhaps I felt such intense panic because my identity was heavily invested in work, perhaps because I experienced every feeling vividly these days, or perhaps because I began to experience feelings about endings vividly.

*   *   *

Fear that there wasn't enough time was now more clearly a fear of death. Whether rage or anxiety or fear of death, my internal process was the same. My stress system was being relentlessly pushed into action in processing any of these emotions, the opposite of what was useful to heal it. Daily I tried to remember that prednisone was a friendly substitute for my own burnt-out adrenals. It bought me precious time to work through the necessary emotional issues, and this had to occur before my organism could achieve its own balance again.

The last page of the design project seemed an important one. I had been thinking about it for days, but nothing had emerged.

Finally, one day when I was leafing through my art materials, I came across a black block print of my hand which I'd made earlier. I looked again. It was meant to be my last page. Once again, I sat, I looked, and I waited. This time the wait wasn't long. As soon as I placed my hand over the print to simulate the experience of making it, words rose within me. They were accepting ones: "I am." As I printed them above the hand, I felt a rush of contentment. It was as if "being" was enough.

The words kept ringing in my head, accompanied by wave after wave of increasing calm. My shell melted. This letting go was as complete as my favorite pre-lupus, summer relaxer: burrowing into beach sand, molding a nest, and absorbing the warmth of the sun and the steady, throbbing sound of ocean waves until their rhythm was part of me. Any need to protect myself *against*, defend myself *from*, vanished. My sense of similarity *to*, connection *with*, mushroomed and the feeling stayed with me for at least a day.

8

Going Deeper

After eight months of therapy, I felt increasingly confident in my choice of therapist and choice to pursue more therapy. In the last session, the object of wrath had been my sweet boss. The state had cut funding. I was appalled when he sat back and accepted, without a fight, the dictate of the administration to eliminate me. I felt abandoned.

Re-enacting this with Ildri, I cried, hurt that my boss did not fight for me. Then I felt enraged, shouting, "I hate you for abandoning me. How could you? How could you?" Again and again I whacked the couch. Before me appeared the image of a three-year-old sitting sad and alone on a stool, my tiny red one stashed under our kitchen table. I told Ildri. She suggested I lie on the mattress.

Lying down made me feel helpless, vulnerable. I became that little girl. My voice changed. The pitch was high and young. I screamed, "Mommy. Daddy. Where are you? Help me." When I cried, my throat, upper chest, and diaphram were tight, as if bound by an Ace bandage. My belly expanded and contracted, but my chest cavity hardly moved. I cried silently, my body knotted in pain.

For a brief moment, my head interfered. My voice deepened. The adult me told Ildri, "I don't know what I'm talking about. I was well-protected as a child."

The pull of these emotions was strong. I became the child again, torn by gut-wracking guilt. How ungrateful I was. How terrible. A bad child. The pain was like a vise some invisible force screwed tighter and tighter. My cries were high-pitched and choked.

Ildri put her hand on my upper chest. Ever so gently, she followed its rise and fall, except that she pushed down at the end of my exhale. Eventually, I broke into deep sobs. They were full-throated, full-bellied, their pitch an octave lower than the last ones. A wave of air rolled from the base of my pelvis, gathering force, through my diaphram and lungs before it moved out again with the steady rhythm of an ocean wave. When my sobs faded, I was exhausted.

I'd always been fearful when I cried the more constricted drippy "coughing" kind of tears that if I cried more, I'd never stop. I'd feel overwhelmed, perhaps hopeless. But that's not what happened. My knotted body relaxed.

From a bioenergetic perspective, one indication of health was the capacity for full breathing. Deep crying took full breathing. This was a breakthrough. I had sobbed, and then finally broken through into sunshine. I had gone into the pain, and I had reached the other side.

Shortly after I returned home, my euphoria disappeared, and something worse happened. The base of my skull began to ache, and so did my shoulders, arms, and elbow joints. This had occasionally happened after a highly emotional therapy hour. The symptoms frightened me. Were they only aches of unconditioned muscles? I thought the symptoms occurred more frequently after feeling angry, but I wasn't sure. Could my battered body tolerate expressing anger any better than repressing it?

Near the end of a therapy hour with Ildri in April, I mentioned my worry that expressing anger physically might exacerbate my symptoms. Ildri said she worried about that, too. After a long silence, Ildri said, "I know!" Her eyes brightened, and her voice turned reverent. "Why don't we ask Alexander Lowen for a consultation? Would that interest you?"

The possibility had never occurred to me, yet it seemed like a logical next step. I was delighted.

Ildri would sit in on my session with him to contribute and as a learning experience for herself. She arranged for us to see Dr. Lowen on April 25, and she would drive.

When we reached his home, Ildri had an individual session with Dr. Lowen while I sat in his waiting room, looking out the window at but not seeing lemon-colored daffodils and tulips and pink hyacinths beyond the terrace.

Then it was my turn. I undressed to my underwear. Watching breathing is important in bioenergetic therapy, and that is done best without clothing. I felt awkward. I was glad Ildri was with me.

The inner office where the three of us sat—they on two straight-back, wooden chairs and I on a simple couch bed covered by a white sheet—seemed the perfect setting for the father of bioenergetics.

Immediately, Dr. Lowen reminded me of my father. When he reached out to shake hands, his hands seemed as outsized as my father's and his grip equally firm. His eyes were compelling.

When Dr. Lowen asked me big questions about myself to which brief answers were expected, I suffered my usual paralysis. Aimless phrases about my relationship with my father, mother, and husband. His habit of saying "Yes" before I finished any statement annoyed me and hinted at a significant difference from my father: Dr. Lowen was pushier and more domineering. Either he knew what I was going to say before I said it or felt impatient with my stumbling. That increased my difficulty in finding words.

"Yes, yes, you were a 'good' girl," he said. "But your feelings are all blocked. That's where the lupus comes from—a longing. You have been fighting off deep, sad feelings for a long time. You hold on for dear life in your jaw. There is more sadness in you than you can possibly imagine, even verging on despair."

It was a shock to hear, "You hold on for dear life in your jaw." No one else talked that way. But this was no kook recommending elderberrry tea as a cure for lupus. I hung on his every word. Finally, someone was making sense of the relationship between bodies and emotions.

To Ildri he said, "You have to get into the whole relationship with her father. That's the thing that has to be worked out very carefully. That's where the hang-up is. She's remaining, in some sense, Daddy's sweet little girl. Her relationship with her father was so close that if she didn't hold on for dear life, it would have been incestuous. It was that close. She said, 'If I lose my head, we're lost.' But the holding is terribly unpleasant, and she wishes to break out of it."

I was speechless. It was all I could do to hear his words, never mind digest them. "Incestuous" was such a wildly inflammatory word.

Turning to Ildri again, he said, "She's got a lot of anger in her about having been betrayed by her father when she got older and had to battle her mother. But she feels guilty about her anger. She's afraid of it. She's got to feel the fear before she can get to the rage. That's why she's myopic—fear is held in the eyes."

How can he be *so* sure, I thought? Many people would scorn the connection between myopia and fear. I was skeptical about his cocksureness; it was the same quality I abhorred in some traditional medical doctors.

He said to me, "You know you have a lot of conflict in you about your father. You're furious at him, yet you love him. Ambivalence looks like this physically: a strong feeling wells up, you bring up its opposite and block the original energy. So it's important to go all the way with a feeling. Like when kicking, go all the way. If you put the brakes on, it'll be felt in the joints which will get inflamed."

I couldn't quite fathom how the relationship with my father was *that* close, but I drank in the rest. No one had ever been this concrete about how emotion related to inflammation in joints or muscles. Dr. Lowen meant that when a feeling got going, like a locomotive down a hill, I put on the brakes and smash, my joints and body received a tremendous jar.

Dr. Lowen must have been reading my mind, for he said, "As you work in therapy, your symptoms may flare up. You'll have to say, 'Okay, what happened? I went with a feeling and got scared at the same time. I blocked.' You'll see that will always be true. You opened up and then grabbed. When that happens, the symptoms flare up because of your harsh blocking. Just take prednisone to quiet them down and start over again."

My body tightened. "'Just take prednisone' is pretty casual. The side effects of prednisone are more serious the longer the drug is used. I'm trying to cut down."

He disregarded this and continued. "You have to open up to your sadness and pain. Do it in a safe place. If you open up to the world with all that pain within you, you'll get hurt and you'll contract. Open up in therapy where it's safe."

"My anger comes out at David and Adam at home," I said. "Any little irritation makes me angry."

"Well, that will happen. Those are your most important relationships. You live in them daily. Anyway, some of your anger is probably appropriate. Just do the best you can," he said. "You've got to keep trying to let yourself cry," he added. "If you don't let it out, you'll stay sick. I give you my word. Lupus is the holding back of that sadness."

He asked me to lie on the couch. I remember that he pushed very hard on my jaw muscles and inside my mouth at the juncture of my upper and lower palate. It hurt, but since my jaw had ached for the past year, I hoped this might loosen it.

When I sat up again, I thought of my greatest fear, the reason I came to see him. "I wouldn't be so afraid of expressing my feelings if I didn't have lupus. Is it dangerous for me to express too much feeling at once?"

"What's that got to do with lupus? It's like saying you're sick so you don't know how fully you should breathe. If you don't breathe, you get sick."

His confidence startled me. *"None* of the exercises would be bad for me?"

"None of the exercises would be bad. None."

Even as the words hit my ears, I thought he was absolutely right, *in principle.* Deeper, fuller breathing was desirable for everyone. But I did not trust his lack of concern for the delicacy of my body. This time I found my voice. "But exacerbation of symptoms could mean kidney or central nervous system involvement," I said. "My life is at stake. My *life* can be as easily diminished by lupus as expanded by fuller breathing."

"Focus on getting your feelings out. That's what will save your life." In parting, he said, "You're a nice, hysterical personality."

I stared at him aghast.

He reached out and touched my arm. "Don't get upset. Hysterical—that's a good quality. I like you."

A strict Freudian would never touch an arm or say, "I like you." There was wisdom in a more disciplined neutrality, but I appreciated his warmth and down-to-earth friendliness.

As I was writing my check in his office, I was already processing our meeting. "Sadness—more than you can imagine . . . ," "Lupus is the holding back of that sadness . . . ," "Fear . . . ," "Anger . . . ," "Rage . . . ," "Despair . . . ." The words kept coming back. I felt panicky. Relating any of these emotions to my father was beyond me. To Dr. Lowen, I was all unreleased feeling. I thought I had been exaggerating my black side. He seemed to be saying that not only was I not exaggerating, I was underestimating its size and scope. For a moment, I stopped breathing. Maybe I was all black demons and grey monsters. Maybe I had a bigger black side than anyone in the world.

On the drive home, I was spent, but I wanted more of Ildri's interpretation. "Didn't Dr. Lowen say my relationship with my father could have been incestuous? My parents understood good parenting. Incest? My father? Never. That's preposterous!"

Ildri thought for a few moments. "From what you say, your father behaved appropriately. Maybe Dr. Lowen is referring as much to the intensity of *your* feelings as his. That your longing for your wonderful Daddy as saviour from a competitive mother was so strong it was difficult for both you and your father. Probably the warmer the bond between father and daughter, the greater the trauma to the daughter when her father withdraws, whenever that happens. You and your father had a special relationship. Perhaps you more intensely felt separation from him as you got older. Maybe you even felt that your whole person had been rejected."

"Yes, you're right."

I was quiet for a while, watching trees and farms out the window. "Well, Dr. Lowen's message is clear. Go deeper into feelings, don't block them. It must be such a strong pattern in me: I expand, I get scared, I contract. When I'm in your office, I can sometimes 'go all the way with a feeling,' as he says."

"In time I think you'll become aware of the details of how your body closes down. Be patient. Just remember that it's fear of an emotion that makes you shut down, not the emotion itself."

For the next four or five days, propped up on my pillow at couch time, I thought more about sadness. Dr. Lowen's lines came back to me: "I give you my word: lupus is the holding back of that sadness." His words prompted me to work extra hard to release tears. Dr. Lowen related despair to sadness, defining despair as a seemingly bottomless pit of sadness.

* * *

The next evening David, Adam, and I ate at a local restaurant. Adam, at seven, was only vaguely interested in reading the menu.

"What do you want, Adam?" I asked.

"A hamburger and French fries. And a strawberry milkshake."

I was relieved. Often Adam's choices were less nutritious. At public school now, he regularly traded sandwiched for Twinkies.

Halfway through the meal, Adam announced, "I want dessert now, Dad." He asked David because he knew I'd say no.

As I opened my mouth to protest, David said, "You can take the shake home with you. What do you want?"

I was angry. David and I had discussed this *hundreds* of times.

"Chocolate-chip ice cream. The biggest size," Adam said.

Usually I interrupted and tried to reach some compromise with David. Tonight, exhausted and in public, I only coaxed, "Eat the rest of your food before the ice cream comes."

Adam went to the bathroom. He climbed on and off his chair a few times. His French fries sat untouched.

"Finish your hamburger before dessert," I said icily.

"I only want dessert. Dad said I could take the rest of my food home."

The dessert arrived. When it was almost gone, Adam looked up at David and said, "Can I have some rock candy?"

David and Adam turned to look at me. "Adam," I said as calmly as I could, "I think you've had enough for tonight." David added, "Mom and I think you've had enough."

Without a second's pause, Adam bellowed, "You don't really agree. Mom made you say that."

My next memory was of David's getting up to pay for some licorice. I don't recall how we got from rock candy to licorice. David returned from paying for the licorice with a dollar bill. Adam

105

grabbed for the change. "It's my money. I'll keep it."

David gave him the money.

I could have smacked Adam. What an obnoxious brat! I could have belted David across the room.

After Adam's usual bedtime wrangle, our bedroom door was finally closed. I started in. "I can't believe what happened tonight. After all the talking we've done. He hasn't eaten half his meal— which includes a shake—and you give him dessert! Where is your brain? And then *licorice*! You're so thick! He demands the change and you give it to him! *You idiot*!" Name-calling and swearing didn't encourage David to listen to me, but as often happened at home, I was beyond even trying to turn my inner burner down.

"It's not the end of the world. He's just a kid. Kids like candy. He'll outgrow this." David's voice softened, "You've got bigger things to worry about. You've got to let the little stuff roll off your back, Donna. This is little stuff."

He was right. I did give food more attention than it deserved. In the greater scheme of things, this food issue was "little stuff." But there was more to this, and I felt determined to pursue it. "Well, food isn't the essence of the problem. It's the dynamic between us. The topic could be anything. In every interaction, Adam plays you against me! We let him split us right down the middle!"

"Look," David said, more firmly but still well-controlled, "I spend most of my day being hassled by other people. I'm just not interested in any more rankling. *Especially* little stuff!"

"What's the big stuff to you?" I asked.

"In raising this child? Honesty. Physical safety. Adam's taking more and more responsibility as he gets older. That's what I consider important."

"How can you settle for so little? What about integrity, a sense of self-worth, kindness, having friends. I want him to identify and develop his talents — eventually to find work he loves." My voice trailed off. How dare I, who could give so little, want so much? I felt cornered.

"In any case, kids learn by example. Example is far more important than words. You only see the results of this approach in the long haul. But I go for the long haul."

"But kids need more than that!" I protested. "*Our* kid needs more than that! He needs limits. He needs to see that there are consequences to his obnoxious behavior."

David cut in quickly, "Then let him learn them in the world. That comes soon enough. Anyway, punishing isn't the way to teach. It only breeds resentment. Don't forget, I was raised just like I'm advocating. I was a rebellious kid exactly like Adam. Nobody paid attention to my antics. And I turned out to be a fairly responsible, honest adult."

"Were you really a rebellious child? Your mother says you were an easy kid. Sometimes I think you encourage Adam to become the rebellious child you only wish you'd been."

He looked ready to say something else, but I rushed in. "Don't you see that Adam's only tactic is to be obnoxious enough for long enough? Eventually he wears us down. He always wins. It's not just at home. He causes ruckuses everywhere. If we could agree, we'd set limits and have a united front."

"I think it's okay if we disagree. I simply don't believe in parents' phonily pretending to be united."

"What about at the restaurant? You said, 'Mom and I think you've had enough,' and Adam said, 'Mom *made you* say that.' Why didn't you answer? When you're silent, what else can he think but that he's right? Is he? I thought you and I agreed that he eats too much junk."

"I do agree. It wasn't worth fighting over at the restaurant. We don't have to agree on everything."

"We come across as hardly agreeing on anything. And I always end up being the bad guy. The heavy. It's not good for you, me, or Adam that I do all the disciplining. It's not good for you to be seen as the angel and me the devil. You *never* do *any* disciplining! *Never*! What's wrong with you? You've got to row your oar, too!" I practically howled.

"Don't tell me about rowing oars! I do *plenty* around here. If you aren't *absolutely* clear about that, you'd better think again. And," he yelled, stomping downstairs, "I've *reached my limit*!"

His red face and strong voice scared me. He rarely shouted. Finally, the sleeping giant had exploded. I actually felt some relief. It was the way I felt as a child on the ranch when an old stone dam, decrepit for years, finally fell. I shook from exhaustion. I remembered Dr. Lowen's words, "You'll do the best you can," and Ildri's, "Remember, it's the *fear* of your anger that wreaks havoc in your body. Not the anger itself." I was more tired for a couple of days, but otherwise held up well enough.

Was David just the well-intentioned but clumsy guy who just didn't understand the psychological side of life and was tired and tuned out from the day's work? Or was he thoughtless and careless about human interactions? When we first married, I thought he possessed a certain kind of innocence. Now I sometimes viewed him as using his lawyer skills to perfection at home. Maybe he was the psychological expert, master of his craft, carefully, calmly, quietly calculating exactly what to say and when to say it to win his case, never wasting a word or gesture.

Perhaps I was the sick, weak wife who was doing the very best she could under difficult circumstances. But did I subtly use my illness to take advantage of him? Did I act out my own anger by getting him to do more of the chores so I could see more clients? Did I care more for them than him? I talked with him or at him incessantly about Adam. Surely he thought I cared more for Adam than him.

Sometimes we did stay in a battle with each other long enough to get to the other side. We examined what was under our angers long enough to allow some vulnerability. I acknowledged how badly I felt about being such a poor example—swearing, screaming, exhibiting the very behaviors I didn't want in my son. David admitted how difficult it was for him to initiate emotional talk, how he actually appreciated my pushing him to get in touch with his emotions. We both confessed to being lousy at setting and enforcing limits and agreed we were often inconsistent, even admitted our mutual helplessness and our need for and appreciation of each other. On rare occasions, we even laughed at ourselves.

9

Doctors, Power and Drugs

In late April, several weeks before school—and my job—ended and around the time I had seen Dr. Lowen, I suspected I had a urinary-tract infection and called my original gynecologist, Dr. Joseph. I returned to him because I wanted nothing to do with anyone or anything that would evoke the memory of my abortion. The emotional wound was still raw. But, having had nothing but routine Pap smears with Dr. Joseph, I knew only that he warmed the speculum, for which I credited him with some degree of sensitivity, and that his personal style was inoffensive. He said he was familiar with lupus. I was too weak and exhausted to quiz him further.

He saw me the same day at the hospital, took a culture, said something about urethral stenosis, and dilated the entrance to the bladder. He sent me off with a prescription for Tetracycline. Questions popped into my head. What if I took this medication and the culture showed a bacteria which required a different antibiotic? Wouldn't I then be putting two medications in my system when one might do? What were the risks if I took nothing and waited forty-eight hours for the results of the cultures?

After two Tetracycline pills, my hands and feet were swollen, red and itchy. I had rashes on my arms and legs.

I had been re-reading Henrietta Aladjem's *The Sun Is My Enemy*, her story of dealing with lupus for many years. She concluded that the medications she was given to alleviate secondary problems in conjunction with lupus were as toxic as the problems they were intended to resolve. Her opinion supported my own conclusion, and I resolved to take no more medication *than was absolutely necessary*. That did not make things easier, for I had no illusion that cranberry juice and yogurt or any of the other remedies I'd read about would solve this problem.

Two days later, the itchiness became obnoxiously annoying. My swollen hands and feet stung and began to resemble red leather. I called the gynecologist.

"The results of the culture aren't back yet. Since it's Friday," he said, "we'll have to wait until Monday."

When I described these symptoms, he said, "Stop taking Tetracycline. We'll get the results on Monday and choose a medication then. I'll call you as soon as I get the results."

Only then did it occur to me to call Chris. When I did, he was irritated that I hadn't called sooner. I was surprised at the intensity of his reaction. He suggested icily that I should check with him whenever I had any kind of physical problems.

Dilation of the bladder is an antiquated procedure dangerous for you," he said. "If you didn't have an infection before, you probably will now. Take Bactrim," he added, although he hadn't seen the culture, or even seen me. I hung up, not moving, hand still on the receiver for a long time. I felt listless and frustrated. This was likely to be a muddled, lengthy process.

Then I looked Bactrim up in *Everyman's Guide to Drugs and Medicines*. I couldn't believe the words I read. Bactrim was not an antibiotic but an antibacterial combination which included *sulfamethoxazole*. I lost my focus, literally seeing red. Every piece of lupus literature I'd ever seen warned against prescribing sulfa drugs to lupus patients. Sulfa could exacerbate lupus. Chris had the audacity to question another doctor's treatment, yet look what he had recommended.

Saturday and Sunday passed as slowly as a week, but I began to relax a little by Sunday evening, knowing there was a plan for the following day. My relief disappeared when I got out of bed on Monday. I felt warm and called Dr. Joseph promptly at 9:00 a.m., too nervous to wait for his promised call. Trying to sound calmer than I felt, I said, "The thermometer reads 102°."

"Just a minute," he said. Let me find the test results." A moment later he came back. "The organism is Proteus, a gram-negative strain bacteria," and, after a pause, "I think we'd better try Chloromycetin. I'll call in a prescription."

I mentioned that I'd talked with my rheumatologist who had suggested Bactrim.

"Sulfa drugs aren't much used these days," he said, "and Bactrim won't work with this organism."

Chris hadn't seen the culture and didn't seem to care what organism I had. But I had to trust someone. However interested and active I was in my treatment, I was not a physician. Instead of calling Chris, I collected the prescription and took a pill, relieved to have some decision made.

Ever in need of some reassurance, I picked up *Everyman's Guide* again before going to sleep.

> Chloromycetin is the brand name of chloramphenicol, a broad-spectrum antibiotic which used to be widely prescribed until its side effects became notorious. . . . Nowadays the use of chloramphenicol is restricted to cases where the disease is even more threatening than the cure. Chloramphenicol can cause severe blood damage.

Suddenly wide awake, I got up and paced the floor. David was asleep, so I went downstairs and began to unload the dishwasher. I could hardly restrain myself from throwing plates and glasses across the room. *Restricted to cases where the disease is even more threatening than the cure.* Was that me? I glanced at the other antibiotics listed; most had far less toxic side effects than Chloromycetin.

Desperate, I did the only thing I could think of in the middle of the night: got out more books. The *Physician's Desk Reference* said three kinds of Proteus were sensitive to Bactrim. None were sensitive to Chloromycetin. Dr. Dubois' three-inch-thick *Lupus Erythematosus* textbook, which I'd recently purchased, had several references to the toxicity of Chloromycetin. Maybe Chris was right.

I woke David up and began haranguing him with my dilemma. He suggested we call Dave, a Boston physician friend and his college roommate.

"But it's almost midnight."

"He'll understand."

I dialed the phone. Our friend was still awake, and after I explained my dilemma, he said, "I think you need aggressive treatment. Chloromycetin is probably worth the risk."

I felt trapped on all sides, afraid to take either medication. Both doctors seemed to have prescribed poisons. Both seemed of questionable competence. I resented being caught in the middle. Not only was I the powerless patient with powerful doctors, I was the powerless woman with powerful men, and sick and weak besides.

After an angry, sleepless night, I called Chris. I told him that Dr. Joseph said Bactrim wouldn't work and that I'd read most lupus patients were allergic to sulfa drugs. "Will you *please* call the gynecologist and get this straightened out?" I asked.

He refused. I was so stunned, I couldn't speak. When I gained some composure, I sputtered out, "Why not?"

"Let's take another culture and make a decision then."

"Are you punishing me for not calling you first?"

"We'll do another culture and make a decision then," he replied. "In the meantime, take Bactrim if you need any medication."

He was dodging the issue. Did doctors so hate to deal with one another? It had seemed a reasonable request.

I knew I would not take Bactrim, and I was momentarily pacified by his taking another culture. A culture took forty-eight hours to develop. If Chris thought it was okay to wait that long to take any medication, I could wait. Then there would be no more mistakes.

The hours passed slowly. I survived without Bactrim. Wednesday, May 10, the day the culture was due, I called Chris again.

"The bacteria is Proteus Mirabulus," he said. "Bactrim works *in vitro* (in the laboratory culture) and should be even more sensitive *in vivo* (in the body). Take two pills two times a day for ten days."

"But lupus patients often have allergic reactions to sulfa drugs," I sputtered.

"These things vary greatly. I've had patients with lupus take sulfa successfully. Bactrim is appropriate to the organism and strong enough."

Since our Boston friend had said aggressive treatment was desirable, I was relieved when Chris said it was powerful enough. But I was still totally confused. Dr. Joseph had said Bactrim would not eradicate the offending bacteria. Chris said it would. Chloromycetin seemed deadly. So did Bactrim. I wanted to scream. If I followed Dr. Joseph's treatment plan, I would, in effect, be deciding to leave Chris. Dr. Joseph looked no more desirable. Whoever he might come up with as a consultant for lupus might be worse. If I stayed with Chris and took the Chloromycetin recommended by the gynecologist, what would Chris do? Did doctors leave patients? At the very least, he'd torment me if any medical problems arose from it.

In the end, I took the Bactrim. At least if I got sick on Chris's regimen, he'd be there to pick up the pieces.

An important change in attitude was occurring around this time. It was a gradual development, and only in hindsight did its significance become clear. I'd learned the limitations of symptom-chasing from my journal experience in 1975 and 1976. Now I was moving toward a deeper, internal understanding that fighting the disease was less productive than pursuing life-affirmative activities. The difference between my old act well/be well stance and life affirmation seemed subtle, but in the latter I couldn't deny I had lupus. Yet at times like this I was confused: Adam and David came first, but was continuing to work, play tennis, and drive to Boston for therapy denial or wisdom? If I'd eliminated tennis, the Boston trip, and some work, I'd have given much more thought to the medical questions.

Knowing my position had been cut, my students gave me a wonderful farewell party. A group of them petitioned the student council for money since state funding for my position was being cut off, giving stirring speeches in my behalf. They were unsuccessful, partly because the student council itself of this community college had no money—but the huge outpouring of affection at both events showed great love, great appreciation for my work and my self.

113

The Bactrim worked. My last work day coincided with the last day of Bactrim treatment. I felt relieved, and proud to have escaped with nary a sign of a drug reaction. I gloated a bit to myself: I must indeed be the exceptional lupus patient.

10

Lost Hope

I was now jobless but free at last. The weekend at the end of May felt like any other; Monday would begin my newfound freedom. I'd keep my hand in professionally by seeing a few clients at home and continuing to teach the Gestalt graduate courses. Since my interest in bioenergetic therapy was growing, I might join the International Bioenergetic Institute's training program which met one weekend a month in New York, beginning in September. In the meantime, I'd be able to exercise more. If I played tennis more frequently, my stamina might increase. If it didn't, I would have time to find more suitable exercise, something uncompetitive, I thought. I would be more available to Adam. The mere thought loosened the stranglehold of my guilt. I hoped to save my best energy for him after he returned home from school and thereby put more joy back in mothering. Maybe I'd be strong enough to work in my basement pottery studio. I could almost feel and smell the wet, grey clay in my hands. The thrill was in watching my original idea for a piece of sculpture transform itself as the material and I met and mixed, the clay informing me of its possibilities and limits. At a point of choice, there was always some tension. Should I do this? Or that? When the solution emerged, tension turned into excitement. The form was then a new gestalt, offering new questions and possibilities. Each clay piece resulted from a series of these cycles. The process never failed to leave me richly satisfied.

When I woke on Monday, however, all I felt was warmer. Mondays were beginning to mean "fever." By midafternoon, the thermometer read 100°, and the old symptoms seemed to be returning. I gritted my teeth, muttering, "Why me? What now?" I dialed Chris.

"Take more Bactrim," he said. The blood drained right out of me. I turned white.

"Bactrim?!" I yelled into the phone. "But, Chris, what if Bactrim *is* the problem?"

"Well, there isn't solid evidence for that yet. Vomiting and fever could just as well be from the infection. You don't have to take it, but I think you'd be a fool not to."

"Aren't there other antibiotics?"

I didn't remember what he said, but he didn't come up with one. I called David, my voice still shrill. "I can't believe this. I called Chris. He told me to take Bactrim. Again. Why doesn't he listen to me? Is he trying to kill me? Am I crazy? Or is he?"

David heard me out. "It does sound like a mess. You could call Dave in Boston again."

"He won't be sympathetic. He told me to take Chloromycetin. I didn't do that."

"Well, Chris is your doctor. He's been on target with everything else. I imagine vomiting and fever could just as well be symptoms of infection as a drug reaction. But it's up to you."

After a long silence, I said listlessly, "Well, I guess I'll try Bactrim. I don't know what else to do."

David picked up the new prescription on his way home from the office. While cooking dinner, I began to feel hot, much hotter than standing over the stove should have caused.

Within two hours, my entire body ached, my temperature had risen to 102°. I felt chilled, although nothing like the wild icy shaking that had occurred the previous March. By the time I had vomited twice, I knew something serious was happening. Why, I wondered, did my difficulties always develop in the evening when Chris was at home? When I called, his response was immediate: "Get to the hospital." Luckily Barbara and Imre were at home.

Within minutes, Imre came to get Adam. David and I weren't exactly veterans, but there was slightly more ease and less panic this round—and at least no ambulance.

The emergency-ward scene was indelibly etched in my memory. There was no chair at the admitting station. David answered questions for me. What did a person do who was alone and too weak to stand? There was a form to be signed authorizing administration of any medication, anesthesia, and treatment deemed necessary. I could refuse to sign it. They could ask me to get my treatment elsewhere if I did not or could, more likely, punish me subtly by pulling the curtain around my stretcher and leaving me unattended for a few days. I signed the form. Chris decided not to come. This was the first time he was not with me in an emergency. Was he punishing me? I was at the mercy of unknown staff.

I shook visibly. No one noticed as I lay down. I begged for a blanket, then a second. I told them I was about to vomit. No one brought a container. There was no receptacle around. I erupted on the floor. They were crabby. I took their nastiness silently—my jaw now seemed like a gigantic vise, clamping in fear, pain, and rage.

Calm yourself. Calm yourself, I told myself silently. Do *something* to relieve the pain. David joined me in the cubicle. I asked him to put his hands on my hurting abdomen. He looked hesitant—I knew what he was thinking—and I said, "You can't understand how that can make any difference, can you?"

"No." But he did what I asked.

His touch called up the reassurance of my father's hand on my shoulder as a child. The contact was instantly comforting. Within three or four minutes David had reached his limit.

I began to think about how and why therapeutic touch worked, a subject that fascinated me. The resident walked in. He asked David to leave the cubicle. I protested, angry that doctors apparently cannot conceive of human support as desirable for a sick person. As David got up, a fantasy ran through my head: They would say, "We're going to asphyxiate her. Please leave." And David would leave.

Damn you, David, I thought. Why don't you fight to stay with me?

117

Weak and disoriented, I was taken to a room and hooked to the intravenous.

During the first forty-eight hours, I rarely opened my eyes. My thinking was totally muddled. It was all I could do to attend to my most basic needs—getting another blanket, making sure the tube flowed freely, making sure what was in the tube was what was ordered. I couldn't sit up or feed myself, but the idea of food seemed revolting anyway.

Within another forty-eight hours, I became slightly cognizant of the outside world. Not only was I clammy from fever but from 80°, dry air blasting through heating units a few feet from my bed and an unbreathing plastic cover beneath the sheet. I opened my eyes more.

The infection had returned. The bacterial organism was the same as before. Fear of the known replaced fear of the unknown. It wasn't much of an improvement.

I was told that Keflin, an antibiotic to which the organism was susceptible, had been flowing in the tube. Then Chris said he wanted to add Bactrim, for reasons I cannot now recall. As the Bactrim flowed in with the Keflin, I began to feel itchy. When it increased to the point where I wanted to scream, they stopped the Keflin. That baffled me, since the itchiness occurred after the Bactrim was added. I told the intern and a resident or two when they came in, and they said, "Tell Chris." I wasn't thinking clearly enough to ask that they reach Chris and ask him to get into touch with me or to have a phone hooked up in order to call him myself. Chris didn't come around. Finally someone stopped the Bactrim.

I was beginning to develop my own criteria for allergic reactions no matter what anyone else said. Bactrim went onto my never-touch-again list.

I thought about predispositions to various antibiotics until a nurse arrived with a new one, the sixth. She hooked up the intravenous. I lay there stone-stiff, expecting disaster.

Kanamycin, it turned out, was my friend. My body didn't react badly and the fever and symptoms went away.

By now, the fifth day, I was able to think clearly enough to request turning off the heat and removing the plastic under my bottom sheet. Feeding myself and taking a sponge bath were the major events of my day. I noticed the gifts of flowers. They'd been put on top of the radiators, so they wilted!

My newly available energy went into talk with doctors, trying first to identify the pieces of this puzzle and then fit them together, but it was maddening. I began reading myself because their answers were so contradictory. One ended a discussion with, "You know too much." When I said, as diplomatically as I could muster, "You don't like my questions?" he grumbled coldly, "Oh, no, I like informed patients," but suddenly changed his language to the most technical of medical jargon so that I could not understand at all.

My books and the doctors agreed on one point: I had had at least one, and perhaps two, drug reactions. Chris was the single holdout, parrying all the questions with, "Perhaps," or "There's always the additional question with you whether the rashes and inflammation result from the lupus or from the infection," and "It's either impossible or very surprising that you could have taken Bactrim for two weeks with no problem and then have a problem now."

I began to suspect that once again he was sticking to his last line mostly because of his ego. He didn't want to admit he might have made a mistake. Given this crazy illness, mistakes would be understandable, but I found his inability to admit error unforgivable.

Chris usually wasn't rigid. The only other time he'd acted this way was during the 1976 abortion when Dr. Pickering disagreed with his recommended treatment. What rankled him didn't seem to be the other doctor's differing opinion. His wall of stubbornness sprang up when I didn't take his word as gospel. His total manner toward me changed.

Now the saga continued. Chris said he wanted to ask the urologist if a cystoscopy, a diagnostic procedure, was needed. Later that day, a doctor walked in and said, "I'll be your anesthesiologist. It hasn't been decided if you'll have a complete or local."

You bastards, I thought. It's my body. Will you never include me in a decision?

One or two bad moments during any hospitalization could be expected, but they began to include the whole hospital staff and seemed to occur all day, every day in mine. The cumulative effect was that I wanted to scream, "Who needs this? You people are toxic! I've got to get out of here!"

A few bold souls would have gotten up and walked out the door. But this hardly seemed constructive when suffering a severe infection. So far during this hospitalization, I'd walked a total of 30 to 40 steps. It would take at least eight times that many just to get to the hospital entrance door.

I felt trapped. Two conditions seemed necessary for me to explode: a just cause and equal power. The angry scenes with doctors and nurses fully provided the first. But I was sadly lacking in power. I was weak and ill with an infection, and threatened by the unknown potential severity of an illness like lupus. I was intensely angry and intensely dependent. For me to protest to a doctor, or any adult standing upright, felt as unwise as taking on a fleet of armored tanks with a knife.

David, as usual, got most of my wrath. I berated him for not being the kind of help I would have been, if I'd been him.

"Look," he countered. "Your situation seems incredibly complex, an unbelievable muddle. I can't sort it out either."

"Well, if you're smart enough to go to Harvard, you should be able to get on top of this! You should be my advocate. You know. Lawyer! Advocate!" I said sarcastically.

"Now wait just a minute. Most of the time you *want* to do it yourself. To you, isn't that *taking responsibility* for your health? And isn't it also your idea of a *liberated* woman?" His degree of sarcasm matched mine.

After we calmed down, David said, "You know, I may be a psychological dunce, but even someone who's very intuitive would have a hard time with you. Just take one dimension, your energy level. First, there's lupus. At your best, you have half the energy you had before lupus. At times you have much less. There are decreases and increases over weeks...months, plus daily variations. Sometimes you look weak to me when you feel okay. Sometimes you look all right when you feel weak. Then you add this infection and its complications. For a few days, you need infant-style care. For a few more days, you need something different. Who knows what you'll need tomorrow. And though you'll get stronger, it may be a *long* time before you're back to your lupus best. Now, that's only looking at your energy level. Can't you see how confusing this is to me?"

A wave of warmth surged through me. "I'm sorry," I said weakly. I reached out for his hand. This conversation gave me a speck of hope.

My thinking was clear during our argument, but I could gather energy for such confrontations only occasionally. Afterwards, I returned to my more typical, mentally disintegrated state.

By the time I no longer needed help feeding and bathing myself and using bedpans, I could hold a pen. My eyes hurt enough that I could do little else. My journal was becoming a way to hang onto my sanity.

About Chris I wrote:

> Trust in Chris seems as decisive as any factor in your healing. His optimism sustained yours. His input of all kinds helped you feel some control over your unwieldly carcass. You no longer trust him. Wading through the medical decisions consumes most of your energy. Every bit of that is well spent. Energy expended in dealing with your deteriorating relationship with Chris is wasted.
>
> You should change doctors. That means changing hospitals. But your 1976 hospitalization was at another hospital. The improvements were minor. Your only real hope is not to need any of these dreadful places.

I made lists: qualities I liked about Chris, qualities I didn't like, qualities I hope to find in a new physician. I made lists of the pros and cons of being in a hospital or staying home. The advantages and disadvantages turned out to be equal.

In another two days, I had enough energy to follow through on a resolve: to reinforce the positive, no matter what. With more appetite, breakfast in bed was a treat. So was absorbing the sight and sound of raindrops falling on the windowpanes, a subtle pleasure I was less likely to pause for when peppier. As a child, eating in restaurants had been special. I still enjoyed choosing food from menus, and selecting meals free of processed food was a challenge. I couldn't concentrate to read, didn't have a Walkman yet, and music on my tape cassette was out because using my own electrical appliances was against the ward rules, so I watched as much television as my eyes would permit. I aimed for programs that tapped positive emotions, and scrupulously avoided those that might tap my personal Strum und Drang.

With equal determination, I told whoever walked in my door about any positive emotion or experience. When I couldn't manage that, I wrote about it. Was the me-before-lupus who found pleasure easily a figment of my imagination? The mechanical way I approached this task seemed laughable, but I had to start somewhere.

The day before I was due to be discharged, a week after I'd entered, I was taken off the intravenous and given Keflex. Antibiotics needed to be taken for fourteen days, so I needed an oral form to take home with me. Kanamycin was the drug in the intravenous, but it wasn't made in oral form. I remembered that I'd taken Bactrim and Keflex together. Chris thought I'd had an allergic reaction to Keflex; I thought it was to Bactrim. Who knew for sure? Keflex seemed worth another try.

On the following day, an ugly, red rash began blooming on my arms and feet, and my hands puffed up so much that I couldn't bend my fingers.

Keflex was stopped. By now I was sure I was allergic to all antibiotics. I left the hospital the next morning with no medication. Chris hadn't yet had time to consult with the infectious-disease specialist to come up with an alternative. Given my track record, that was totally irresponsible from a medical viewpoint, but I couldn't bear the hospital for another second. If I hadn't written down all the medications I'd ingested, I couldn't have remembered them, never mind when I'd taken each or what the reaction was. It was all an ugly mess I wanted to forget.

* * *

My world at home was very different from the hospital. I could forecast the scenario. One walk downstairs would prove to be my major activity of the day for a while. After that, preparing a meal might be the crowning event—if my energy lasted long enough to execute what I had planned—or a burden which reduced me to tears if it didn't. For the past year since Brenda had moved, I had a weekly housekeeper, Duffy. She was warm, peppy, and bright and ended up doing far more than cleaning. Unfortunately, she had moved away to start summer school a week before I was hospitalized. We therefore had no help at home.

Chris called shortly and suggested the next drug alternative: nalidixic acid. My drug books didn't say anything terrible, but when I took it I was terrified anyway. As each hour passed without a problem, I gradually relaxed.

As soon as I relaxed, however, I discovered I had a vaginal fungus infection. Would the trauma never end? Fungus infections are a common side effect of antibiotics and easily treatable, but I didn't know that. No one had reminded me that I could get one. I called Chris, read books to see what natural means of treatment might help, called in his prescription, arranged for it to be picked up, and worried. Who could predict what an ordinary fungus infection might do in my body? Adding this new medication to nalidixic acid, prednisone and Plaquenil, an anti-malarial drug used in lupus, it seemed my whole day was consumed in taking medications.

That first night at home we received a phone call from middle-aged friends who had worked long and hard to adopt a baby. It had died a few days after birth. I was jolted out of my self-pity. Hearing a tragedy worse than my own shrunk my own problems down to size.

* * *

Twelve days after I left the hospital, I went back again. The symptoms were the same. So was the confusion. No one knew if I was having a drug reaction, more infection, or both.

Eventually they concluded it was infection. "Acute oophoritis," inflammation of the ovaries, and "acute salpingitis," inflammation of the Fallopian tubes. Chris said, "Since the organs are all close together down there and the tissues are quite penetrable, it's not surprising for an infection to spread."

Could these reruns could have been avoided if I had taken that very first antibiotic, Chloromycetin? Would nothing put out this fire? What if I were being given the best treatment possible and even *that* didn't work?

I was put on another antibiotic intravenously, the seventh: Cleocin. Why not Kanamycin, the antibiotic with which I'd had no problems? Chris gave me some explanation which made sense, but I still held my breath and waited for the worst.

David brought Adam to see me every day. At first he ignored me entirely. Then he conveyed that life was a lark: "Dad and I eat out every night. So far we've gone to Friendly's, Notis Pizza, McDonald's, Barbara and Imre's, and Nana's. I *always* get dessert."

I shuddered. In homes, he was at least offered a vegetable before dessert.

Adam interrupted any sentence I addressed to David. "Let me go to the soda machine. Can I have a candy bar? Let me have a dime, Daddy. I'm hungry again."

The single disciplinarian bone in David's body had vanished. He jumped as quickly to Adam's "I'm hungry" as he might ordinarily to "I have to go to the bathroom now, Daddy."

I said, "Dad keeps some apples in the car. Next time, why don't you see if you can remember to bring them up to my room."

"I don't want apples. And don't tell me that psychologist stuff."

I felt too helpless to say anything more. Was I being petty? Undoubtedly. Even my son had more power than I. Feeling I had so little control over my life dragged my spirit downward.

I almost can't write what happened next, for it seems absolutely incomprehensible. As usual, I needed an oral antibiotic to complete the fourteen-day treatment at home. Chris prescribed *Bactrim*! I can't remember what he said. It must have been something like, "If you had a drug reaction last time you were hospitalized, it had to be a reaction to Keflex. Bactrim was obviously not the problem." He must also have made some case for Bactrim instead of other drugs we hadn't tried. Somehow I let myself get talked into it.

All I could think of was getting out of this hell hole. "Just let me out of here," I pleaded to the skies. "Let me get well. Then I'll get a new physician."

* * *

I wasn't home more than six hours when the symptoms began.

I didn't think. I didn't feel. I just dialed the phone. David and I drove to the hospital silently.

With each hospitalization, my spirit and my battered body fell far into a deep, black abyss and crashed to an unseen bottom. Each time, the abyss loomed bigger and blacker and deeper. It took longer and was harder to pick myself up. Each time, I lost some hope. By now, the end of round three, I'd lost confidence in the natural healing capacity of my body and had no confidence at all in doctors.

Much later I concluded it was the extreme swings from relative strength to acute weakness within a short space of time that banished my hope. I was riding a diabolical roller coaster. Just when I found my feet enough to begin to feel hopeful again, crash, another round of despair-producing events.

* * *

We had planned with some excitement to go to England in July. It was out now, almost forgotten. My bedroom was the only place I felt remotely safe. Cape Cod, where we were to spend our vacation in a month, seemed a long two hours away. The thought of a three-hour drive to see Dr. Lowen overwhelmed me.

At least once a day, as a slender thread connecting me to sanity, I reviewed the data: my primary problem was lupus. My mixed-up immune system didn't easily fight ordinarily treatable infections. Some of the symptoms during the infections could have been allergic drug reactions. I probably didn't feel the symptoms of infection because the prednisone was suppressing the inflammation of lupus and any other inflammations. I could find no simpler way to say it. I was often lost by the time I got to the end of this recitation and had to start at the beginning again.

There were few journal entries that month. One was:

How different this hospitalization would have been if the doctors and you admitted your mutual helplessness. Disagreements occur among bright, educated, thoughtful people, even those with medical training. Your situation was very complex. There were legitimate questions about diagnosis and treatment. Dispel any remaining illusions: just because it's allopathic medicine doesn't mean things are clear and simple.

11

New Paths

In August we went to our house in East Falmouth. David did repair work on the house and played tennis. I exchanged my bed at home for the couch at the Cape.

One of my fantasies about this vacation was that Adam would hang around the couch to get reaquainted. Instead, he was in and out of the pond all day without supervision.

I tried to forget my fear. But by mid-afternoon the second day, it had escalated to terror. Every hour was a nightmare. Each sound outdoors made me jerk. Sometimes I lurched toward the door. I saw myself staggering outside barefoot, arms uplifted, screaming, "Help! Someone please help! Please save my drowning son!"

I thought an adult should be at the water or that a six-year-old needed a life jacket. David disagreed and wouldn't support any rules. Was this my own helplessness projected onto my child? My own fear of death? Or was David right? I couldn't sort this out at all.

I kept telling myself, "If you can't change the situation, change your focus. Worrying is the wrong kind of stress." Mental relaxation techniques, even simple breathing exercises, didn't work. Although I had tried using guided imagery techniques drawn from the Simontons (the Texas oncologist and his wife who taught them to cancer patients) with clients and students, I couldn't coax myself to stay with them now. Only books diverted me from worry and pain. I read on the couch for the fifteen-minute stints my eyes and brain could tolerate. I found research articles but they were hard to digest. Often the best I could do was to copy significant sentences or paragraphs, hoping to review and absorb them later. My pen sometimes dribbled off the page mid-sentence as I drifted off to sleep, only to be jolted awake half-dreaming of Adam drowning.

One study I came across was about depression in lupus patients. Finally, a study about lupus! Depressed patients with lupus, the authors claimed, had "an unusual need for activity and independence," which was "a denial of the guilt-provoking wish for maternal affection. Activity warded off depression in such individuals by representing the ability to provide for one's own needs."

Depression seemed a normal reaction for anyone unable to care for even the simplest of physical needs, and didn't activity also ward off depression in people who weren't sick?

Something about the article hit home, however. I was beginning to feel my own need for more nurturing. I had an intense drive to prove myself by staying active, hanging in, and underneath that a deep longing to be taken care of. The two sides had been constantly at war since I became ill. If depression in lupus was related to lack of nurturing, there was no substitute for filling the need. If I aimed only to become active and independent once again, I'd mask the issue, not resolve it.

Seen positively, the extreme dependence and inactivity of lupus provided me with an opportunity to receive all kinds of nurturing more directly and fully. Illness was a way of dismissing false dichotomies and divisions, an inner "breakdown" or "crackup" necessary for self-healing. My troublesome facade would melt. A richer, stronger me would eventually emerge.

Was there a lupus personality? I still wondered. Two clients with lupus had been referred to me recently. Between appointments as I tried to decide whether to take them on, I worried about them constantly. I should be in their homes, pitching in. Soon I began to see what other therapists had told me would be true: this early in the illness I didn't have sufficient detachment to be properly helpful. I referred them on. My initial impression was that we were different personality types, but we had common emotions. They were angry and self-blaming, too. They explained these emotions similarly. Lupus was often invisible, and severe exhaustion was a prominent symptom. People therefore thought lupus was in your head. You began to doubt yourself and were simultaneously angry at the world for not believing you when you said you were sick.

* * *

For a few days, I couldn't stop thinking about belief and its part in healing. When I still had some confidence in antibiotics, the results had varied. When I had completely lost faith in both medications and my physician, I took the sixth antibiotic with no problem. That made me ready to join the physicians' side: how much the patient believed in treatment was irrelevant.

I could have more accurately concluded that in the absence of a pattern, no conclusion was possible. Or that my results simply reflected my particular belief: trust in medications was a subtle factor which raised the odds for healing. And changing the odds from 49 to 51 could make the difference between life and death. In *Health and Healing*, the physician Andrew Weil said beliefs are the major factor affecting the success of treatments. According to him, if I believed 100 percent that prednisone would cure me of lupus, it would. If I believed totally in snake venom, it would, too.

An article in the American Medical Association Journal described a Filipino woman, married and living in this country, with severe lupus and kidney involvement. She believed she became ill because a rejected suitor had put a curse on her. To cure her illness, she believed she must return to her native country and find a witch doctor who could lift the curse, which she did. When she returned to the United States, her incredulous physician found no evidence of lupus. Two years later she remained free of symptoms and laboratory evidence of lupus.

Beliefs were often attitudes and opinions borrowed from others, but this woman's were gut-level, based on her experience. They had some internal logic. They penetrated the verbal, intellectual level to the deeper strata of the mind. These beliefs were the kind that counted.

Since I believed blocked emotions were so significant in my illness, that raised another question. Why didn't I just have a nervous breakdown? That seemed the most imbalanced part of me. "That would be intolerable! I'd rather die first!" welled up in answer to my question, as my body stiffened. Death was preferable to insanity. Such an instantaneous, intense reaction suggested how totally unacceptable mental illness was to me.

Conclusions of past studies are now in question, but they indicated that the proportion of schizophrenic patients who died from cancer was much lower than that of the general population. Some have theorized that the schizophrenic's lack of ego boundaries — ability to switch personalities, to become John Lennon or Jesus Christ without conflict—operated to prevent physical disease. A personality such as mine, with a high degree of ego control, reflected the opposite. Could a combination of strong ego, iron will, and intense desire to hold on to reason and mental functioning combine to prevent mental break-down?

* * *

Rebecca sent an article from *The New England Journal of Medicine*. It was about Norman Cousins' miraculous recovery from ankylosing spondylitis, another connective-tissue disease also thought to be autoimmune. Creating his own treatment plan, Cousins discovered that ten minutes of belly laughter gave him two hours of pain-free sleep and that his sedimentation rate—a general measure of infection or inflammation—dropped a significant five points after each laughter session. He also took massive doses—up to 25 grams intravenously—of vitamin C which also lowered his sedimentation rate.

I began the article with skepticism. How accurate a gauge was the sedimentation rate in measuring inflammation? Might his sed rate have decreased without vitamin C? But the diseases and treatments were very similar. I was amazed that Cousins found a method for measuring results, since I hadn't found any. His use of the sed rate particularly interested me since every time lupus acted up, my sed rate rose. In recent years it had been the only measure consistently reflecting lupus flares. I had even thought about taking massive doses of vitamin C before I read Cousins' article. By the time I had finished reading, I felt exhilarated. Cousins' combination of science and psychology made more sense to me than anything else I'd read. I slept with the article virtually under my pillow.

I called Rebecca more than once to sort out my excitement at Cousins' take-charge approach. In one conversation, I said, "Probably it's less important that Cousins' measures—sed rate and sleep—were scientifically valid than that he believed they were."

"You think so?"

"I'm starting to. Remember Dr. Simon, the lupus specialist I occasionally see in Boston? The one who said there was no proof of Selye's ideas about stress?"

"Yes."

"I saw him again early this spring. I asked him if he, like Cousins, thought positive emotions had a positive or stimulatory effect on the immune system. Knife-sharp as before, he said, 'Many studies have been done with rheumatoid arthritic patients. Happy patients felt less pain than depressed patients, but the inflammation, when measured by laboratory tests, was the same.' I recall the exact words. His tone of voice so unnerved me, I didn't hear his full response the first time and had to ask again."

"Now I remember. His first comment stopped you for about six months. This last one stopped you for about two weeks."

"When Henrietta Aladjem's lupus went into remission, the doctors called it a 'spontaneous remission' or 'the placebo effect.' They'll say the same about Cousins, too. So what ! If non-chemical healing methods can be that significant, it's even more essential to use them."

"That makes sense to me," she said.

We were lost in our thoughts until I said, "Research will demonstrate far more body-mind connections than we can even imagine. But it will be decades before the hard data is in. In the meantime, I'm more willing to trust my own sense of things."

"You are," she agreed.

I was already on to the next subject. "Cousins had demonstrable results within two weeks. Maybe that's why he had so little inner resistance to doing his healing activities. Most people find it hard to eat better, to stop smoking, to lose weight."

"I always lose weight fast at the beginning of a diet but can't stick with it later when pounds come off more slowly."

"Results can change beliefs, too. Everyone doesn't start out believing in a treatment they try. In *The Words To Say It,* a French writer, Marie Cardinal, said she'd bled continuously from her vagina for years."

"That sounds horrendous," Rebecca said.

"She had tried many doctors and many treatments. Nothing had helped. In desperation, she began psychoanalysis. She wrote, 'At the core of my being, I felt this treatment would have no more effect on me than cauterizing a wooden leg.' On the day of her first session, the bleeding stopped. It never returned. "

"That's amazing."

"Results like that made it easier to stay with three-times-a-week psychoanalysis for several years. And she had very little money."

"I might need dramatic results to invest that much time and money."

"It's so hard to act when you don't feel rewarded. Faith is essential then. To you, what is faith?"

"Something like a deep, internal conviction," she said, and then paused. "Clearly, it doesn't come from external proof or evidence. If I have evidence, I don't need faith."

"It does seem that when I have a lingering doubt about something, sooner or later it happens. Then I say, 'That proves it. My doubt is true.' It's a vicious cycle."

"The mind is so powerful," Rebecca said. "So powerful."

12

Type A Healing

Summer over, I saw five or six clients and taught my graduate course. I taught experientially, and one open-ended evening when I asked for client volunteers Jay came forward. He was 45, worked for a large insurance company, and had just married for the second time. "I want to talk about my marriage," he said. "I'm always waiting for my wife—like I waited for my mother—to do something. Then I get angry if she doesn't. Or if she doesn't divine my wishes, I get angry too." His brow wrinkled. "But that's not her problem, is it? Often I don't know what I want. So how can I tell her? I'm so stupid! " With each sentence, his voice became louder, higher and sharper.

I placed a big pillow in front of Jay and said, "Put Jay there. What would you say to him?"

"I don't even want to talk to him," he said, closing his eyes and moving his hands as if to push the pillow away. "He's so stupid." His hands smacked the pillow.

I said, "If your hands could talk, what would they say?"

"Stupid! Idiot! You don't even know what you want. You are retarded!" He yelled as he whacked the pillow again and again.

Eventually, one movement became a punch, the next, a slower, easier, stroking motion.

I said, "Your hands are doing something different now."

"They're ambivalent. They'd say . . . they'd say," his voice grew quieter and lower, "you're not all bad." Jay started to turn his face away, as if the feelings were too much.

"You mean you care about this guy?" I said quickly.

"Yeah. I care about him a lot. A lot."

"What are you feeling?" I asked.

"Nothing."

"To me your eyes look sad."

"No. Nothing. My mind is blank, too." His eyes looked glazed and unfocused. His hands still appeared to move unconsciously, delicately molding indentations in the sides of the pillow, as if it were a tiny baby, and he was following its contours at the waist. He gently lifted the pillow and then carefully lowered it. He touched its upper half, as if caressing the baby's head. His hands repeated the gestures: patting, soothing, caressing. I looked into the face of this tall lean man. A tear rolled down one cheek, and then the other.

"Yes, I'm sad," he said. "I'm so sad. I don't know what I want. I don't even know who I am. That's sad." He paused for a long time, then started touching the pillow again. "You know I had a teddy bear when I was little . . ."

Only a few minutes of classtime remained, so I gently stopped Jay and asked him to close his eyes and sit with his feelings for a minute. Then I told him to look around the room.

"Joyce is crying," he said, in a voice suggesting that a soft-hearted response from her doesn't surprise him. "Joanne's eyes say she knows what I feel." Then in an amazed voice, he said, "Rob has tears in his eyes." Other group members were crying too.

I imagined that our hearts had picked up each other's rhythm and beat in unison. Mine was melting. I'd been as self-critical as Jay. As he reconnected with his heart, I reconnected with mine.

These classes were so rich. How could I not teach? Wasn't it in pursuing such passions that we coaxed healing our way? Although the classes met at night, and I had to recuperate most of the next day, it seemed worth it.

I was action-filled in other ways too. I arranged for more psy-chotherapy: double sessions with Ildri; a monthly week-end bioenergetic training program in New York; and monthly sessions with Dr. Lowen to coincide with my drive to New York.

My therapeutic activities one week in early 1978 were representative. By this time, my jaw muscles hurt only intermittently. My shoulders, however, ached daily. On Thursday, I saw Ildri and talked about my conflicting feelings toward Adam. I somehow ended up swinging my arms like forceful pendulums, saying, "I love you" with a sweet voice and "I do not love you" with my eyes. On Friday, I saw Dr. Lowen. I can't remember what we talked about. Sometime during the hour, he hit the top of my shoulders in short, hard, karate-chopping motions with the sides of his hands. The blows felt good but hardly made a dent in the tension. I yearned to sob, but barely cried. Saturday and Sunday were the New York training days. I volunteered as a client at some point during the weekend. The trainer showed me more stretching motions lying backwards over the stool. I reached my arms above my head while lying over the stool. The pain increased. When I stood up, he said, "Can you find a position which releases the pain?" I moved around a bit, gravitating toward the same position I did on early, sleepless mornings at home. I hung my head as far forward as possible, chin on my chest. Now, my arms involuntarily lurched forward, and my palms cupped to cover my head, as if to ward off a blow. My breathing probably had been expanded on the stool. I sobbed. I felt very young, humiliated, and ashamed.

Never before had I made the emotional connection between my shoulders and feelings of humiliation and shame as completely and directly as I did that weekend. The pain also disappeared for a while, as it did after each of these other events.

* * *

My dreams were no longer random, innocuous stories from which I awakened motionless. Late in 1977, the old pattern of awakening with my arms straight above my head recurred more frequently. I could never remember my dreams on those days. I asked Dr. Lowen about this. He said something about guilt over sexuality, that I couldn't touch myself "there." I awoke with one of two feelings when my arms were up: that I was being strung up for punishment or was drowning. Was Dr. Lowen right or did I still see lupus as a punishment? The words accompanying the drowning feeling, "I've got to get out of here," resonated more powerfully. Get out of my house? My marriage? My body? At times, they all seemed desirable.

Virtually every day, even when I couldn't remember dream content, I awoke gripped by raw emotion and, except when I found my arms jutting overhead, tightly curled in the fetal position. Finally, toward the end of the year, when I awakened one morning with my arms flung up, I remembered my dream:

> I'm trying to get to a bus station in a strange city, like New York. I'm not sure which is Greyhound and which is Trailways. I start out walking in just enough time. I get panicky. Am I going in the right direction? Is there enough time? Four hoodlums try to stop me; somehow I evade them. I begin walking with another woman. It turns out to be a long way. I don't know if I'll get there in time.

My first reaction was disappointment. Secretly, I hoped this dream would unlock a particular childhood trauma, the trauma. Quickly I saw that part of me *still* longed for a magical answer, as if there were one dream, catharsis, or insight which would solve the riddle of my illness.

Merely remembering this dream was progress, and it reflected increasing synchronization between my day and night life. Was I going in the right direction? Did I have enough time? These two questions haunted me every hour of every day.

Bus stations suggested movement and, since they weren't the safest places, walking to them required independence. Home made me think of my Worcester house but could also mean my childhood home or my inner self, although the latter didn't occur to me then. That I wasn't sure which was Trailways and which was Greyhound suggested I couldn't distinguish one means of movement from another. When my safety was threatened by four thugs, I apparently faced the situation calmly and reasonably. I found a way to escape and did it. When I recognized that I needed support, I chose a woman. We walked. I again chose an independent means of moving.

Dr. Lowen said, "Keep paying attention to your dreams," so

I collected fifty and sent them to him. In the seven he picked for me to analyze, a common theme was retreat. If the places I withdrew to were seen collectively as the illness, there was a pattern: When I expanded out into the world, I felt too vulnerable, and retreated. The illness was a haven. The other theme, as in the bus station dream, was that although frightened, I moved, forward and independently.

* * *

I began massage again. I needed to be loved—held and touched —on demand. How could any adult arrange that?

Theoretically, being loved was simple. When love was offered, whether by husband, friend, acquaintance, or even by a stranger, it flowed into me. I converted it into healing energy.

Practically, it was still hard. My difficulties on the receiving end hadn't vanished. The scene in Ildri's office, and more recently in the bioenergetic trainer's office when my arms bent toward me instead of reaching out, was representative. The needier I felt, the more painful it was to ask. Even when I could comprehend being so disgustingly needy for weeks or months, I could not imagine it for years. After being ill for three years, I felt like an insatiable bloodsucker, and in addition, one who would perish if rejected.

My friends' offers of help often spared me asking. Rebecca usually came to my house. Eventually it became understood that she would, so we didn't have to negotiate every time we saw each other. My friend Pat in Boston almost always initiated phone calls. Suppers with Barbara, Imre and their children were mostly at their house. Receiving such "unearned" love was still difficult. I felt stabs of pain and guilt after getting my "reasonable ration." I still heard a voice harping, "Get up. Move. Give. Repay it now."

Yet, increasingly, I moved beyond that. When Rebecca and I spent an hour together, I still secretly divided the time in half, just as I'd done in The Struck Cafe in 1976. But when it was my turn, I no longer saw my black pain oozing across the table. Instead I felt like an infant. Rebecca's attention was my milk. I sucked greedily. That presented a new problem. The more I imbibed, the more anxious I felt. When she got up to leave, I felt I'd been ripped from the breast.

I allowed these feelings even more with Ildri. A year ago, I anguished about separating from her during the last five minutes of our session. Six months ago, I felt it for the last fifteen minutes. Now my anxiety about parting began when I entered the door.

The anxiety showed itself graphically in massage. I'd found a new household helper, Laura, earlier in the year. Her younger sister had lupus, more severely than I. Three years later, she died. Laura was one of the few people who really understood what living with abominably limited energy was like. She was always on the lookout for alternative healing paths and interested in whatever I did.

When Laura began to study massage, I became her first client. She was familiar to me. She built a fire in the fireplace. Even in late spring, I appreciated that. She spread the blanket on the floor. She closed the shutters to create a warm and cozy nest. All *without my asking*. This was much more important than whether her technique was Reichian, polarity, Shiatsu, or Swedish.

For several weeks during the first half-hour of the massage, I was so anxious that I might be left emotionally and physically opened and unsatisfied, I dared not let myself receive her touch at all. The energy I should have used to take in I gave out in a steady stream of "That's good," "I like that," and "That's wonderful." I was afraid. Would she stop if I didn't give her constant reinforcement? Eventually I dared to risk saying nothing. She didn't stop. She rarely left me before I was ready. That was miraculous.

*   *   *

Every month or so I tried to meditate but found it so frustrating that I decided to stick with contemplation instead. I'd take some idea written in my journal, close my eyes and let my intuitive side respond.

*   *   *

As I'd worked more, tennis as exercise became too difficult. It had to be planned in advance and involved other people. I substituted bioenergetic exercises. They could be adapted to my strength on any particular day, could be done at home, indoors, at any time of day, and they added the special emphasis on emotional release.

After opening my torso, which always felt good, I often worked with my pelvis and legs. Afterwards, pain there often disappeared for awhile. It reaffirmed the principle I'd discovered in 1977 of focusing on strengths rather than obstacles. Instead of moving a sore shoulder, it might be better to see if the other shoulder or opposite hip was supporting its share of weight. The key was *support.* Muscular support was as necessary as emotional support for eliminating blocks and encouraging energy flow.

* * *

When I had vision problems and needed to use my eyes less, I tried using music more consciously. In *Tuning The Human Instrument,* Steve Halpern reminded me that music was energy. Speaking its own vibrational language, music could rebalance and realign every organ, system and cell. Halpern said the body reacted to sound whether we heard it consciously or not.

I discovered that before I could listen to music Halpern said was healing, I needed music that matched whatever emotional state I was in. If I felt sad, the sounds had to reach my sadness. Joan Baez, Judy Collins and Edith Piaf usually did the trick. It didn't matter if the song was about personal loneliness, broken romance or the woes of mankind. When I was agitated, the vibrations had to match that rhythm in me. That required music with a fast tempo and stronger beat.

Once the music matched my rhythm of the moment and touched its source, my heart, it set up a support. That word support kept cropping up everywhere. I could then move to sounds which soothed or revitalized me: slower rhythms, less distinct melodies, and more harmonious and mellow sounds — often those of flutes, harps, and bells.

* * *

Work took on even greater importance as my healing activities increased. The more self-absorbed my days were, the more I craved getting out of myself. It was therefore easy to ignore my promise to myself to take on only ten clients, and soon I had twenty-five.

* * *

139

I wrote in my journal:

> At times I'm beginning to perceive the interrelatedness of it all. Exercise affects my mind and my spirit as much as my body. What I need to heal myself physiologically is also what I need psychologically; what I need systemically is also necessary at a cellular level. The concept of holism is beginning to have meaning.

The effort required to act was so great, I hardly saw what I was accomplishing. I was in a process of choosing. The choices were important ones. They involved problems I wished I didn't have, but I did have choices, and I made them. Since I was more aware of myself than in 1975, I saw more choices. I was choosing methods I believed in and forms I could be successful with. I could do dreamwork on my own and as my energy permitted. While I needed teachers for visualization or meditation, I could contemplate successfully on my own. Seeing a familiar form, contemplation, in a new light was freeing. I did massage right this time, too. I found a skillful masseuse who was also sensitive and able to respond to my special needs. Since I believed health involved a complex of factors, I'd sought a combination of healing methods. Although I hadn't identified nutrition as a separate category, I was working as hard to cut out junk food for my body as for my mind. I wasn't choosing so many methods that I couldn't do any well. In fact, I was putting together a very solid alternative healing program for myself.

The point is that, however briefly I experienced the power, *choice was empowering.* Feeling I had more choices made me feel less helpless.

* * *

When I saw Dr. Lowen in November for my monthly session, I said, "The extent of my resistance frustrates me. Everything is such a struggle. Mothering. Marriage. My healing activities. I have to *force* myself to begin bioenergetic exercises. I have to fiddle around for fifteen minutes before I can concentrate enough even to begin."

Dr. Lowen crisply admonished, "You must stop struggling.

Give it up. Do what's pleasurable."

"You mean I should stop my healing activities? I don't understand."

"You seem grimly determined to carry on even when faced with problems you can't resolve. You must learn to accept defeat as a part of life."

His words seemed important. They weren't sinking in.

"It's hard to stick with these healing activities, week after week and day after day. If I feel strikingly better for a few days, I want to stop exercising or listening to music or eating carefully. I get tired of being locked into a rigid, constrictive program. When I get discouraged, I want to slack off, too. Whenever I lower the medication, I get more symptoms temporarily. That's expected, but it's as if every time I feel better, the reward is a punishment. Even after my body stabilizes on a lower dose of prednisone, my inner experience is that I *never* get much better. I take less medication but feel somewhat the same." I stopped to think more about that. "That's the hardest part."

He said, "I can imagine it is."

I said, "Furthermore, I can't tell when I'm genuinely weaker and shouldn't exercise from when I'm depressed and would feel better if I did. Even on a 'good' day, no matter how carefully I do the exercises, I sometimes hurt more afterwards. No matter how many relaxation exercises I do successfully one day, more symptoms sometimes reappear the next. I feel like a puppet with a hundred strings, each one being pulled in a different direction."

"You want results. Results don't always come in when you need or want them. Your body still needs months, maybe years, to renew itself. You have to be patient."

That was one of Rebecca's familiar lines. I still had little patience.

*   *   *

Near the end of 1978, laboratory data suggested lupus was in remission. I wrote in my journal: "I feel grateful for my health now." On the same page, I wrote:

> I never feel well. Not even close. I *never* have more
> than half the energy I had before lupus. My body still feels

constantly locked into overdrive, heart thumping fast, pores expanded, pupils dilated. My skin is always clammy. My breathing is still shallow, my mouth as dry as sandpaper, and my muscles tense. Every day.

Was I sick or well? Was I healed from lupus but just mentally off balance? There had been times when my lupus laboratory work didn't look good, and I'd felt my lupus best.

I wrote in my journal:

> My unconscious is still my more frequent reality. If health comes only when the personality finds some balance between the conscious and the unconscious, I am still a ways from health.

I was adding on more health activities of the right kind but still clinging to the old framework. It was inconceivable to me that eating, exercising, massage, and stress reduction could be the sole or even primary focus of my days. I had never counted those hours and still did not. Yet my priorities could not be family and work and rest and exercise and other remedies. It was that simple.

I kept remembering *"act radically,"* a journal note I'd written after reading Norman Cousins' article. Real revolt, true revolution, is to break away from a pattern, to inquire outside it. My changes were never revolt. They were merely heightened activity, a more valiant struggle *within* the same pattern.

Eventually, the fuller import of Dr. Lowen's admonishment about struggle began to sink in. I was identifying my despair but not fully accepting it emotionally. Instead of saying, "Okay, I'm defeated. I have failed. Let me proceed from there," I chronically protested, "I'm not defeated. I'm *not* defeated. You can't defeat me." That denial produced a desperate kind of willed action that kept me tense and was self-defeating. Was it a matter of will, or had I still not yet hit bottom? Had I still not accepted "defeat as part of life" as Lowen said?

13

Trust and Betrayal

On New Year's Day I was washing up the supper dishes when my neighbor Sally called. "Adam took Johnny in the woods this afternoon with a box of matches. They could start a fire! It's been cold, but it's dry. I don't want Adam teaching these things to my son."

"What?" I said in amazement, not because I couldn't hear or hadn't understood, but because I felt overwhelmed by what she was saying. She repeated it, this time with rising anger in her voice.

"I'm sorry," I said. "I'll talk to Adam. He is older. He should know better. It won't happen again," I promised, with a certainty I didn't feel.

David came in from outside and I told him. All my hopelessness about controlling Adam poured out. David listened quietly, and then got himself a glass of juice. "Didn't you light matches when you were a kid?"

"Yes, I did! But that's irrelevant! I wasn't anything like Adam! He's way more provocative, on the edge of trouble all the time!"

"What did your parents do?"

I thought back. "They made me light a whole box of them on the back terrace, as a punishment," I said wonderingly. "Pretty odd punishment."

"Did you ever do it again?"

"I don't think so."

Adam won't do it again."

"How can you be so sure? What's our punishment?"

But too late: Adam opened the front door on a straight line to the refrigerator. My anger and David's patience were going to have to lead this round.

"Adam!" I lit in. "Mrs. Wartenberg just called and said you'd taken Johnny into the woods and lit matches. Is that true?"

"It was Johnny's idea."

"Adam, you're eight. Johnny's five. You know you aren't supposed to play with matches. A littler kid doesn't know better. You're responsible in a situation like that."

"Johnny does things like that all the time. You'd be surprised at the things he does. Anyway, it's winter. You can't start a fire in this cold."

"Yes, you can," said David. "It's very dry now. Anything flammable will burn. It doesn't matter how cold it is."

"Yes, it does!" yelled Adam, now cornered.

"Adam, you're not even listening! Stop fighting us and listen! You always cause trouble! You never behave! You're bad! Absolutely hopeless!" I grabbed him by the arm and smacked him on the seat three times, hard. "Never, never, never do that again!" David stared at me stonily, disapproving. He didn't believe in spanking.

Adam didn't shed a tear. We all stood in the kitchen, shaken, not knowing what to say. Finally Adam broke our strained silence. "Mom, I'm not a bad kid. I'm not a good kid. I'm a medium kid."

I suddenly grabbed him and hugged him, closing my eyes to hold back tears. I spank him, he doesn't cry, I thought. It's I who cry. I wanted to wring his neck, but he was also vulnerable and oh, so resilient.

*　*　*

My eyes had become myopic every time I saw Dr. Lowen. If merely seeing him stimulated feelings that were otherwise submerged, something was happening. It made me angry that the unconscious, over which I had so little control, could have such power.

144

I remember returning home after those New York weekends feeling renewed, but David said I came home physically exhausted. A three-hour drive on Friday and a three-hour drive back on Sunday was much more than I drove any other time. That meant extra hours of sun or glare or eyestrain at night. Perhaps my eyes were affected simply because they were overstressed.

They were a weak system anyway. At fifteen, I had burned my left eye severely with the alkaline solution from a home permanent. I was hospitalized, kept completely immobile for a month, and out of school for two months. I began wearing glasses to correct vision in the injured eye and slight myopia which had developed in the other eye.

Dirty snow clumps in April meant spring, but on the drive to New York to see Dr. Lowen, I mostly thought about my eyes and what they were revealing. Acute myopia suggested that I saw only what was up close. "Distance" made me think of future and past time. "Past" brought associations with my father, perhaps because I was driving to Dr. Lowen's.

When I arrived, we talked about my father. "Did your father protect you?" he asked.

"Yes," I replied emphatically.

"Not so," he said. "That's a delusion. Your mother was a frightened little girl herself. When you were born, she didn't want a child yet. Having a girl was even harder. You turned to your father for protection and nurturing. To a point he responded. But somehow you felt tremendously disappointed by him, abandoned, even *betrayed*. The feeling was so deep you felt you could die. The only way you could survive was to deny the betrayal, to conclude, 'Some day he will love me. Some day my prince will come.'" And, after a pause and in a softer tone of voice, he added, "You must give up the delusion that your father was there for you."

My thoughts stopped.

"Lie down on the couch now. Reach up with your arms. Do it slowly enough so you can feel your body sensations as you reach."

At first, I held my breath. Gradually, I began to lift my hands from my chest. I was surprised. My arms were full of feeling. The higher I lifted them, the more I felt. Although my jaw and the rest of my body felt tight, my arms trembled. I began to breathe more easily. Eventually my hands throbbed slightly. My fingers tingled.

"Put your head back a little," he said, touching my forehead. "Let your mouth soften. Just let go. Reach up with your lips."

Soon my lips began to quiver.

"What do you see?" he asked.

"My father's face." I was shocked. Despite my resistance, I saw his face, his warm, loving eyes.

"What do you feel?" he asked.

"Loving," I said.

"Anything else?" he quietly said.

I didn't want to admit what I felt. I finally dragged out, "Longing." My eyes filled with tears.

"Say, 'You weren't there,' to your father."

I opened my mouth. Nothing came out. He could see that I was struggling.

"Try it," he coaxed. "Say, 'You weren't there,' to your father."

I opened my mouth again. A tunnel of pain the width of my neck moved from my mouth down to the center of my chest. Time stood still. No words came out. My face moved from one pained expression to the next. Emotions I never showed the world were all on display.

"Why don't you sit up now?" he eventually said.

As I sat up, I felt dizzy again, even more disoriented than before. This time I saw an image of some walls of rock I'd examined with my college geology class in the foothills of the Colorado Rockies. We'd driven there to examine the upended rock. I remember feeling amazed as I looked at thousands upon thousands of layers of rock, millions of years old. I felt awestruck now, as if I'd glimpsed layers of lifetimes of feeling inside me. But the feelings were too much. I couldn't stay with them. I rushed back into my head. "Why my eyes and why now?"

"Seeing clearly and fearing what you will see is the issue which is now in the foreground."

"But," I countered, "maybe it's just too much driving, or general over-exhaustion, or because they're weak from the childhood accident."

"They could be weak; they probably are. But they'll improve to the degree that the conflict can be resolved."

As we ended that session, Dr. Lowen said, "The next teaching seminar at my Institute will be about the relationship between the psyche and somatic illness. Would you like to be the 'presenting patient'?"

I hesitated. We discussed the pros and cons briefly, but it seemed a unique opportunity. I said, "Yes."

Four days after I left Dr. Lowen's house, everything more than a foot away was a blur. I considered the secondary benefits: at least the myopia caused me to withdraw from the outside world, and after I had the confidence that prednisone would eliminate the problem, the withdrawal was pleasant. Instead of a revved-up prednisone high, this was cozy, painless and womb-like, the same enclosed sensation I felt when sitting in my warm house as the first soft snow fell. When a voice deep inside accused, "See, you're out of control," instead of panic, I felt relief. The paradox was stunning: lupus as retreat, however painful, from stress and tension. It was the same observation I'd made when analyzing my dreams in 1978.

* * *

Four days before Dr. Lowen's seminar, I got the flu. I would need to talk that night and it had settled in my throat.

I called Dr. Lowen. My throat hurt so much that I measured every word. "Flu," I croaked feebly, "might not remain flu in my body. I can't decide if coming to New York is worth the risk."

"How long have you had it?" he asked.

"Three days," I responded.

"Any fever?"

"One hundred and two the first day. One hundred yesterday and today," I said.

"I think you should come. This seminar will be very important to you," he said without hesitation and with his usual authority. "The bug's probably reached its peak. You'll feel better by Friday."

As soon as I hung up, I was furious. I had intended to use him as a resource. He responded as an authority. Did he want me at the seminar for his purposes? Did he have any concern for my health? I felt used.

David cancelled my Wednesday and Thursday appointments.

I went to bed for two days, getting up on Friday only in time to dress, grab a snack, and get in the car to drive to Dr. Lowen's. By this time I felt somewhat stronger. I could speak without sharp pain, although my voice was weak and raspy. I left home feeling guilty that David had had to wait on me so much. I'd virtually ignored Adam for three days.

When I reached Dr. Lowen's house, I was steaming. "I needed your help to sort out the pros and cons of whether to come, not to tell me what to do. You acted as if your mere suggestion that I'd get better would actually make me well." If I stopped, my courage might dissolve. I continued quickly. "I don't think you gave a damn about me. And you're my therapist. Your main concern should be my health and life! You cared only that your seminar would be less interesting without a live patient! That you wouldn't look so good!"

"Yes, I did attend to my own needs." His tone of voice implied that that was exactly what he should have done.

I felt hateful but said nothing.

He was silent, too, for several moments. Then he said, "On second thought, I think you're right."

That totally disarmed me. I was so shocked I almost broke into tears. If I had believed he was genuinely sorry, I would have cried. But I suspected his response was also a strategy to pacify me. A hostile patient would not make tonight's presentation easier.

The clinical seminars and our training weekends were held in an office building a few blocks from Grand Central Station. The large rectangular room and two smaller rooms were free of furniture and had thick carpets with lots of colorful pillows. Six or seven rows of folding chairs had been set up in a semicircle at one end of the big room for the seminar. The audience was limited to members of the New York Institute of Bioenergetic Analysis who were practicing therapists or trainees.

Dr. Lowen and I sat on folding chairs facing the audience. The recessed lights, except those on us, were turned down to signal that it was time to begin. I was suddenly grateful that the ten people in my own training group and our trainer, Ed, were in the room with me.

Dr. Lowen suggested I pull my chair closer to his. I was struck once more by how similar he seemed to my father—their muscular,

agile builds and their direct, warm eyes. I was struck by a difference, too. Instead of asking me to move closer, I thought my father
might have pulled his chair closer to mine. Was that delusion again?
To give the audience a feel for who I was, he began asking me about
my childhood, current life, marriage, and so on—the same kinds of
questions he asked at my first therapy session with him.

As the evening progressed, Dr. Lowen articulated his central
thesis: I converted unconscious or unrecognized emotions into
physical symptoms. "The illness," he said, "is almost like a physical
hysterical symptom." I recalled Freud's famous patient, Anna O.,
whose paralyzed limbs, poor vision, coughs, muteness, and
headaches disappeared as she recalled the first time the symptom
had appeared and relived the accompanying emotions. I guessed Dr.
Lowen meant that instead of an anxiety reaction which resulted in
a paralyzed arm, my illness was organic *and* was also an anxiety
reaction in my whole body.

He asked the audience, "What are the forces in her personality which could lead to the illness?" A few people responded, and he
described my father-oedipal story and the bioenergetic reaction.

"What has to happen for her to get well?" he asked the audience.

That one, too, he eventually answered himself. "Her outer
structure—emphasis on rationality and reality—has to collapse.
Then her body won't have to do all the reacting. She has to give
up the delusion that her father will rescue her. When she does, she
will go into despair. Despair will manifest itself in deep crying,
which is her way out. She has to feel it, to go to the very bottom of
it. Then she will stop struggling, and healing can begin."

He continued to talk to the audience. I was lost in thought.
Rationally, David was a good choice as a husband. But why hadn't
I chosen someone with whom my emotional connection would be
more like I claimed to want? Had I known that opening my heart
more was too risky for the twenty-five year old me? When I tuned
in again, he was saying something about crying deeply so "the
pulse would break through the pelvic floor into release." "Opening
into pleasure" and "the trap door opening and breaking out into
sunshine" were other words he used. Such phrases still made me
lose my bearings.

"How can we get more access to my tears?" I asked.

"Once you get to the point where you know where you have to go, I'll put so much pain in you, you'll have to cry. I will keep it going until you break down."

Whoa! I thought. You sadist! Don't you even come *near* me! My body closed down entirely from the shock of his words. Once again, I felt he'd taken advantage of my vulnerability, but I was too overwhelmed to say more than, "No. Not here. No! I don't want to do that tonight."

Going over this experience later, I thought that if I confronted him about this incident, he would soften his statement and agree that my body needed particular care. But why should I have to police him, of all people, on this issue?

I also thought he would be more interested in my own understanding of my illness. I had foolishly imagined he would say, "You've lived with this illness for four years. What are *your* ideas about its genesis? What do *you* think needs to happen for you to get well?" But Dr. Lowen's emphasis was consistently on his truth, and what he was teaching me and the audience was that this very Freudian set of insights was *the* truth. I felt awe and respect that he saw some portion of my essence so clearly. But his truth was not quite my truth.

I had wanted to throw out other questions to the therapists in the audience, to see if any therapist had worked with patients who had lupus. I wondered what experience other therapists had with their patients with physical illnesses. Was exploring symptom as metaphor helpful? Had dreams predicted illness or the onset and location of symptoms? How else had dreams been useful? I even wondered if my fear of doing hard and deep body work was merited or if it was only the kind everyone has in depth therapy: fear of the buried, unreleased feelings.

The evening ended around 10:30. Out-of-town students of the Institute were allowed to sleep overnight during training weekends. I dropped onto a mattress in one of the smaller rooms, my body an exhausted knot, and did not sleep a wink. I didn't participate in the next day's training and finally relaxed enough to sleep around noon. I dozed most of that day and night and part of the next, rising in time to make the journey home.

In my mind, I could not help returning to a moment in the presentation that seemed significant. Toward the end of the evening, I wanted to hear from the audience. I said to Dr. Lowen, "We haven't given them a chance to talk much. I know only what this guy thinks." I pointed to the only person who had spoken frequently throughout the evening, a burly, mustached man sitting toward the front.

The man responded, quietly, "What *do* I think?" The audience chuckled. I didn't understand why. Then out of the blue, in a loud, harsh, piercing voice, he continued, "I'll challenge you. Do you know what I think? Can you say it?" And after a grand pause, as I sat open-mouthed, he taunted, "Or," pausing again, "would you like to let that chance slip by?"

Not knowing what provoked all this, I concluded that bioenergetics had its share of dopes. I said, quietly but firmly, "Yeah, I'd like to let it slip by."

"Like a lot of other things," he mocked, even louder.

I still said nothing, but rage shot out of my eyes. If eyes could burn, that man would have been scorched.

Afterwards, people told me he was Stanley Keleman, probably the second most prominent bioenergetic theoretician and clinician in America, who had himself trained a whole generation of bioenergetic therapists on the west coast. He was in New York to lead a workshop at the Institute the following day. Members of my training group said provocative confrontation was his typical style. They thought that he was just displaying his own neuroses—smart people can also behave stupidly—or that his anger was meant to say to Lowen, "Move over, I'll show you how to do this right."

All I knew was that this rush of rage through my eyes seemed important. Was this the right feeling in the right organ (blocked eyes) but directed at the wrong person? It was safer to burn a stranger than Dr. Lowen and, certainly, than my father. Although I had begun to identify and express anger at Dr. Lowen, more often I'd shied away from it. Plenty of anger remained unexpressed.

My immediate reward for the New York venture was a week and a half in bed. This time my eyes became swollen and sore, but my vision never became myopic.

* * *

As I watered the greenhouse plants in May, I felt as bedraggled as they looked. The rest of the spring and summer was a roller coaster of symptoms. When I saw Chris in July he said that my blood complement—one of the measures of lupus activity—was low. I was to go back onto prednisone, 15 milligrams.

We left in early August for two weeks at the Cape, and I was determined to use it well. I pictured cheerful activities, not just lying on the couch: I would pick wildflowers for the table and walk on the beach when the sun went down. I would lie on the sand and really listen to the ocean. I would sit on the dock of the pond and watch our tanned, tousled-haired boy wade into the sandy bottom of the pond to catch frogs.

I also hoped to have some pleasant night-time dock talks with David. Since he'd been in therapy, our conversations had livened up. I was particularly interested when he shared what he'd discussed in therapy, which he described as a place to air his grievances against me. I couldn't see that he was getting closer to the deeper-level intimacy issues involved, but since all our conversations seemed more animated, I didn't think much about that. He was considering ending the therapy in the fall. I regretted that, but the drive to Boston was very time-consuming, and I wasn't in a good position to protest much.

My images dissolved in two days. A fluttery abdomen became sharp pain and urination became difficult. I went to the emergency room at the Cape Hospital after calling Chris and learning he was on vacation; they gave me Keflex for what they diagnosed as a urinary tract infection. But the symptoms didn't go away. I returned to Worcester as angry-looking blisters were beginning to erupt along the back of my right leg and over my right buttocks.

Chris took one look: "It's shingles, an inflammatory condition involving the nervous system. It typically affects only one side of the body at a time, not unusual with lupus. Prednisone is sometimes used, but you're already on that." He launched into a tirade about the Cape hospital having given me Keflex, when a culture taken there indicated a urinary infection.

* * *

I saw Dr. Lowen once in September and twice in October. In one of the October sessions he said, "I've never been able to get the arthritic patients I've worked with to fully express their anger. My attempts have generally resulted in a worsening of the arthritis, and they, consequently, stopped the therapy. They couldn't express any real anger because they were too frightened or too guilty. So, instead of getting the energy into their hands and limbs, they withdrew it. That led to shock and an exacerbation of their illness. It's the same problem as yours. We'll just have to keep working through your fear and guilt."

At another point in a session, I asked, "At the seminar, what did you mean when you said you would put so much pain in me, I'd have to cry?"

"What I meant was that when you're *completely* convinced that you need to feel the depths of your despair, we'll find a way, even if it means I have to force it," he said.

*　*　*

I turned thirty-eight in September. I decided to have a party, to take some initiative in creating a celebration. It turned out to be a graceful, flowing evening. My friends brought most of the food, and the dinner was a delightful melange, aesthetically pleasing, nutritious. I'd asked each guest to make a gift of a cassette tape of music she loved. The selections ranged from classical to folk to New Age, all delightful.

Afterwards, I had a better understanding of my difficulty in asking friends to help. It was more than my inability to ask. A chronic illness with exacerbations and remissions presented special difficulties. I had to decide when I needed help, ask, decide when I no longer needed it, tell the friend, decide when I was in need again, and ask again. No dependable routine developed for either of us. Also, friends tired of years of giving. However much I needed to learn to ask, they needed to be able to give in ways they wanted. Considering all these factors was exhausting. No wonder I often chose not to ask.

The party also reminded me that indeed I had the rich friendships so longed for in that first hospital bed in 1975. It wasn't so much that I hadn't had friends then as that I felt their caring more richly now. I no longer felt chronically needy. I could accept some love and nurturing. Massages needed to last only 45 minutes. I was no longer anxious about separation when I was with Rebecca or Ildri.

But I blamed myself for every little mistake of Adam's. I became convinced his behavior resulted from having a crazy mother. What if my despair, rage, and paranoia leaked into him and became his?

Dr. Lowen helped me see it differently.

"You are wrapped up in saving him because you need to save yourself," he said matter-of-factly. "You'll be able to change Adam only as much as you change yourself. If you focus on Adam, then you go back into your old role as protector, but you'll sacrifice part of yourself. If you focus on helping yourself as a person, then you'll be there for Adam, too, because you are his mother."

"You mean that if I want to raise a healthy child, I should heal the child inside myself first?"

"Yes."

I felt immensely relieved. For once, I didn't mind his cocksureness. I wanted to jump up and embrace him. His words kindled a burst of hope.

14

Facing Death

In October, I finally changed doctors. Before Barbara and Imre moved, they had introduced us to their friend "Lutzey" Leb, a hematologist, and his wife. We saw them a few times at Barbara and Imre's house. I liked Lutzey and even talked about my illness at a dinner party. He seemed interested. I mentioned my desire to change from my rheumatologist, Chris, as my primary physician and my reservations about changing. Although I knew there were still a lot of unknowns, his responses reassured me.

David and he began to jog together. One day he asked how I was. David said, "Not so good."

"Have her call me," he said.

That was just what I needed to hear. I saw him in his office the next day. When I mentioned I didn't have the energy to talk with Chris if I stopped seeing him, he said, "Let me take care of it." He told me what he would say, diplomatic and honest words. His phone call to Chris allowed me to make the transition. When he didn't pressure me into any kind of commitment to him, I knew he would be my new doctor.

Late in November, I had more blood tests because my blood complement had risen significantly. I didn't feel the least bit better.

I saw Dr. Lowen the first week in December and made another appointment for the 19th. I hoped keeping closer tabs on myself before a vacation would ward off another holiday disaster. Vacations required enforced intimacy; maybe I upped the pressure on myself to be cheery, vibrant, and fun, especially at Christmas.

Soon I was again anxiously marking off the days on the calendar until vacation. My journal had no entries after the 13th, and I had to be in bad shape to give that up. My eyes took on a slant and gradually became puffier over the week. There were days of nausea and weakness. I felt better on the 18th and thought I would drive to Dr. Lowen's, but the next morning I could hardly move. Was it lupus, the flu, or an infection? Lutzey and I decided to call it flu until there were other indications it was something worse.

Christmas week we had planned to go to Vermont with my sister Karen and her husband, Jay. We'd stay at an inn near our friends, Elvin and Lee. Since I felt better the day we were to leave, Lutzey encouraged me to go. I was peppy and calm enough to take in the scenery and felt enlivened watching the greys and greens slither deeper into each other as we drove higher north.

The mountains were almost bare, but David and Adam skied on what snow there was, hiked, and played all day. I stayed in bed and joined everyone for dinner at night. The more limited my energy, the more I was savoring the few pleasures I had. Delicious inn food and the good company of my family and friends were enough.

After the third day, I definitely felt worse. The base of my skull throbbed with pain, and my face ballooned. My eyes swelled almost shut, transforming me into a creature from outer space. Food and friends no longer held my interest. I felt no fury, not even "why me?" I only longed for help. I called Lutzey.

"How long will it take you to drive back to Worcester?" he asked, knowing I minimized problems.

"About two-and-a-half hours," I said, feeling less tense just to hear his voice.

"I'll be at the hospital to admit you when you arrive," he said quietly.

It was Christmas Eve. As they put the sterile white johnny on me, I felt relieved. That meant I was sick. I would be taken care of, I could collapse.

Lutzey consulted this hospital's chief rheumatologist, Dr. Pindera. He took one look at my bloated face and eyes and said, "I think she has kidney problems."

"I'd better call in a kidney specialist," Lutzey said.."I'll call Dr. Roth, the head nephrologist here. He's very competent."

When protein was found in my urine, the doctors surmised I had lupus kidney involvement. Dr. Roth came into my room and called for a kidney biopsy.

The new medical trend toward recognizing patients' rights to have full knowledge of diagnoses and procedures was coming into vogue. My first taste came when Dr. Roth breezed in the door with his entourage of five students shortly before the biopsy procedure. He said, "In a kidney biopsy, the skin, muscles, and tissues are penetrated with a needle to reach the kidney. The needle is a special one which enables us to remove a core. The primary complication can be internal bleeding."

He said more about the odds of internal bleeding and the possible extent of damage. I heard the word "death." By the time he finished his speech and said, "Do you have any questions?" I was reeling. His words felt like a fist between my eyes. I who worried about everything had not thought much about the risk from a biopsy. Yet hearing the worst was far better than being informed of nothing.

Kidney biopsies, I later read, are not considered worth the risk by some specialists, but when Lutzey had recommended it, I didn't have enough energy even to raise the question. The only thing to do was to submit and to relax as much as possible. During the next few hours, I used every breathing technique I knew. Repeatedly I visualized myself being wheeled smiling and unscathed from the operating room.

The anesthesiologist came in with a needle for a local. I pried out of him that it was a "caine" drug. He was unaware that lupus patients are frequently allergic to them. Given my track record, I thought I had as much chance with that medication as with any other, so I said nothing. I breathed even deeper as the needle went in. I steadfastly reran the image of a smiling me on the stretcher.

The next jolt was seeing a medical fellow I had never met holding the biopsy needle poised above my back. When despite cool coaching from Dr. Roth and attentive silence from the remaining cluster of residents he missed the kidney in his first two attempts, I had just about run out of calming strategies. Fortunately, his next puncture was successful.

The biopsy results were back in two days. When Dr. Roth came in, he said, "The biopsy showed that your kidney has been affected by lupus. The technical diagnosis is diffuse proliferative glomerulonephritis. It's easier to say lupus nephritis. Unfortunately, it's the most serious kind of lupus kidney involvement." He continued to talk, but I had already stopped breathing.

I looked over at David. He looked gray. We both looked back at Dr. Roth as he continued, "Prognoses vary. Some people recover well. The best treatment for you seems to be more of what you've had. First, we'll give you large doses of prednisone intravenously. Then we'll raise your oral prednisone dose to sixty milligrams daily. I have other drug possibilities in mind, too, but we can talk about that later."

He continued to talk. I missed more sentences until I heard, "Loss of the kidneys is possible. That's not what we're aiming for, of course, but if the disease progresses to end-stage renal failure, dialysis or transplantation are possible. Dialysis involves going to the hospital about three times a week for several hours. Losing a kidney doesn't sound good, but in fact, you won't have any lupus problems in your kidneys afterwards. The success rate is very high for transplants, and the new kidney usually works very well."

Then I heard the word "death." It had the same effect as when I'd heard it when Dr. Roth discussed the biopsy. I didn't hear anything more. All at once my muscles and bones seemed to come unhinged and float into space, all separate of one another.

I started listening again when Dr. Roth said, "Do you have any questions?" He looked at each of us.

"Well, probably," I said slowly, "but I can't think of them now."

"It's a lot to take in all at once. I'll be back tomorrow, and you can ask questions then."

After Dr. Roth left, David and I looked at each other and out the window. I saw neither David nor the view. We sat in silence for a long time. Finally I said, "Did he say recovery was possible?"

"Yes."

"And that so was loss of the kidneys?"

"Yes."

"And so was death?"

"Yes."

"The way he said it made possibilities sound like probabilities. Was it just me? When I'm this weak, I tend to hear the negative more strongly."

"His style was sledgehammerish. The doctors are new at this patient's rights business." David hesitated. "I think he meant to convey that death was possible, not that it was probable."

"I hope so."

When Lutzey came, I cried. Instead of making a quick exit from my room or injecting me with some "chin up, old girl" routine, he simply said, "I know you're discouraged. I would be, too." At his instruction, no doubt, nurses dropped in every so often, quietly attentive, offering their best. I flipped from disbelief and terror to tears most of the day. Lutzey checked on me again in the evening. Whatever he said about lupus nephritis made recovery seem possible if not likely.

Nonetheless, I felt continual shock and anger. How could this be? Why didn't I identify these problems during the fall? I had assumed puffy eyes were a companion to blurred vision. That puffy eyes might imply kidney problems had never occurred to me. If I'd had any inkling, I would have opened my *Merck* manual to read under *nephritis*: "Edema develops in most cases. It may be noticed first as puffiness of the face and eyelids...."

Why had none of the doctors noticed the kidney problem prior to this? When Chris was still my doctor, why hadn't he said something? Despite the strain in our relationship, he was usually open with me. He must have mentioned the possibility, or else he said what Lutzey and Dr. Roth said now, that since there was no evidence that patients benefited from early aggressive treatment, he would have done nothing different anyway. That made me feel as helpless as ever.

Yet again, despair returned. After the 1977 hospitalizations, I was sure I'd reached the depth of the blackness. I was sure the pit had bottomed out and that the only place to go was up. Now I found myself in a blacker, deeper abyss, a looming coldness. "I could die. I *really could die*," I heard myself lamenting. Dr. Roth reminded me he had seen many more serious cases. The point here is that I faced death, not that I was, in an objective sense, near death.

Yet, when things were at their darkest, there was an opposing force at work: luck. Luck came my way and left its imprint. Fortunately, it had an equally strong pull. From the second I entered, this hospitalization seemed less toxic than all the others.

Chris was in Vermont for Christmas. Despite having switched to Lutzey, I still felt involved enough with Chris to feel obliged to call. His absence spared me guilt. Lutzey, being Jewish, was more available than usual. At St. Vincent's, most of the doctors and patients were Catholic. Everyone wanted to be at home for Christmas, so the hospital was uncrowded. The staff on duty was skeletal. Except for essentials, I was not disturbed and could rest in peace.

When the nurse was pushing my wheelchair toward my room on Christmas Eve, I worried about what a lousy Christmas it would be for Adam. Rebecca called to say she had invited David and Adam for Christmas dinner. That spared me asking her to include them, for which I felt almost as grateful as for the invitation itself. When Adam reported a day complete with turkey dinner, jolly family, and brightly lit Christmas tree, I relaxed completely.

Now, five days later, whenever I wanted company someone walked in the door. When I wanted contact, but not company, which was more frequent, the phone rang. When I had a problem to resolve, whoever called seemed the perfect person to help me sort it out. The instant I needed something to occupy my mind, my Boston friend, Pat, called and mentioned that *The King and I* was on television. I didn't watch much since my eyes hurt, but listening was enjoyable. The instant I was able to read again, another friend, Mara, walked in with a 1941 issue of *Life* magazine, of special interest to me since I was born that year and big pictures and short articles were all my eyes could tolerate. Everything seemed perfectly synchronized.

Lying there and thinking more about death than ever, I realized my last wish would be to see the people I cared about. They all called or came, partly because they were the only ones left in my life. That I had these nourishing friendships was about the only positive thing that did not seem accidental. I had worked long and hard to create this wonderful network.

This hospitalization continued to be different. A few nurses still thought patients would have mental breakdowns if told their temperatures, but not one nurse hassled me about wearing my own nightgown or about my habit of keeping my door shut. I even knew the electromicroscopist who analyzed my kidney biopsy. His kindness in calling to explain the results and to assure me they had been forwarded appropriately and immediately was one more small, but significant gift.

On the second day, I told Lutzey my only complaint was that the old peoples' moaning all night kept me awake. Could I change rooms? He saw to it immediately without suggesting that I was being difficult. Another time, when I expected him to come in at the end of the day, I woke up with a question I knew would nag at me until I had it answered. Determined to avoid unnecessary stress, I called his office. His secretary said he would return the call. He called shortly, and as if he had read my mind said, "I knew the sooner I called, the less time you'd spend worrying."

Toward the end of this hospital stay, everyone reminded me I should get a second opinion about the kidney. I agreed, even though it meant more doctors. Just as I was rousing my courage to talk with Dr. Roth or Lutzey about that, Lutzey walked in and said, "I think you should get a second opinion. Would you like me to talk with Dr. Roth about that? I presume you'd like to use your Boston lupus specialist, Dr. Simon?"

"Yes."

"I'm sure that would be fine with Dr. Roth."

In other hospitalizations, multiple doctors added to the confusion. In this instance, two doctors worked well. Dr. Roth delivered the facts. Lutzey helped me digest them. He was a wonderful emotional support. Expecting a doctor to be both a technical and relationship expert, the more so when my life was threatened, was a formidable expectation for any one human being. Without design, Lutzey had also become my advocate. My relationship with him was becoming reassuring.

After three or four days of intensive, intravenous doses of prednisone, sixty milligrams of oral prednisone were prescribed. My head spun. That was more than I had ever taken and guaranteed marriage to the drug for at least a year, probably longer. I was determined to get its maximum effectiveness. Each time they hooked up a new intravenous bag, and thereafter when I took pills, I made a fervent, silent plea for its best use inside me.

When Dr. Roth came in to discuss treatment, he said, "I recommend that you take Imuran for two years in addition to prednisone. Imuran is a cancer chemotherapy drug. It's also used after kidney transplants to prevent the recipient's immune system from destroying the new kidney as a foreign invader. Like prednisone, it halts inflammation and suppresses the immune system. The major risk of Imuran," he said, "is the possible occurrence of lymphoid cancers and bone-marrow damage. As you know, the possible side effects of prednisone are much more numerous."

"I've had so few side effects from prednisone, it's easy to discount them. But *cancer*, what an outrageous thing to have to worry about from a drug."

"There isn't hard research data yet, but I believe Imuran is more effective than prednisone alone."

"Your idea is that if we add Imuran, prednisone can be tapered faster?"

"Yes, and that you can eventually be sustained on Imuran alone."

"Which could possibly give me cancer?"

"True, but no choice is without some side-effects." He paused and then said, "If I had to take prednisone or Imuran on a long-term basis, I'd choose Imuran."

"You would?"

"Yes."

"Well, let me think about it. When I'm this weak, my mind isn't so clear. I'm not sure I heard all of what you said or that I'll remember any of it."

"I know how weak you are. You seem to be following what I'm saying."

"Let me talk with David."

"Okay. What I'd like to do is start you on it today. But it can be discontinued within three weeks without problems. That gives you three weeks to make a decision."

After a week in the hospital, I still needed bedpans and nurses to feed and bathe me. Yet since I didn't need any technical hospital care, Lutzey and Dr. Roth were considering sending me home. I had never been this weak.

When Lutzey came in, I said, "Before I go home, I need your help in planning. Right now I can barely move. But I've never taken so much prednisone. I can feel it beginning to rev me up. I imagine it'll soon make me think I have more energy and strength than I do. My tendency is to do too much too soon."

"Even with so much medication, you may feel quite weak for a long time," he said.

"I might?"

"Yes."

"How active should I be when I get home? Give me some explicit guidelines. Please take the decision out of my hands."

"Don't work for a month. Spend *most* of each day resting. Blood will flow better through the kidneys if you're lying down."

My mouth must have dropped open, for he added, "Yes, I know that's a conservative stance." He paused, winked, and said, "It's consistent with my European training!" He knew a Europhile like me would be reassured by those words. My blood flowed better already.

The day I left the hospital may have been New Year's Eve, but the new year was the last thing on my mind.

*　*　*

Even though David and I were veterans, the transition from total care in an institution to none at home was always a jolt. I could foresee where problems would develop between us and initiated discussing ways to avoid them. David knew my peculiarities when weakest: for example, that arriving home to a messy house upset me. He neatened it up so I would not burst into tears when I walked in the door. I cried anyway when I saw the sad state of my plants. Even though they gave me more than I gave them, they withered under anyone else's care.

My good luck continued. Rebecca was on our doorstep with a whole supper. Exactly when those leftovers were finished, another friend appeared with a pot of soup—not just any soup, for which I would have been grateful, but one with sour cream, tomatoes, onions, and garlic, some of my favorite winter flavors. It had to be luck that she arrived the day we ran out of food, and she didn't know me well enough to know that her choice would be so pleasing.

The closest thing to a minor trauma occurred the day after my return. I felt icy cold and assumed it was because my system was so delicate. I wanted more blankets but felt too weak to get them. More luck! Pat arrived with a box of fresh raspberries, my favorite fruit. She said it was freezing inside and that our furnace might be off. Since she owned a huge Victorian house with a couple of apartments, she knew about heating problems. Sure enough, the furnace was off. The temperature outside was close to zero. Pat knew just where the water gauge was, diagnosed the problem, and called David, who called the repairman. Even the repairman came within fifteen minutes. I rejoiced in my good fortune, aware that it was fortune.

I wrote in my journal:

> What I observe about life irritates me. My psychological state does influence my perception. I notice positive events more because my mental state is somewhat improved. But that's not all there is to it. Fewer bad things and many more positive things are actually happening to me this time. It's the experience of more positive moments, *most of which resulted from luck,* that helps hope take firmer root within me. I've done nothing to deserve the good fortune any more than I had done anything earlier to deserve the bad. *That* is a tough lesson.

* * *

After a week at home, I was weaker than I had ever been. I stepped into my terrycloth bathrobe to go downstairs, aware of its weight and of the weight of the left, then the right, sleeve of my nightgown. It took effort to slip my arms through, straining to pull the zipper closed its entire twenty inches. My slippers were kicked under the bed. I had to kneel to find them. It took so much energy, I cried.

Years of illness were taking their toll. I was regaining strength less quickly than ever before. The advantages of a strong constitution and thirty-odd years of a well-balanced lifestyle had evaporated.

* * *

I had one week to make the Imuran decision: Tuesday, January 15, was the deadline. My mind worked so slowly. I could deal with only one question at a time. Since organizing my thoughts and making even one phone call could do me in for a day, a week seemed like an hour.

Lutzey, knowing that nothing reassured me like technical data, had armed me with articles from recent medical journals. Dr. Roth gave me a chapter on lupus nephritis from his soon-to-be-published book, which said that although optimal treatment was controversial, a combination of prednisone and azathioprine (Imuran) was recommended.

I did not reach the same conclusion so quickly. My handbook for prescription medicines noted an "unusually frequent occurrence" of the lymphoid cancers from Imuran. I took advantage of already-scheduled doctors' appointments, carefully deciding who could best answer what, so I wasted no words and needed to talk with each person only once. Everyone—Lutzey, the rheumatologist who'd been consulted, Dr. Pindera, and the other doctor friends whose opinions I trusted—repeated Dr. Roth's comment almost word for word: "If I had to take prednisone or Imuran for a long time, I would choose Imuran."

Their answers were all conditional on being able to eliminate prednisone. Most implied that it could be tapered faster if Imuran was added, but when pressed, no one would even say it was probable. Given that fact, I could not understand why they all said they would take Imuran anyway. I felt that for me to take an anti-Imuran stand would be like David's taking on six Goliaths. I began to doubt myself, using all the old lines: the doctors had more training, more knowledge, and more experience. Maybe my brain had gone soft.

* * *

Although I had much more support, less unnecessary stress, and more positive emotion available than during any other crisis, I remember never being more out of control than when I was in the midst of the Imuran decision. Adam was never more out of control either. My terror of death, the life-or-death quality of that decision, was with me every second. As if that weren't enough, Adam caught a cold. His pattern of catching a cold after I returned from the hospital had become as dependable as my getting sick on vacations. The only warning I had been given about Imuran was, "Don't catch a cold or flu." Upper respiratory infections were dangerous when taking immunosuppressants. One minute I was bidding Adam come closer when he wanted something, reasoning that when he had a cold, I probably would get the bug anyway since we lived in the same house. The next minute I was pushing him away.

One afternoon I let Adam invite a friend over to play. I knew it was a stupid decision. Adam's friends were wild monkeys like himself. Despite my attempt to establish rules in advance, the house became a shambles. In their play, the boys even broke a baluster on the stairs. Their noise, wanton destructiveness, and my impotence to control it crazed me. Although I could barely stand, by the time David arrived home I was screaming—yes, hysterically— "Get him away from me!" I had slapped Adam in the face several times. Bruises in the shape of my fingers remained on his cheek for several days.

One of us, Adam or me, had to get away for the weekend. Months earlier, we had reserved this weekend to go to a different Vermont village and inn than the one we'd stayed in before Christmas. Dave, one of the doctor friends in Boston whom I often informally consulted about lupus, had arranged it. Only because he would be there did I feel safe enough to risk the trip. Miraculously, our former housecleaner, Duffy, was in town. One phone call on Friday brought her a few hours later to care for Adam at home. We arrived at the inn to discover that there was a mistake in the reservations. The innkeepers' marvelous solution was to give us an entire house filled with lovely antiques, guaranteeing quiet.

When we arrived home Sunday evening, Adam, mincing no words, said, "I love you, but it was better to be apart. I had a fun time."

* * *

Time was running out. It was January 10. Decision Tuesday was four days away. My last resort was my Boston lupus specialist,

Dr. Simon. I called him and presented my case step by step and hesitantly.

"Dr. Simon, this is Donna Talman. Dr. Roth sent you my biopsy results. Thank you for looking at them. I saw your letter to him saying you agreed with his diagnosis."

"You're welcome."

"I have a decision to make, and I'd like to ask your help."

"Go ahead."

"Well, as you know, I'm taking prednisone. Since prednisone has to be tapered so gradually, I'm committed to it for however long it takes to get off it. As I understand it, my doctors hope that adding Imuran will make it easier to taper prednisone. But no one will even say it's probable." I paused, but only for the second it took to inhale. If I stopped longer, I feared I'd lose my thoughts.

"My thinking is this: prednisone is still effective in my body. Drugs sometimes lose their effectiveness, and that could happen in the future with prednisone. Why add a new drug when an old one is effective? That's adding unnecessary complications. Even if this particular kidney episode is resolved, I could have another some day. I think I should take only prednisone now and keep Imuran in reserve for such a time."

"I agree with you," he said. "I wouldn't use it either." He hesitated and then added, "For all the same reasons."

I almost dropped the receiver. I was as shocked as when Dr. Lowen agreed with my criticisms of him. I could barely hold back sobs.

As soon as I found my voice, I said, "I can't tell you how relieved I feel. As I told you, everyone else wants me to take Imuran."

"I'd take the prednisone. And for exactly the reasons you've mentioned."

"Well, thanks a lot."

"Sure. Call me if I can be of more help."

I could have asked Dr. Simon to call Dr. Roth. The whole process of getting extra opinions was complex. Dr. Simon had just been officially consulted for a second opinion about the kidney biopsy. In that transaction, he responded by letter to Dr. Roth. Now I was only calling him informally as a resource in helping me make a personal decision. Thus, I certainly wouldn't ask him to talk with Dr.

Roth or Lutzey, nor would I probably tell Dr. Roth that I'd consulted him. That might be seen as playing one against the other.

By the 11th, I had no doubts about the Imuran decision. Even without Dr. Simon's support, I'd have had the courage to stop taking Imuran.

This decision was made as I'd always aspired to make such decisions: not from fear, not from misplaced hope, and taking into account both facts and feelings. From that deeper, inner place of knowing, beyond facts, this was the right decision for me.

It felt tremendously liberating to trust my intuition and to make a sane decision. My intuition had always been excellent, but in this illness, I hadn't trusted it easily or consistently. Instead, I'd often tried to make health decisions with my rational mind. Like the millions of cancer patients struggling with chemotherapy decisions, I eventually learned that all the facts can rarely be marshalled and are rarely black or white. My intuitive and rational sides thus often got locked in battle, and I was left paralyzed. When I couldn't choose, energy that would have been better used in healing was drained in the conflict.

This time I did it right. First, I accepted that there weren't any perfect decisions. Second, I made a decision. And finally, I did not look back. My confidence and determination were increasing.

Letting Lutzey tell me how much to do at home wasn't abdicating my own responsibility either. In that instance, my decision was to let Lutzey decide. After that, the process was the same: I committed myself to his prescription without looking back, which was empowering.

I noticed other changes in my emotional state. Even though only three weeks had elapsed since my biggest crisis ever, the blackness was already lifting to glimpses of light. My despair was easing. My body was drained, but my psyche was regaining strength. Positive emotions were creeping back, like wary forest visitors to a clearing.

Was the change an act of will? Had I been scared badly enough to stop "indulging" my emotions or to stop "feeling sorry for myself"? I still heard that voice over my shoulder admonishing me to do both, but now I talked back better. I had faced fear and rage before, not once but again and again in recent years. I moved through the emotions faster. I recognized the feelings faster. I had clearer insights into them. I dealt with them more fully and quickly. And, having been the same route many times already, I knew feelings were transitory. They could not devour me.

Perhaps my years in therapy were finally paying off. I was no longer lost in an emotional abyss. Although my father issues hadn't been tied into any neat packages, I had sufficiently tapped into my reservoir of childhood feelings so that they weren't all-consuming. I could invest energy in other directions.

Even this wasn't the entire story. I had five years' experience in dealing with this illness. I had five years of expanding awareness. I had a vast repertoire, not just of ideas, but of tested methods to nourish my health. My spirits rose partly because I knew which actions counted, and I knew how to use each miniscule amount of energy as it returned. Within the limits of my weakness, I moved smoothly from awareness to action. I acted on selected fronts, more vigorously and more quickly than ever before.

* * *

These last few free days in the month of total rest Lutzey had prescribed offered me the first moment during that January to contemplate old couch-time issues. I wondered where the kidney involvement left me with regard to Dr. Lowen's statement about my myopia: "Maybe that's where your personality problem is at this moment…. Seeing clearly and fearing what you will see is the issue which is now in the foreground. Your eyes will improve to the degree that the conflict is resolved." The edema around my eyes and blurred vision often did coincide, but maybe they were separate problems. But if both the edema and blurred vision were only symptomatic of my kidneys, it made his whole argument seem either ridiculous or at least so incredibly complex as to be useless. I wrote to Dr. Lowen after I returned from the hospital.

He responded kindly and quickly, but did not mention eyes. Instead he wrote, in part:

> In many illnesses, accepting the possibility that one could die is often the turning point of the illness…. In the face of death, one unconsciously gives up the neurotic

struggle to maintain a facade, which makes more energy available for combating the disease.

Overcome with emotion, I stopped reading. My jaw dropped open. What beautiful, powerful sentences. He captured my struggle so well. Then another emotion surfaced, equally intense. I clenched my fists. I was furious! Profound insights were easy after the fact. Hadn't I hired him, after all, precisely so I wouldn't have to reach a point near death in order to "give up the neurotic struggle"?

Soon I cooled off and accepted Dr. Lowen's gift more graciously. His words were deeply insightful. They highlighted another pivotal moment in my healing process. "Giving up the neurotic struggle to maintain a facade" seemed related to accepting the illness. I realized I'd never really understood the concept of acceptance. I had related it to death. Acceptance had meant "giving up," that is, resigning myself to be sick the rest of my life or to die. How could I "give in" to lupus, say yes to it, *without empowering it*?

This kidney crisis forced me to see how closely related acceptance of death and of the illness were. I was pushed to the edge, and somehow facing the possibility that I could die resulted in "giving in." Previously, despite saying I didn't believe I had all the control, I'd acted as if I did. If I just made the right decisions, had the right attitudes, found the right methods, and did enough of them faithfully enough, I'd get well. If I never ate a bite of "bad" food or never had an impure thought, lupus would vanish. Suddenly, I understood on a far deeper level than ever before that I didn't have all the power, that no matter what decisions I made, I could die. That was the bottom line. Greater surrender to mortality was the kind of giving-over most of us needed to do, even when well. We needed to admit we don't hold all the cards, that the body isn't a machine, that there are mysteries, twists, and turns of existence beyond us.

I felt immensely relieved. Less afraid to die, I was less afraid of making wrong decisions, and in fact desired more to live. Apparently, facing death was a necessary prelude to rebirth. The next time death stalked me, either literally or symbolically, I'd greet my fear sooner. My denial and the physical contraction that was part of it would be smaller.

15

Commitment to Act

Once home from the hospital after the kidney involvement, I made an outline of the aspects of my life I would strengthen to heal myself. I called it:

Prescription for Health

Physical rest. Rest for ___ hours a day. Write no more than ___ hours a day. Work no more than ___.

Emotional rest. At all costs, *avoid* stress. Forget about "coping effectively." When you can, stay in emotional neutral. Accept that negative feelings will creep in. If you can't turn them into assertion, find delicate and fast ways of expressing them.

Psychotherapy. You have less need for insight and emotional catharsis. Use therapy for support to help you carry out this plan. (Dr. Lowen would not be good at this, nor would he be interested; Connecticut is too far to drive.) Find a local therapist.

Exercise. No ifs, ands, or buts! Exercise every day. Get up in the morning *in order to* rest and exercise.

Music and Massage. Keep using them.

Nutrition. Eat more legumes, fiber, fresh fruits, and vegetables. Avoid red meat, salt, sugar, preservatives, caffeine, and alcohol. Increase vitamin supplements. Learn about nutrition used at the level of drugs.

Visualization. Visualize at least two times a day. Give yourself two months to develop imagery and two more to solidly establish the habit.

Although one doctor friend suggested rest might be old-fashioned, Dr. Marian Ropes in *Systemic Lupus Erythematosus* said a conservative approach was twenty hours of bed rest daily for many months. This time I wanted to err on the side of moderation. I thought I could eventually manage three hours of work a day, four days a week, and convinced David that amount was reasonable, although in hindsight, I was *still* over-ambitious.

While the contents of the prescription weren't new, my level of commitment would be. As 1978 had been about the process of choosing, 1980 would be about commitment. I'd commit ferociously. I'd find the necessary supports to get me through my rough spots. I'd suspend my judgments. Like Norman Cousins, I'd make my healing plan an act of faith.

* * *

Since this hospitalization, my entire body had become extremely cold-sensitive. Before bed at night, my hands, head, and especially my feet were freezing. My sleep was restless and light. Almost every day I awoke between two and four a.m., waking David up unintentionally. My back was invariably cold. I also felt anxious, and my back muscles were very tense. It seemed as if energy couldn't flow up my spine. David wasn't a natural cuddler, but I often asked him to hold me. His soft, warm front side thawed my tight, icy back. No matter how short the time was, I felt less apprehensive and, at least temporarily, felt lupus muscle pains in my arms, chest, and back subside. If he cradled me long enough, my body seemed to absorb the slower, stronger rhythms of his. Once or twice I fell back to sleep after being held. Usually I was wide-awake, if not for the day, for another couple of hours.

During these hours, I wrote in my journal and worked on visualization, first picturing the disease process. In lupus, fighter cells mistakenly think the nucleus of the cell — DNA—is foreign, and attack it. I visualized my fighter cells as soldiers with guns and bayonets, and my suppressor cells as expertly trained space-suited robots with very keen eyes. To solve the immunological problem I decreased the fighters, increased and strengthened the suppressors, and made enemy viruses and bacteria orange, few in number and feeble. Only when the suppressors identified real enemies were fighters allowed to leave their stations to attack.

After picturing how the medication worked in my body, I reviewed my notes to understand what caused symptoms. Whenever fighters attacked DNAs, groups of nonfunctional cells were created. These clumps of useless cells led to inflammation and clogging of bodily functions. The clumps and inflammation were what I felt as symptoms.

I needed to flow those clumps out of my body. I visualized my kidneys: two big, soft, rosy kidney beans. I saw gray, lumpy places in the kidney tissues. I flushed a special yellow super-liquid, fortified with all the nutrients needed for healing and metabolism, through my entire body to cleanse and nourish all cells on the way to the kidney, and to dissolve the clumps. I pictured the residue draining out through the ureters, long tubes leading from each rosy bean to the bladder and out of my body. As I looked again at my kidneys, they seemed healthier: red-pink, plushy, and porous.

I felt ecstatic. I had come up with healthy imagery on the first try. In succeeding days as I used it, it was harder. The gray lumps originally had the consistency of aspirin. First they became pasta-like and then eventually turned to cement. The more I willed the substances soluble, the harder they turned.

I kept lecturing myself, "Your resistances always become monumental before they give way. Keep visualizing those cement clumps. The power balance will reverse itself. Let your will work *for* you. Be patient. *Be patient.*" Eventually, the balance reversed. The clumps looked like the soft, gray froth left by receding waves on a beach.

* * *

As soon as I felt strong enough to sustain firm touch, I began weekly massage again with Karen, a new person.

Massaging sore muscles helped. With a very careful touch, Karen moved the muscles surrounding an inflamed place to open conduits and re-route energy, rather than touching inflamed muscles and joints directly. She added polarity techniques, when we discovered they dependably reduced inflammation, particularly when I had more symptoms after lowering prednisone. In polarity all the soft tissues are very gently but deeply kneaded in a pattern that stimulates and balances energy flow. Months later, when I had more strength, Karen included Feldenkreis movement. Parts of me that I wished massage could reach, but never did, seemed softly released and opened by these movements.

Toward the end of each massage, Karen concentrated on relaxing me. By this time, my mind, absorbed by her touch, had stopped wandering. She used feather-light strokes of lymphatic massage to stimulate lymphatic drainage. My drifting off to sleep was a big victory. Skillful as Karen was, it was months before I fell asleep four times in a row.

Karen practiced a form of meditation which included chanting. She played one of her chanting tapes as background music during massages. From my experiments with music, I knew how powerfully sound affected me. The slow, full, repetitive sounds of the music may have slowed my breathing and pulse as much as her compassionate words and attitude and her expert touch.

* * *

As soon as I was able to drive to my Cedar Street office, I looked for a new psychotherapist. Sue was a woman who had struck me as particularly kind and unassuming when I knew her in the Worcester Women's Coalition years earlier. She soon became a fixture in my life. Ildri would have been the best choice, of course, but the drive to Boston was too much. Sue's office was a block away from mine, and she was willing to come to my house if I couldn't get to her office. She seemed amenable to helping me monitor and stick to my **Prescription for Health**. She was willing to keep asking me the same tedious questions: Did I really work only thirteen hours? Was I visualizing? Did I count as hours in my day those filled with chauffeuring, meal preparation, and eating? Was I keeping the right balance between home chores and office work? Was I exercising? What was I doing with anger and sorrow and fear? Was I remembering pleasure? How could I nourish hope?

* * *

Ever since I left the hospital, part of my middle-of-the-night awake time was focused on nutrition. I read that the stress of immobilization caused a marked loss of nutrients in the body, so my losses would be greater than previously. I had been, and would be, on my back longer than ever before. Hourly, I felt the cumulative drain on my body. A sip of wine without food left me nauseated. A few second's exposure to cigarette smoke did, too. One cup of very weak, black tea kept me awake all night, systems pumping even faster than usual. While the average person might not feel or show the effects of toxic substances unless exposure was either intense or prolonged, I showed it instantly. If they could affect me so quickly and powerfully, might not nutritious substances do likewise?

My need to take prednisone again also heightened my interest in nutrition. I read that it robbed the body of calcium and phosphorus, depleted the adrenals of vitamin C, and the entire body of vitamins C, A, and potassium. Looking in a mirror was another reminder of the ill effects of prednisone and lupus. Since this hospitalization there had been a dull, gray residue in my hair. Every morning, when I could manage, I washed it out. Within twenty-four hours, it returned. One of the functions of skin is elimination. If there was that much residue in my hair, there must be volumes more inside.

Chronic constipation became the final incentive. I'd had it for months before being hospitalized. It was all the more puzzling since, contrary to everyone's belief, it wasn't disappearing as I became more active.

I began exploring nutrition, vitamin supplements and vitamin C, since I'd been so impressed by Norman Cousin's megadoses of vitamin C and Linus Pauling's work. But would vitamin C create kidney stones? How does prednisone interact with vitamin C? A thoughtful librarian at the medical school library did a computer search for me, and, astoundingly, offered to bring it to my house.

Unfortunately, the literature offered little. Norman Cousins had already uncovered most of it. The doses administered were far less than I was considering. I found no information about the interaction between prednisone and C.

Dr. Roth made an appointment for me to see Dr. Pindera, chief rheumatologist at the hospital, to get his opinion about adding the equivalent of fourteen aspirins daily to the prednisone. The theory was that we could decrease the prednisone faster. So I saw him in January, and he thought the aspirin was fine. He said nothing about side effects. Unthinkingly, I suddenly decided to ask this man a dietary question.

"I've been to an orthomolecular physician who recommended taking bone meal and dolomite as calcium sources," I said. "I want to make sure the volume is equivalent to the calcium supplement you prescribed when I was in the hospital."

His face reddened. He puffed up as though he might levitate. "Any physician should have known the answer to that question!" he boomed. "If he doesn't, he should have a *Physician's Desk Reference* in his office and look it up. Who is this person? Are you sure he's competent? You can tell him I said that!"

Why hadn't I thought to look it up in my own *Physician's Desk Reference* at home?

He continued, "Bone meal? What is the amount of phosphorus in bone meal?" He looked at the five residents and interns who were seated near me. Then he said, sarcastically, "Do you think it would be harmful to her?"

One said he didn't think so.

He returned to me. His voice was tight and sharp. "Bone meal? The only bone meal I know about I put on my lawn. I've never heard of its being given to humans. Does Dr. Roth know you're taking this? What does he think?"

He then had the nerve to suggest I should make another appointment with him. He curtly noted that it took three or four months to get one. This was one medical prima donna I did not need. For once, I felt secure enough to act on my feelings. I stood up and walked out.

I walked out for all the other times I hadn't been able to leave an obnoxious doctor. I felt exhilarated. Later I wondered if I set up this confrontation to test how narrow and rigid this doctor really was.

This experience left me more aware of medical politics. The holistic physician looked at the totality of the body, beyond particular symptoms. That conflicted with a specialist whose life work was involved with a system or complex of systems. Because the holistic doctor was an M.D., I thought he'd work with the specialists I required in a way that a homeopath or acupuncturist trained outside the system wouldn't. That was unrealistic. But he didn't want to be in hospitals where drugs and surgery were the main treatments, and allopathic physicians wouldn't rush to include him. Many holistic physicians had trained in family medicine and were dedicated to being generalists. But there seemed to be an additional element of snobbery involved. Specialists often implied that doctors choosing family medicine weren't smart enough to make it as specialists. The holistic physician I had seen had little more credibility with them than I did.

*   *   *

I moved into action again. My feelers on the subject led me to believe Dr. Roth was anti-vitamin, but I thought I'd better let him know what I was up to. More important, the hospital staff considered Dr. Roth a walking reference book on kidneys. If I approached him with my best, maybe he'd offer his. Maybe he'd see me as an interesting patient, not a difficult one. Approaching him was also a matter of candor. Whatever his response, I'd know I had tried my best. I'd know where I stood. Both meant less turmoil.

Before my next appointment I wrote him a long letter, complete with references, detailing how vitamin C might help my adrenals produce cortisone, increase the effectiveness of prednisone, decrease aspirin toxicity, and generally detoxify.

Dr. Roth's comment about my whole vitamin routine, which I had also sent him, was, "I don't think they'll do you any harm. But they won't do you any good either." He was unable to resist a concluding zinger, "You could take me and my family on vacation for a week with what you spend on vitamins." I should have reminded him that the cost of one day in the hospital was more than the cost of my vitamins for one or two months.

Nonetheless, I felt encouraged and wrote Linus Pauling. He said vitamin C would not interfere with prednisone and that C stimulates the adrenals. I decided to keep taking bone meal and slowly to increase my intake of vitamin C.

Clearly, I was on my own, my own treatment coordinator. That style was the most natural one for me. It is still the only option for most patients who choose to combine alternative and allopathic methods.

* * *

The Cape vacation in August was the first one that worked the way a holiday should since I had gotten sick five years ago. David and I occasionally found our way down to the dock, often walking back up to the house with our arms around each other. Adam played happily; I worried less about him. We returned to the crisp rustle of September rested.

But over Thanksgiving my body set up a relapse. Should the prednisone be upped again? I had gotten down to ten milligrams a day, plus the Plaquenil and an aspirin-like anti-inflammatory. I didn't want to increase it—prednisone masked weariness, allowing me to go on speedy energy rather than real strength. Lutzey supported my reasoning. "If you're determined to try it, go ahead. You're aware of the trade-offs. I'll be here to monitor you."

Not taking Imuran had been a new kind of choice a year before. I felt these other methods were strengthening my body, and I wanted to give them more of a chance.

By the end of the month I wasn't better. But I wasn't any worse. This time I was wise enough to see that as progress.

Rebecca said, "I don't see how you stay optimistic."

"I really have been putting less emphasis on results," I said. "They aren't certain. Looking at them doesn't sustain my hope."

"That must push you back to the old question: how to keep going when you don't get results?"

I nodded.

"Well, when you first read Norman Cousins' article, you concluded faith was important."

"I still think that. And I've had more faith this year. I've been much more patient. I've trained myself not to measure progress so relentlessly. You and I haven't had a talk like this for a long time."

"That's true."

"I've had a rule. No matter how discouraged I am, no matter how rotten I feel, do my remedies. Dig in my heels. Not too exciting, but it works. Right now breathing exercises are all I can handle for exercise, but when I do that, or visualize, contemplate an idea, or listen to healing music, I feel virtuous at the least. When I feel virtuous, my sense of well-being increases."

" Faith and hope really do creep back?" Rebecca asked.

"Yes. Of course, I used to think that if I had faith, I'd get what I wanted: cure. Now I read that faith means that whatever happens I will come to see as right."

Her brow wrinkled. "That business of something to learn from? That some good will come of whatever happens?"

"Even if it's not what I see as good right now." I stopped for a long time to digest what we'd said. "But I still like to measure. So instead of measuring how many symptoms I have, I'm measuring my success in carrying out my Prescription for Health. That is clear and does nourish my optimism."

After Rebecca left, I pulled the **Prescription** off the bedstand to review it.

Physical and Emotional Rest. During the year, I said "No" to overwork. No more teaching graduate classes, no more bioenergetic training. As part of the training, I'd begun to drive to Hartford to receive supervision from a psychiatrist. I eliminated that. My M.D. co-therapist Mark started a weekly peer-supervision group of psychiatrists, psychologists, and social workers which I wanted to join but didn't. I told every new client of my illness; they were less troubled than I expected them to be. In the coming year, I would rest one week a month, plus all of August, and prepare my clients long in advance. "Avoiding stress" as distinguished from "coping effectively" was my watchword. The minute I convinced myself I could handle normal levels of stress, I set myself up for failure.

Psychotherapy. My therapist and I had discussed the rage I'd felt at everyone during the summer of hospitalizations in 1977. The intervening years offered even more distance and, therefore, a larger perspective in which to see those situations. There were good reasons for dealing with the feelings as I had. Writing in my journal meant I stepped back and examined situations. I wasn't denying or suppressing feelings. I gave them time to mature. The broader vision that resulted allowed me to eventually dredge up some compassion for the people I felt angriest at.

This year I was angry less often. Adam could still incite me to violence, but even with him my feelings seemed less exaggerated, and I felt I had more choice in how I expressed them.

I'd been quick to catch myself criticizing when I felt insecure. Sue and I had followed that pattern carefully throughout the year with different incidents and individuals.

We discussed my therapy with Ildri and Dr. Lowen. I thought Ildri had given me a wonderful, dependable, motherly love and the support to work deeply quickly. Since the relationship was longer and I trusted her more, I felt her loss more as time passed and regretted not having worked through my separation from her. I concluded Dr. Lowen and I had worked as rapidly as possible. Being ill created a pressure to gather dramatic insights and release emotions quickly, and the infrequency of our sessions added to that pressure. It was difficult to separate the egoism of Lowen and Keleman from their valuable work. Their strong sense of self made it far easier to get angry at them than Ildri.

Music and Massage. They'd continued to be pleasures.

Exercise. By the end of September, and prior to the relapse I was doing some form of exercise at least three times a week. When I didn't walk or attend a drop-in Stretch and Strength class at the Y, I did bioenergetic exercises or Hatha yoga.

Nutrition. My eating habits were steadily improving. I'd become as much of a purist about simple salads as I'd been about bernaise sauces. My pharmacist helped me concoct the same liquid brew of vitamin C that Linus Pauling had given to cancer patients (except mine was sugarless). Soon I was taking twenty-five grams daily.

Visualization. By the end of the year, I visualized twice a day. I'd made a tape recording of my imagery. That support, more than anything else, helped me visualize more frequently. The more successful I became in concentrating on the imagery, the more I looked forward to visualization time. But it was still a struggle. I wasn't in a deeply relaxed, alpha brain-wave state very often, so I didn't gain the maximum benefit, but I'd regained some ability to focus my mind. Sometimes I fell asleep in the middle of the tape, which was good too.

Some parts of the visualization had become quite meaningful. The detoxification imagery kept expanding and changing. Each day when I finished those scenes, I felt a wonderful sense of relief and release. I also liked the beginning relaxation phase. In listening to my own directions on tape, the quality and pace of my voice were as important as the words. I focused on becoming aware of my breathing, holding my breath, slowly tensing muscles from my toes to my head and releasing them part by part. Then I breathed into each part. I felt the air flowing into me and expanding the tissues. After ten minutes of this, I may not have been as relaxed as my graduate students claimed to be when I led them through similar routines, but I was more relaxed than when I began.

Visualization directions had suggested imaging a natural setting as a meditation sanctuary. Mine came to be a soft chaise lounge next to a rippling stream on a lush, green, grassy oasis. This scene was no place I'd ever been, but midway through the year, I suddenly realized it was like my grandmother's big weeping willow which I'd spent hours sitting under.

Support wasn't a category in the **Prescription**, but it could have been. I'd been able to ask for help more often and more easily. I'd received what was offered more fully. I had a broader understanding of what support meant. My paid helpers were just as important as my friends. The indirect support of a voice on a cassette tape was almost as effective as being led in person. Exercising at the same time in the same room with the phone off the hook and the family trained not to disturb me was an important form of support, too.

In years past, I'd been frustrated by my inability to act. Wondrously, a more conscious commitment and deeper faith moved me into a year full of actions.

16

Including Spirit

In March of 1981, I developed a kidney stone. It was calcium oxalate, the very kind Linus Pauling said he'd never seen from vitamin C. The doctors argued about whether it was from the megadoses of C or vitamin D and calcium, but I wasn't angry at them. I'd chosen to take C. Both rheumatologists had recommended D and calcium, but they had explained the risks. That had been my decision too.

Prednisone was increased before the stone was removed, but I bounced back quickly afterwards and it was reduced to twenty milligrams.

I laid off vitamin C but continued to work with nutrition. Over the years I had tried different vitamin combinations, at first based on my own reading, particularly Adelle Davis, and more recently under the holistic physician's guidance. I never felt noticeable benefits, and my digestive system always felt more scrambled. Yet I was convinced I needed more than decent food and a multi-vitamin to correct deficiencies and re-balance my immune system at a level that could heal such a serious disease.

I'd stumbled upon information about macrobiotic and wheatgrass diets. John Gunther's book about his son, *Death Be Not Proud*, had introduced me to the Gerson nutritional therapy program.

Karen mentioned a similar one run by a man named Kelley. In that one, dietary preferences, health history, psychological behavior, and lifestyle data were collected in a 1,000-item questionnaire, and, along with blood and urine samples, synthesized and analyzed in computers to arrive at an individual program.

In all the programs, assimilation and detoxification were as important as food and supplements. Likely I had difficulties with assimilation, and I was more constipated than ever. Although I had tried everything, absolutely everything the doctors and everyone else suggested, nothing helped. I thought there was nothing seriously wrong, did not want to use allopathic medicine for this, and thought one of the diets could help. I favored Kelley's program because I was most comfortable with a diagnostic system similar to Western medicine. It was also intensive. The special enema used to cleanse the colon, liver, and gall bladder would guarantee at least a temporary respite from constipation.

Kelley's program seemed philosophically sound. While it included vitamins to correct specific shortages, it went way beyond vitamins-to-match-the-symptoms. As well as anyone, Kelley seemed to understand synergism — that, for example, daily exercise improved digestion, which improved the emotional state, which lessened pain and increased appetite. From that, he speculated that increased nutritional consumption created improved immune activity, which caused more rapid cell turnover, which caused increased elimination, which, in turn, created a need for greater consumption of nutrients.

Absolutely pure and fresh foods were required. Leftovers lost considerable food value. Fresh, raw fruit and vegetable juices were emphasized because they were more concentrated and easily assimilable. Megadoses of vitamins, minerals, and particularly enzymes were taken around the clock. Local water might contain substances that weren't in the diet, so distilled was used. Diets ranged from vegetarian to ample meat or fish, depending on one's metabolism. I was impressed with the concept of metabolic types. Everyone couldn't be vegetarian nor everyone a meat eater. It made sense that not only did we have unique hereditary, environmental and absorptive factors, but that as the body was affected by the nutrients, nutrient needs changed. Thus the program was re-evaluated and adapted every six months.

I kept musing on the idea that the more radical the change in lifestyle, the more likely the healing. "Acting radically" could mean many things, but at the time, I thought most essential was that healing activities become the way I defined myself. By the end of 1980, I'd cut down on work and healing remedies had gained in importance, but they still weren't primary. I thought this nutritional program would be the final step: healing would become the center of my life. And it proved to be so.

* * *

Spirituality was not a topic I made any rational decision to focus on. No will was involved. It was merely the next magnet to attract me. Whatever I picked up to read, I found myself glancing longer at sentences about spirituality. I jotted down memorable passages. In my own bookshelves, I was drawn to books on Eastern philosophy and read them with new eagerness.

My "I am my body" philosophy was becoming less and less comfortable. For someone with a body like mine, it was too depressing. I longed for a new one. One analogy suggested that if a body could be likened to a car, the soul was the car's driver, and that just because something was wrong with the car didn't mean something was wrong with the driver. Simple explorer that I was, that seemed a powerful insight.

A client, Margaret, brought the subject to the fore. Bioenergetics had taught me to applaud the look of health: bright eyes, lively coloring, mellifluous voice, graceful strides that moved with garments rather than against them, easy gestures. Defining health in this way seemed all the more seductive as our society became fitness-obsessed.

But then there was Margaret, an under-five-foot, 75-pound wisp of a person who had polio as a child. She wore a heavy brace from her neck to her thighs, other braces on her legs, and walked with a cane. Her twisted back jutted one shoulder up at an opposing angle and several inches higher than the other. She breathed through only one-quarter of her lungs. Her voice was weak, her eyes not particularly clear, her movements choppy, and her coloring sallow.

Although I was her therapist, I often sat humbly in her presence. She seemed beyond the kind of suffering in which I'd been so immersed. It wasn't that she didn't feel angry or afraid, or even at times sorry for herself. She was bereft when the only person who had ever fit her with a painless brace died — an expert craftsman who cared enough to keep trying until the fit was right. When she thought her employers expected her to do more than she felt she could, her anger had a plaintive "why me?" quality. For her, travel by plane required many extra arrangements and added expense. She was as frustrated by the continual mistakes and ineptitudes of the airlines as I had been by those of the hospitals.

About some aspects of her suffering, however, she seemed immune. I suspected she was always in a fair amount of pain. When I questioned her, her answers were vague. I thought she was denying but eventually concluded she was so accustomed to pain she was no longer aware of it. She had surgery after surgery since childhood and was forced to live in residential schools during the school year. She had lived so long on the edge, it no longer seemed like the edge. Margaret had dealt with her handicap so intensely, so often, and so long that she seemed unafraid of pain and even of death.

Despite choppy movements and weak voice, I would describe Margaret as graceful and strong. Somehow, from somewhere, she emitted vitality, a fragile but potent vigor. Margaret was more than her body. In knowing Margaret, I perceived a definition of health which included a spiritual base.

My masseuse Karen was also especially interested in the spiritual aspect of existence. Increasingly during massages that fall, the subject came up. My curiosity increased enough that I accepted Karen's invitation to tag along to her meditation center. She offered the extra help I needed to make it possible: driving me literally door to door.

From the moment I saw the grounds of the center and walked through the door, my impressions were positive. The center was in an elegant mansion on a large estate. I liked the idea of a home built for rich people now being used by large numbers of people.

Chanting, meditation, talks, videos of Swami Muktananda, and a vegetarian lunch were on the schedule. Modern technology in the form of a video seemed incongruous with the other activities, but for someone as mildly eccentric as me, sitting crosslegged on the floor was a more appropriate style than sitting in a pew, even though I needed the support of a wall to sit for any length of time. We sang the same chant Karen played during massages, Om Namah Shivaya. Sanskrit was alien, but since I had already experimented with sound as a mode of healing, I understood and quickly experienced its therapeutic value. Singing together also brought back happy memories of church camp as a child.

At the end of the program, many people went up to the altar to bow before the Guru's picture. I felt uncomfortable, but since I had learned how important good teacher-guides were, I took the bowing of the devotees in that spirit.

As we drove home, I reviewed the day. There had been no pressure to conduct the chitchat of ordinary social situations or to interact in the heavy emotional encounters of professional workshops. The food was served by people who cared about food and their work. Most of the participants looked vital, not spacey or emptily mellow, as I had stereotyped meditators to be. The place exuded a reverence for life, even a quiet sense of celebration. "Avoid stress" in my Prescription had now been expanded to "Be around healing energy." The gentle, positive energy in this place seemed just right.

* * *

I began to attend a Sunday evening meditation group at Karen's house. Long before the half-hour of chanting was over, sounds caught in my dry throat and my voice turned raspy. Yet I liked chanting , and it felt relaxing. When we closed our eyes for meditation, however, I was still aware only of my exhaustion, my roving mind, the aches in my back and legs and whatever else hurt that day. Occasionally I could follow my thoughts as if I were reading a ticker tape, but they never stopped for even a second. Yet I wasn't terribly worried. This was my phase of grand resistance. I was about ready to set out a few flower pots of acceptance on that stubborn wall!

Back home I didn't even try sitting meditation. I was still weak enough to prefer lying in bed. I'd circumvent my wall by listening to tapes of Sanskrit chants. They served as background music while I read, wrote, rested or was up cooking dinner.

David saw chanting as another of my "things." He asked that I listen to tapes when he wasn't within hearing distance. Adam said, "You carry a parasol. You wear strange clothes. You eat yukky food. Now you listen to weirdo music in words nobody understands." When he invited a friend to the Cape for the weekend, he called me aside. "I want to ask two things. Don't play those chanting tapes. And don't floss your teeth in the car."

One day, reading a book on Eastern philosophy, I came across the words, "God is the inner self in each person." I felt elated. The language fit for me. For the first time in my life, the word "God" had meaning. Many times during my youth I had undoubtedly heard the Biblical words, "Behold, the Kingdom of God is within you," but that language left me cold. As a searching person, I'd rejected rote learning and belief without internal understanding.

During a massage shortly afterwards when I'd been listening to Karen's Om Namah Shivaya tape, I turned to her. "I've been hearing these words for months," I said. "I never remember their meaning."

"'I honor my inner self,'" she said.

For the second time, I had an extravagant moment of recognition.

"What's happening?" Karen asked. "You woke right up."

When I recovered, I said, "Apparently, I have to look at the same idea in 500 different forms before I find a way to internalize it. God, inner self, love — they're all the same thing!"

Without hesitation, Karen said, "Yes. I think so."

I closed my eyes to let the idea settle in. Eventually, I said, "Your Siddha yoga books talk a lot about love."

She quickly interjected, "Yes. Love as a state of being, though. Not needing an external object. You know, the source is inside us."

"Your books also use 'universal energy' as a synonym."

"That should appeal to you," she said.

"It does. One of my clients talks about universal energy. He feels the connection through nature, trees, for example. They're rooted in the earth and extend out into the world. They cycle water, carbon dioxide, subatomic particles, and so on. Since he's a physician, these descriptions appeal to his scientific self."

She looked surprised. "A doctor?"

"Yes. Sometimes he visualizes the lines in a grid connecting himself to the trees. Other times the connection is less tangible, more of a feeling. Sometimes he blends into trees, sometimes trees blend into him."

Karen said, "How interesting that a doctor thinks this way."

"Well, he said he never told anyone about this before."

* * *

Curiously, my interest in sex had waned after the kidney crisis. At first that could be attributed to sheer weakness, but I wasn't more eager as my stamina increased. Mostly I thought this was temporary, some kind of transition. I wasn't becoming so "pure" that I was letting go of earthly pleasures, as someone suggested. I surmised that the same energy used in the charge and discharge of sexuality was being drawn inward, that a kind of recycling was occurring deep inside me. As I thought more about it, sex seemed one way to lose or get beyond oneself, to abandon the ego, and spirituality seemed another. Spirituality still hadn't offered me the same ecstasy as sex, but for the moment, a spiritual path seemed to be choosing me.

My choice of words—energy being drawn inward and spirituality choosing me—seemed significant. I hadn't willed this either. Perhaps this hiatus from sexuality demonstrated I was somewhat less driven by the need for intensity, more fulfilled through ordinariness. Time would tell. I was curious what would emerge next.

* * *

Since I was having some success with visualization, I stuck with it, but my understanding of meditation also broadened. It was focusing the mind. It was emptying the mind. It was contemplation. It was watching thoughts in a detached manner. Again, it was *and*, not *either/or*. Through visualization I was learning to focus my mind and to watch with detachment. I ran images through my head and observed what occurred in my body without interfering. That was more learning than I understood and gave myself credit for at the time.

When I felt strong enough to sit up more, I still didn't sit for meditation. I chanted. It sidestepped my mind chatter. When I sang with a tape, I felt the support of other voices. When I rocked to the rhythm of the music, my agitation diminished. When I chanted while cooking or doing chores, my not-enough-time voices were stilled. Slowly, increasingly, my throat was less dry less often. My sound became more full-bodied and clear; it was healthier.

I stopped hassling myself about my difficulty with sitting meditation after I talked with more meditators. Some told me that when a person's mental and physical imbalance was as great as mine, meditation masters sometimes recommended suspending sitting. A heavier (meatier) diet and vigorous exercise were often prescribed. The theory was the same as in bioenergetics: tension and imbalance came from conscious and subconscious interference with the meditative process, not from the process itself.

* * *

Around this time I spoke on the phone with Althea, a woman who'd had lupus longer and more severely than I and who had used many alternative paths. During our long conversation, she said, "We are powerless, at some point, to change our bodies. I'm committed to achieving the highest degree of health of which I am capable."

I said as little as possible to keep her talking. I wanted to hear this wise woman out.

"Getting your spiritual act together is important. You've got to appeal to the gods for help. Lupus is bigger than you. When you get in touch with the 'beyond the beyond,' or whatever you call it, all remedies work better."

Althea was right. But it wasn't that if I'd "found God" six years earlier, I'd be well. Spirituality was one of many healing factors. It made sense only because I had built a foundation on which this insight was the capstone. Of course, once I understood, it seemed ridiculously simple.

* * *

Looking back at my handwritten notes, I was surprised that my Prescription for Health included, "Write no more than ___ hours a day." Seeing that sentence reminded me that this spring writing had taken on a greater and different importance.

I suspected this more comprehensive writing would bring with it healing qualities, perhaps major ones. Yet it could, like work, as easily kill as cure me. It was a successful diversion from worry and pain and I was developing the same passion for it. It had similar drawbacks. Writing required the same kind of emotional energy. It meant re-experiencing the emotions of the illness: fear, panic, confusion, hopelessness, irritation, anger, sorrow. That was the antitheses of the emotional rest I had prescribed. Like work, I could get so involved in it, I would easily skip eating, visualization, or exercise. Fortunately, by this time I had some confidence I could limit my investment in writing so that it could work for me.

At first I found myself tightening up and forcing words out. Performance anxiety, I thought. I was writing for an imaginary audience, for one more authority figure perhaps, or for all the ones I had so far encountered.

Very quickly the outer-directed motives dissolved. When my writing came from inside, my performance fears evaporated. I hoped my thoughts might be useful to someone else, but it was sufficient to be doing something meaningful only to myself. In fact, it was absolutely exhilarating to be so self-motivated. I was doing work of my choice, at my own pace, in my own way. Few people in their entire lives have such freedom.

As I wrote about my parents, I realized that the love I felt toward them was now much less ambivalent. In fact, if I had begun writing about them in 1980 and depended solely on my memory, I would have written a different story. If they contributed to what I may have missed in childhood, they should be credited for what they gave me. I was able to survive the interminable wearing-down from lupus partly because I entered it with a fairly solid personality foundation. My parents' philosophy of self-reliance and strong-willed optimism gave me the courage to think for myself and, eventually, to persist despite few rewards. I didn't minimize their gifts of good health habits and a nutritious life style. My parents exemplified a good balance between work and play, solitude and companionship.

"Less ambivalent." The words were telling. I wanted to be sincerely acceptant. I hadn't come full circle to forgiving my parents in the deepest sense. Most people never did. But I certainly knew the difference between expressing anger, being polite, and forgiving one another.

I was closer to forgiving myself, too. To love myself, I had to forgive myself; to do that, I had to know myself. By this time, I knew myself quite well.

17

Integration and Health

So many times in recent years I thought I grasped a more holistic view of health and illness, only to discover that I was far short of genuine understanding. Years ago I had thought, within the doctrine of specific etiology, that a specific, isolated cause could be found for each medical problem and that this, in turn, would suggest a specific, isolated cure. Quite quickly I concluded that the causes of my illness were multiple, though genes and viruses probably played a part.

Yet I was still thinking allopathically: instead of one specific cause and matching cure, there would be three or four causes which I'd match with three or four cures. My healing methods would fall into neat categories: methods for the mind, methods for the body and, eventually, methods for the spirit. I applied methods in an allopathic way for a long time, each as an antidote to a particular symptom. I might take more vitamin C when my joints became inflamed or do more relaxation exercises when I felt greater emotional stress: always reacting to a symptom, hoping to vanquish it.

Gradually I began to grasp more about a way of looking that included the whole of my being—a concept of holism. By 1978, I began to fight less against the illness and more *for* health. I eventually de-emphasized the symptom-and-crisis orientation and embraced one which went far beyond simple crisis resolution. I began to see that any one healing activity affected far more than one aspect of me. Did massage belong in the "body" category only because it soothed sore muscles? It also brought me more in touch with my emotions; more recently, it had become my best means of deep relaxation and seemed to help unclog my digestive system.

Thus my healing methods began to overlap and intertwine. Images I had earlier only while visualizing occurred spontaneously during yoga and massage. When I breathed deeply during yoga, I could see oxygen being sucked in through my nostrils and flooding deep into my lungs, to my abdomen and pelvis. When Karen massaged my body, I saw snake-like intestinal tubes rhythmically kneading foods, sorting wastes from nutrients, and propelling nutrients to my cells. When I was preparing dinner, the sounds of the chants spontaneously welled up in me. My body was affecting my mind and spirit in positive, not just negative ways.

When I understood how even one approach could affect all of me I understood why grasping principles was essential. Holism was not merely a series of methods. When I had conceptualized it that way, I imagined I was slow to get well because I hadn't come upon the right methods or enough of them. Now I understood the importance of my attitude: any technique pursued with the aim of quieting and balancing could be healing.

Not only could methods change, but since the dynamics in my body kept changing before a new balance and harmony was reached, different methods needed emphasis at different times. Changing my diet radically in 1975 couldn't have hurt, but it would not have been sufficient to resolve my emotions. Although I felt nutritionally balanced and adequately exercised in 1975, by the time I achieved more emotional harmony in 1980 I had become nutritionally imbalanced, and daily exercise was an absolute necessity.

That internalized insight quickly illuminated others. Another facet of the old allopathic way of thinking had been that when a symptom was gone, I would stop the remedy, and when I got well, I would not need any remedies. The change in my attitude was first evidenced in massage. Previously, in between crises whenever I was the least bit stronger, I considered skipping a week, as if it were still an undesirable crutch to be dispensed with soon. Later I recognized the thought almost instantly as a remnant of an undesirable old attitude and caught myself before I acted on it. Why abandon support that was so pleasing? Finally the old attitude slipped away entirely, without any struggle or effort. I might even have a weekly massage for the next twenty years!

That attitude began to extend to my other healing methods. I no longer caught myself saying, "When I get well, I'll stop eating so carefully, or chanting, or visualizing." I might slip for a few days or change the form of an approach slightly, but these "methods" had become a part of my life, my spirit and body.

*   *   *

Another school year was almost over for Adam. It had gone well. He adored his fifth-grade teacher. Since I could see changes in Adam and in my relationship with him, I called his teacher with less trepidation before school let out in June. The verbal report was equally as positive as the previous year's.

When I was tired, I still lost sight of all progress, but usually both Adam and I felt more optimistic. His optimism still seemed stronger and more solid and triggered mine. When I got angry or discouraged about his behavior, he'd remind me he had made a lot of progress and I should give him credit for it. He never tested my support, for he was sure of it by now. He seemed to be outgrowing his publicly rebellious side. He accepted punishments with more loud backtalk than we would have liked, but he did accept what was meted out, and David did more disciplining. That worked better for all of us.

I remained available for him after school. He began regularly to check to see if I was there so he could announce, "I don't need you." Occasionally, though, and increasingly, there were some special moments of contact. One day when I sat in the rocking chair waiting for him after school, he came in. At my invitation, he sat on my lap. He kept flicking his finger across the page of the book I was reading. "I'd be glad to put down my reading to give you my full attention," I said. "But often when I do, you don't want my attention anymore."

He fidgeted a bit more. "You know, I don't want you to take

this as an insult, but..."

I prepared for the insult which usually followed.

"It's hard having a mother who can't do athletic things like the other mothers." And, after a long pause, "It makes me feel different."

I thought about this for a minute. "What is it like for you to have a mother who has lupus?"

After a short pause and with his voice on edge, he said, "Sometimes you get angry at me because you don't feel well. You take out your anger at being sick on me."

What could I say to the truth?

After another pause, he added, "I've felt sad for you that you have to be sick. It's not fair. It makes me angry." And then, rather quickly and more quietly, he added, "I worry about you."

"What do you mean?" I said.

"You know," he said impatiently, "I was worried you might die. I worried a lot." While I was still searching for a response, he continued, "If I had one wish in the world, it would be for you to get well. I know you'd like to not have to think about getting well so much."

"I'm much better," I said. He's only ten years old, and he's mine, I marveled. Tears came to my eyes. Adam noticed and became squirmy.

"I'm soft," I said.

"You mean sensitive," he corrected me and laughed cockily. "You see what I learn in school," he said and ran off.

I lived for moments like those. They gave me hope that Adam had begun to act like a child who could show love to others, who knew he was loved. Whatever damage I had done, it appeared to be less than I imagined. Perhaps my mothering had not been a total failure after all.

* * *

That summer, Adam, David and I finally visited our friends in Switzerland. Finally I felt safe enough to be farther from home than the Cape. One overcast afternoon we drove outside Geneva to a tiny lake in the nearby mountains. The next day I used the experience in visualization and later wrote it in my journal:

As we walk around the lake, our congeniality sends waves of warmth through me. I feel the presence of the water at my side. Through occasional glances, I make its acquaintance. We sit at the water's edge. Words become fewer and farther between. Soon our sharing is wordless. The silence has texture. It becomes a cuddly blanket wrapped around me. I feel comforted and bask in the sensation. When it slips away, I refocus on the silence and the blanket. The comforted feeling returns.

I concentrate on the glassy sheen of the lake. There's not a ripple on its silver-gray surface. I visualize the lake inside my eyes. They feel cooler, and the muscles behind them begin to let go. My head, throat and mouth slowly soften. A gentle throb starts in my throat and spreads through my head. My lips begin to tingle.

I let the lake flow into the rest of me. The water floods through, purifying and nourishing organs and tissues. The water moves in harmony with the beat. As I breathe in and out, slowly, gently, the throb spreads through my torso and then into my arms, legs, and back into my head.

I see myself as my cells, millions of them, different shapes, colors and sizes, all gently vibrating and expanding and contracting to the rhythm of the throb. I feel wave after wave of pulsation.

Several bodily states felt restorative: gratitude, confidence, joy, hope, strength, peace. Usually they intermingled, but somehow gratitude was pivotal. When I felt my throat throb and felt that beat spread through the rest of me, softening and melting me, I was healing. I had no doubt about it.

The content in this visualization wasn't new. In fact, the imagery was far simpler than usual. But I was more focussed and more relaxed, able to spin the sensations out, letting them deepen and flow more fully than ever before.

Two months later I had a comparable experience while doing yoga, and another during chanting — in which I couldn't tell where I ended and the sound began. I felt deliciously blissful afterwards.

The next time I saw Rebecca, I described these events. I ended by saying, "I thought I'd given up needing results, but I'm getting hooked on another kind. After the visualization in Switzerland, I wanted more like that. Now that I've had a beautiful chanting and yoga experience, I can feel my greedy little mind revving up."

"You'll keep upping the ante, wanting a more spectacular experience all the time?" she chuckled.

"Yes. Instead of demanding that my symptoms disappear when I sing or do yoga, I'm demanding that I have a deeper, more expanded experience. It's just attachment to a different kind of results."

"It's still making your efforts contingent on rewards," she reflected.

"Yes. And it raises another of the big questions again. If crisis isn't what moves me, or a goal like conquering or achieving, what does?"

She laughed. "I know what I'm supposed to say. Service, gratitude, that kind of thing."

"Well," I looked at her, "do you believe it?"

"I understand it intellectually. That's all so far."

"I can't remember where I read it, but I wrote in my journal, 'Saying a heartfelt thanks stimulates humility, which stimulates hope.'"

"Humility," she pondered. "I suppose I feel more humble when I'm grateful. I'm acknowledging that I need other people. I feel less separate." She laughed again. "Of course, 'heartfelt' is the key. I'm still concentrating on *feeling* thankful, not just thinking I should feel it."

* * *

One evening David and I drifted into a conversation about how lupus had affected our family. I said, "We're three willful personalities who venture out into the world with home as a solid base to return to. We haven't become a team. How long has it been since we've raked leaves together or had a family picnic?"

David argued, "I like our emphasis on individuality. It has more to do with our genes and values than lupus."

"If I had more energy, I'd aim for more cooperation."

"You'd try," he said in a tone of voice suggesting he wouldn't extend much support.

I continued, "A chronic illness with exacerbations and remissions creates more than one set of family dynamics. As I see it, at my sickest, you're the single parent to a special needs and a 'regular' child. When my symptoms lessen I get cast in the role of the mean, rigid parent with two boys ganged up against me. When my symptoms become more invisible, you're dependent on my word to know how much help I need. Occasionally, I take advantage of you, and regardless, you get tired of putting out. You feel resentful and act out."

"That dynamic also occurs when you become the over-committed disciplinarian. I definitely want to be left out of that," he said.

"When my health is best," I said, "we play more balanced roles. Adam doesn't see you as the source of all fun, edible food, practical help, and material things."

"He never sees you as the source of edible food," he laughed.

David looked ready to pick up his magazine again, so I said, "How else has lupus affected us?"

"I wish we had more couple friends like we used to," he said.

"I do, too." I paused. "But Adam has benefitted from our friendships. He sees a whole range of successful life styles, not just middle-class couples with two children."

"He's learned a lot about how illness affects life," David said. "Adam might have backed away from that new friendship with the boy who has diabetes if he'd had no experience with disease. Adam's unsympathetic when you're ailing, but whenever Aidan is crabby, Adam says it's because Aidan doesn't feel well."

"Yes," I agreed. "Adam also knows that no matter what happens to me, you're there. That stability must be very important," I said, as a wave of gratitude rolled through me. "I've also felt that security too. Did you know that the findings in psychoneuroimmunology suggest that creating safety in intimate relationships helps the immune system?"

"That makes sense," he responded.

I didn't know where to take the subject, so I moved on. "Adam thinks we're classic workaholics, and he's still all play. If we played more, would he work more?"

"I don't know about that." He looked at me. "Anyway, tennis

or skiing are out. With your vision difficulties, even movies are tough."

"We haven't yet found new activities we both enjoy. But you've spent untold hours editing my writing. You're enduring all stages. For me, that time together is a very meaningful form of connection."

His voice tightened. "It's better than screaming or yelling."

I frowned. "David, really, why do you help me with the writing? You always do it, yet you grouse."

There was a long silence. Then he softly pushed out, "I do it because I care about you and because my helping you seems so important to you." By the end of the sentence, his voice had changed to a tone which conveyed, "Enough of this soft stuff."

18

To Meet Each Moment

In January 1982, almost seven years to the day lupus had been diagnosed, I saw Dr. Roth for the first time in six months.

Dr. Roth's first question was the usual one: "Well, how are you?"

Choosing my words carefully, I pronounced them slowly: "I have never felt better since I have had lupus."

"To be very honest, ever since I've known you, you have always looked like a mildly ill person, even at your best. This is the first time I've ever seen you looking normal and healthy."

"I know. I like my unpuffy face. My eyes look clearer. My hair is growing in again."

"I never thought I would get you this far. How much prednisone are you taking?" he asked.

"*None*. Just for symbolic purposes, I took the last pill on December 31."

"Wonderful," he said. "Are you still taking your other medications?"

"Yes."

He caught me by surprise when he said he wanted to see me again in two months to check my kidneys.

A ping of anxiety struck. "Lupus can become active in the kidney even though I don't have any symptoms?"

"Yes, it's something we should check, particularly since you've stopped taking prednisone. Also, your last x-ray showed a calcium chip in one of your kidneys. We should take another x-ray to see what's happening there."

Hearing this increased the humility and caution I already had. Although we had not designed a plan to taper my other medications, I knew it would take approximately two years. And that was two years *if* there were no other problems. Another kidney stone might necessitate surgery, and that would, at the minimum, slow the tapering schedule. The longer I was on medications, the more likely a candidate I was for their side effects. If I had to eliminate a medication because of side effects, we would have to change our entire course of action.

As I left, he said, "Your progress is wonderful. But don't forget that the pattern of lupus is to come and go. Don't be shocked if you get sick again."

* * *

Shortly after I saw Dr. Roth, I attended a workshop with Richard Moss, whom I discovered through his book, *The I That Is We*. A Stanford-trained physician, he runs retreats which emphasize the radical transformational potential of life crises and works frequently with physically sick people. His workshops include sound, movement, meditation, dream analysis, and a whole range of other energetic approaches.

At an appropriate moment in the week-long group, I described the two-day orgasm, soaring temperature, and pericarditis when I first became ill and ended with, "I was fairly unconscious about what was going on. The only thing I knew was I felt incredibly wonderful and then, wham, the shock."

Richard sat in silence for a minute or so. Then he said, "Did you know that the *kundalini* energy kills some people? Indian literature describes some people dying within 48 hours of its activation. It sounds to me, Donna, that your orgasm awakened that energy in an unprepared vehicle."

I said, "I came across the idea here and there in books. Do I remember correctly? *Kundalini* is another manifestation in humans of what I call universal energy?

"Yes," Richard said. "It lies dormant at the base of the spine until it is set in motion. I received a letter recently from a woman who'd been meditating for a number of years, and suddenly in the middle of meditation, the *kundalini* broke through and went up the back of her spine. She spent a year afterwards in a wonderful state of freedom and bliss. Then, for the last ten years, she's been severely ill."

Richard seemed lost in thought. When I glanced again, he was smiling.

"Why are you smiling?" I asked.

"I'm smiling because life is a mystery, and in one sense, it's oh, so easy to be ill with pericarditis or lupus. It is so much harder to be in the mystery, isn't it? Isn't it paradoxical that one person pursues what we think is a higher state of consciousness only to find themselves ill? Another person is ill and does the same thing and ends up getting well. It is so mysterious, so *totally* mysterious."

"It is," I agreed.

He looked at me. "I personally think it's not just Western medicine that is primitive and archaic. So is what we call holistic medicine. And so are these ways I am teaching you to understand and follow energy. We haven't the vaguest idea what we're talking about."

"What do you mean?" I asked.

"What is health, anyway? I truly don't know how we decided what 'normal' is."

"Well, I don't feel very sick," I said.

A member of the group spoke up. "You certainly don't look sick. You're a picture of health."

"Precisely," Richard said.

"But, wait," I protested, feeling a huge pang of anxiety, "sometimes I've looked well enough and been sick."

"Oh?" he said. "You have been?"

I didn't even try to respond. We sat silently for several moments.

"We haven't yet begun to define the human being in wholeness," Richard continued. "There's no question that people end up with things called diabetes and lupus and multiple sclerosis, that when you do a tissue biopsy, that diagnosis is verified. But that label simultaneously says something and says nothing. It only says something to the rational mind. To the soul it says virtually nothing."

He paused and his voice softened. "It just says, 'Here is one more of the infinite possible combinations of human experience.'" He looked at me. "Are you following?"

"Yes."

"It's as if to say that being without the diagnosis equals health, as if to say you can go from a very linear, limited cause-and-effect mentality to a more three-dimensional holistic mentality without consequence to the body."

"I suppose that is fairly ridiculous," I responded.

"The hospital diagnosis of lupus represents a statement that comes from the one-millionth percent of who we are. We let ourselves be defined by the millionth percent and are unavailable to the other 99% of what we are. We don't begin to have an inkling of the kind of strength and love of which we're capable."

He paused for some time. Then he said, "You don't know what's next. You don't know what will produce what in you. Crohn's disease, lupus, loss of a child, financial ruin, they are all perfectly valid ways to give us a momentary glimpse of the mystery, perfectly valid. They force us to look at love."

"It's taken me years of living with questions I couldn't answer and forces I couldn't control to learn that," I said.

"Love is so essential," he quickly replied. "Without it, we're just going to undo the whole world anyway."

There was another long silence. No one in the room seemed to move even a muscle.

After a while, Richard looked at me again and continued, "So that's why I smiled. Don't try to get anywhere, Donna. Just see what you can do with an honest meeting of each moment as best you can."

"I know," I said, "you really haven't got any answers."

"Right. Just stop and say, 'I am here,' and set aside the idea of getting anywhere. That person who wants to get somewhere is only a millionth of who you are."

Epilogue

1990

When my pre-lupus friend Lois, known more for her honesty than tact, visited recently from California, she said, "You look lovely." After a more careful examination and in a surprised tone, she added, "You actually look more attractive than you did before lupus."

Absence of sagging skin and few wrinkles are, of course, less important than how I feel about myself and therefore act. I look softer, less guarded, and that reflects less fear. A tight face has become a more relaxed, expressive one. Guarded, questioning eyes have turned receptive, at ease with wordless communication. My voice has a richer tone. A generous self-appreciation has come with maturing.

Besides looking well, I feel well, too. I have fewer aches and pains than my friends and with an afternoon nap, match my contemporaries in energy. I exercise regularly, either walking, cross-country skiing, or playing tennis. I do some combination of chanting, meditation, yoga, and visualization daily, have a weekly massage, and over the years have continued to explore healing modalities ranging from acupuncture to workshops in shamanism and Native American healing. I stopped the Kelley program in 1983, when their measures suggested substantial progress and when

I felt I no longer needed such intensity. Recently, I've been utilizing the Indian system of Ayurvedic medicine which adds small amounts of herbal preparations to a recommended diet. My digestive system has never worked better.

I have still had occasional lupus exacerbations for which I have taken prednisone and, in the past three years, haven't been able to eliminate it entirely. One possibility is that as prednisone is withdrawn, my adrenals have not picked up the slack properly. I keep diligently coaxing them to function fully again.

How has the illness transformed me? A decade and then some is, in fact, an excellent vantage point from which to answer the question. It is so hard to interpret one's own progress. Sometimes I realize only in retrospect that an important shift has occurred. Other times a change I think is finalized crops up as a lapse into old thought patterns and behavior. But there are some changes I am sure of.

I am a better therapist. I have less need to expend energy separating client issues from my own, to have clients need me. I've had more professional training, a little more therapy. As each year passes, I know myself better, am better balanced and more integrated.

Because of lupus, I know suffering and am thus more compassionate with others. I have more to offer in crisis. "Is the problem too heavy?" or "Do I have what it takes?" aren't questions anymore. Murderous rage, abject hopelessness, stark terror are known qualities. I'm less afraid of those emotions in myself and in others. The remaining question, "If I help, will I ever get away?" is still with me, but I keep confronting it. Before lupus, I might have noticed a few ways to help a sick person; now I invariably see a multitude. It would be easy to use lupus to avoid involvement, yet, more than before lupus, I have the courage to get involved while simultaneously allowing myself to set limits on my time and involvement.

A quiet *joi de vivre* fills a substantial chunk of most days. Occasionally I touch into remnants of the deep grief I was experiencing ten years ago, but I rarely feel angry. Fear is still with me, but it's clearly more related to the death of my ego than my physical body. Increasingly, there are entire days when, for no specific reason, wave after wave of gratitude pulses through me.

In 1982, I still believed that struggle and suffering were inherent in the process of solid and substantial change. I was still wrestling to understand the underlying principle: we struggle and suffer when crisis and pain—at base, the fear of death—are our primary motivating forces. The more our source of motivation becomes positive, the less we suffer. Today, I don't need a symptom or news of someone's cancer or the latest disaster to renew my appreciation for life. A mountain view does quite as well. And the subtle can have as much effect as the dramatic: a single leaf can feel as powerful as a stupendous panorama. Overall, of course, it's a matter of changing balance. More often I'm moved by the positive, more often nature or dance or song touch me deeply enough to reconfirm my connection to the universe.

I am more humble. However well I hid my feelings of superiority because of my former physical health and fitness, I felt it. I used my supposed mental health in the same way. Never again can I use those superficial standards to measure human worth. Confidence in the way my body functions does increase my self-esteem, but it has been liberating to discover that a sense of self-worth can also come from simply appreciating myself as a human being.

The simpler life I have adopted is now genuinely satisfying. Success, achievement, and materialism drive me less. Living a life in which relationships, connection to nature, seasons, and activities basic to existence come first, attracts me more. Taking time to cook with fresh foods is rarely a chore, nor is talking on the phone with my parents or visiting David's ailing mother. Recently I've craved fresh air, sky, trees, and earth beneath my feet enough to brave many days of walking to my office in 20-degree weather. I also limit work because I am more attuned to subtle cues of tiredness and more able to give myself permission to respond to them. I may not live this way forever. Obtaining a doctorate would require major changes in lifestyle, and some day I may make them. What I am wholeheartedly grateful for is having a choice. Voluntary simplicity is far more pleasant than enforced, but when lupus has forced simplicity upon me, I've found ways to savor it then, too.

I do seem to live more in the now. I think about whether I like what I'm doing at the moment and rarely miss opportunities to express affection or appreciation. Conversely, only in the past few years have I dared to extend my time frame beyond the hour-at-a-time view it took me years to learn. What's different is that I see it as a luxury. I don't take daydreaming about trips or toying with options for work and play for granted. Nor is thinking about the future a substitute for enjoying today; generally I can do both.

I am more the kind of mother I have wanted to be. Adam's quiet but convincing words at the end of a recent squabble were reassuring: "After all, I am growing up to be a fairly decent young man." Although mothering older teenagers is still complex, I am often content taking each day as it comes, doing what I see needs doing, and leaving it at that. I am pleasantly surprised at my contentment.

David insists, adamantly, that lupus has not changed him much, except to make him more accepting of changes around him. He has, however, learned not to postpone play. He is furiously planning trips; surprisingly, they are often dangerous white-water ventures. I can't say I play more today. When I took up photography last fall, I did it with such fervor most people would have called it work. My boundaries between work and play continue to blur, and it's still the rhythm and balance between them that gives me greatest satisfaction.

One qualitatively different way I do take better care of myself is by staying at my meditation ashram for a week or so each summer. We sleep up to six in a room in buildings that accommodate hundreds, and the day begins at 5:00 a.m. Part of each day is spent in direct, often basic, labor—cleaning, tending gardens, preparing vegetarian, cafeteria-style meals. For someone who covets solitude, detests crowds, and avoids cafeteria dining, the ashram is a strange choice for vacation. Yet I always leave intellectually stimulated and emotionally nourished, with my values clearer and, I hope, my motives purer. Shared chores reconfirm my ordinariness, and simple labor is an appealingly direct way to contribute to the common good. More than ever chanting and meditating simultaneously reaffirm my uniqueness and my connection to other people. Each moment in the ashram reminds me that it really is possible to live in that more open-hearted state every day.

The feeling that there isn't enough time plagues me less. I

believe in my own version of reincarnation: if I can't complete my spiritual journey in this lifetime, I will be reborn at the level I have accomplished. To a former competitive-achiever for whom every second counts, that belief helps, but it wasn't adopted for expediency; it simply makes more sense to me than heaven and hell.

Before lupus, I did not think so consciously about the meaning of life. Shortly after I became ill, I believed life must have inherent meaning, and my task was to find it. Following that, I saw only the inherent meaninglessness of the universe, and the thought left me paralyzed. If life had no meaning, why live? Today everything seems grayer, and finally I understand paradox. The illness has no inherent meaning, but I can make it meaningful. I want to get well, yet my chances may be enhanced by being less obsessed with that goal. I cannot say I am cured, yet in most ways, I have never been healthier. I don't have all the power, and I don't use nearly all I have. None of those apparent contradictions throw me as much as they used to.

I ask fewer questions these days, significantly fewer about cause and effect. Symptoms and emotions interconnect, but I am less clear about the extent to which my emotions stimulate symptoms or are in response to symptoms. Perhaps I gave emotional blockage as a causal factor in my illness greater importance than it deserved; on the other hand, the powers of the mind still seem so much vaster than I ever imagined. What yogis demonstrate in controlling their bodily functions is probably possible for most of us but requires an incredible commitment of time and energy. I am not much clearer about where my "can'ts" end and my "won'ts" begin, where acceptance ends and resignation begins. The illness has been as much a journey into unknowing as knowing.

That doesn't mean my questioning has been a waste of time. To outgrow the need for questioning, I had to question. And tomorrow, if I get cancer, have a heart attack, or become severely depressed, I'll ask many of the same questions. I like to think I'd move faster, be clearer, and have a broader perspective, but the process would be similar.

Some of the changes in me are, of course, related to lupus. But it is impossible to tell the extent to which they are related or if they are at all. Understanding suffering and feeling more humble seem directly connected to lupus, but knowing that chance is part of life, being more aware of mortality and more accepting of fate, are common mid-life realizations. Privileged circumstance has been a significant factor in my choices. Without David's salary, I'd make others.

The most significant change is my perspective of change itself. I see that transformation is rarely instant, dramatic, and permanent. Change is more often subtle, slow, and compromised with loss. The process of integration, the tolerance and self-tolerance of maturity, is always incomplete and imperfect. To believe otherwise breeds arrogance and despair. Healing, with or without physical illness, is a lifelong task, and I am more committed than ever. Messages in a recent, beautiful dream were: I am giving myself over to the healing process at an even deeper level, and I am healing, much more than I can even imagine.

That I am alive today to pursue healing is a gift from the universe. It's beyond my understanding. I'm fast coming to echo Joseph Campbell's conviction that, ultimately, it's grace that matters most.

* * *

My parents came to visit recently. I had mentioned the book and my concern about their reaction to it many times before they arrived. They stayed first at my sister Karen's, where they read the earlier chapters with her input and support. Then they came to Worcester.

The first morning Dad and I sat together at breakfast. Without my asking about the book, he said, "Your description of how lupus affects everyday life is excellent. It should be very helpful to others."

"I hope so," I responded.

"I think you were too hard on your mother. During your childhood, she contributed to your well-being more than I. After all, I was out of the house all day." His voice became stern. "You were too hard on David, too. He took care of you in the best way anyone could. He was *very* tolerant. You should have been more grateful for that."

"I know, but I couldn't. I didn't feel it—and forcing it didn't work. What would you have done?"

"Well, it's a difficult dilemma. Illness seems to bring out negative and exaggerated reactions."

After finishing the last of his poached egg, Dad said, "I think Ildri took advantage of you. You were weak and vulnerable. She pushed you to emphasize the negative."

"You know, she really didn't." I glanced at him. His jaw was set. This was a familiar cue. I wouldn't get anywhere discussing this further.

"I felt more kindly toward Dr. Lowen," he added. "He seemed more fair and honest, although psychotherapy is a field I know little about; it has a tremendous amount of gray areas."

Dad and I went for a couple of walks. Intermittently, I slipped in questions like, " What do you think causes these autoimmune illnesses? Years ago, when you had colon cancer, did you ask any of the questions I did?"

All I remember hearing him say was, "Have you ever been to Mexico City? It's in a bowl surrounded by volcanos. . . . What are your property taxes in Massachusetts? . . . In this book about Kenya I was reading last night. . . . Medical malpractice insurance seems prohibitively expensive here. . . . Did you hear the story about the schnauzer who wouldn't mind?"

Another morning mother and I sat alone at breakfast. She, too, thought Ildri had forced me to cry and had emphasized the negative. She thought Dr. Lowen overemphasized sexuality. I could see the roots of my own critical nature in their responses. Mother's voice became quiet as she added, "If you'd really had a bad childhood, that would be one thing."

"I know," I held up my hands, signaling her to stop. "Yesterday I saw one client who'd been sexually molested by her father and another who had no parents. Four women in one therapy group had children who died. Relative to many people, maybe most, my childhood was pretty idyllic, by whatever standard you use. But we each need to know ourselves, no matter who we are. Having a history and making sense of it isn't just for people with the most painful stories."

My mother also said, "It's hard to hear myself described as a wicked stepmother. Saying I lie on the couch all the time makes me look lazy." Mostly, however, she made editing comments and asked questions like, "What did you mean when you said one day I pushed you to be perfect, and the next day I did the opposite?" or

"What about amending this sentence about your father's never having arguments with his brother. 'Never' is an exaggeration."

I said, "I'm amazed at how you and Dad are going along with my book. I thought you'd both be upset. I thought you, especially, would think I'd been much too hard on you."

She dried her hands on the dishtowel after washing our dishes. "Well, I do think you're sometimes inaccurate. And sometimes unfair. But I see what you're trying to do. It's not to be critical. And it is *your* story."

The day they left, we sat at the table eating breakfast together. I said, "I thought you'd be more interested in talking about some of the ideas in the book. Dad, last year you even sent me a sheet relating levels of illness and levels of stress."

He said, "Well, as you know, it's not that I haven't thought about these topics. But causality, for example. It's so complex."

Mother added, "Maybe a latent virus was involved in your lupus. You had an extremely bad case of chicken pox at a later age than most children."

Dad glanced out the window briefly and then turned to me. "You know, I'm seventy-five years old. I've lived a very full life. I don't want to think about these subjects anymore. I just want to enjoy each day."

"I understand." Suddenly I did. Why make them probe?

After they left, I called my sister Karen. "Was I crazy to be worried that Mom and Dad would be angry about the book?"

"No, not at all," she said. "I thought they'd see it as quite hurtful, as washing dirty linen in public, and so on. I had all the same thoughts you did."

"I'm relieved to hear that."

Her voice sounded sympathetic as she continued. "But you've done a lot of spadework over the years. You've been carefully laying the groundwork for these discussions. You enlisted my support a long time ago."

"You've been wonderful at all levels. I think you know how much I appreciate it." My throat softened, and the increasingly familiar wave of feeling streamed through me.

"There's a lot to timing. Mom and Dad have had to deal with huge changes in their economic circumstances and their own health problems in the past decade. They're older. At this point in their lives, they're making their peace with the world. They're seeing everything from a more accepting perspective."

"Yes," I answered. "Their generous gesture makes me want to give something back, not only to them, but to whomever crosses my path. In fact, it's time to reach out into the world more. The best thing is that it's a desire, not an obligation."

Appendix

Guide For A Self-Help Prescription

At the onset of the illness, what would have helped me more than anything was "how-to" help with the decision-making process. Which decisions take precedence? By what criteria can choices be made? What are realistic expectations? How can I grasp principles and gain self-knowledge faster? It was the process of change that I needed to learn as quickly as possible.

What follows is what I wish I'd had. The ideas are general and therefore adaptable to your illness, your personality, your specific situation. You may want to alter some steps, eliminate others, or tackle them in another order. The healing process is not static, nor are the steps sequential. The process is more like a spiral, requiring the recycling of issues again and again. With each round, issues are seen from a deeper, broader perspective. My intention is that these suggestions take into account the reality of being ill and still help you maximize what is possible for you, help you accept that many things may be impossible *and* that more is possible than you think.

Choosing

Empowering comes through choosing. There are always choices. They may be about a problem you don't want. They may be between the lesser of evils. Nonetheless, you have choices. The more self-aware I was, the more choices I saw. The more choices I had, the less helpless I felt, and feeling more in control really did stimulate optimism.

The goal worth aiming for in every decision is to make it not from fear, not from displaced hope, but from knowing yourself so well that it is perfectly clear what choice to make. This is tremendously difficult, so be patient. One of the first decisions I made with that level of certainty was not to take Imuran for the lupus nephritis.

Educating yourself about your disease offers a sense of control. Your physician may be your main source of medical information. Second and third opinions can help, although at first may seem more confusing because you may then need to make more choices. Libraries and agencies such as the national foundations for lupus, arthritis, multiple sclerosis, and other illnesses are eager to provide information. If you're too weak, in too much pain, or too upset to digest what you might discover, is there someone who can do this for you and whom you can consult when you're ready?

Healing takes time. As our measuring devices become more sensitive, we will probably confirm that each aspect of the body, mind, and spirit affects every other aspect in greater or lesser measure. Healing depends on *hundreds* of factors, intertwined into a complex web of interactions in which connecting threads move in both directions, and the flux keeps changing. Many people undoubtedly make wise choices, work very hard at healing, yet still do not live. Dare to ask how much time and energy you wish to invest. The higher the priority health is given, the more likely you'll get results. But since you cannot know results, throughout your illness judge yourself only on the *intent* and *care* with which you make decisions.

The effects of changes in life habits are slow to show. In one study, people with diverse illnesses who recovered from hopeless prognoses took about ten years. Trust that the process works, even though you can't know if you will be given the gift of time.

Wise choices reflect beliefs. To help you identify your beliefs, try asking, "What will help heal me?" or say "I'll get well if I . . . " several times. Write down whatever comes to mind first, no matter how irrational it seems. Read your list out loud to someone else or to yourself. Which answers evoke the strongest feelings? Identify the emotions. What scares you? What makes you feel a greater sense of control? Which answers are attitudes and opinions borrowed from others? Are they from parents, books, or conventional wisdom? Merely being aware of your beliefs helps. I had to see that my act-well-means-I-am-well stance was denial before I could change it.

The body heals best when you act on convictions that have some internal logic and stir you emotionally. Conscious beliefs and attitudes may differ from those beneath the surface. In the early years of my illness, I thought I believed I'd get well, yet my attempts at visualization then suggested part of me did not. Dreamwork, artwork, and visualization techniques helped me penetrate through my verbal/intellectual screens to deeper levels. Dialogues—with symptoms, with the illness, with dreams, with yourself before, during, and recovering from illness—help bring hidden feelings and beliefs to the surface faster. Even though I'm trained in these techniques, it's hard to use them by oneself: I've used them far more effectively with the help of another skilled therapist.

Illness is also a process of developing beliefs, and many change over time. Before the lupus-nephritis crisis, I believed that if I found enough of the right methods and used them faithfully and flawlessly, I'd heal. When I was forced to face that I could die no matter what I did, I was pushed to question that belief and then modify it, to acknowledge that I didn't have as much power over life and death as I'd thought.

Contemplating, "You don't get what you want; you get what you believe," spurred me to keep looking closely at my values. If you pray, imagining that you get what you ask for is a way to test your belief. If you are seeking fearlessness, see what happens in your body when you say, "I am fearless." When my belief is shaky, my chest tightens, my breathing catches, and my throat constricts.

Open yourself to new ways of physical, emotional, and spiritual nourishment. Many alternative methods work in conjunction with allopathic medicine and are low-risk. Physicians and the disease foundations won't educate you about alternatives, for their interest is in methods based on hard science. Alternative systems are interested in sharing data about the results they have achieved. *Cancer Survivors* by Judith Glassman describes case studies of people using different healing methods. The authors of current personal-experience books have often used alternate methods.

In *Planet Medicine*, Richard Grossinger discusses different levels of medicine in a way which expanded my thinking:

> Meditation, Prayer, Self-Reflection
> Activity (T'ai Chi Ch'uan, Chanting)
> Diet and Herbs (Homeopathy, Ayurvedic Medicine)
> Healing by the Senses (Touch, Vision, Hearing, Dreams)
> Bodywork (Massage, Adjustment)
> Acupuncture
> Surgery, Radiation, Drugs

The higher on the list, the more active the person treated has to be, the more they have to take on responsibility for their healing. The lower on the list, the relatively quicker and more mechanical the treatment. An illness treated by radiation or drugs is dealt with in a matter of months, days, or even seconds, yet the side effects are often greatest from these most "invasive" methods. The more active levels seem slower, but you may become centered enough from these methods for your body to access its own healing strength. Psychotherapy combines self-reflection and healing by the senses, and bioenergetic therapy adds bodywork to that. If you have to take a strong steroid drug, you can also take a homeopathic remedy to off-set side-effects and build strength.

Today most cities have homeopathic physicians, acupuncturists, doctors of chinese medicine and naturopaths, as well as holistic health centers — but word-of-mouth is still a main source of information about practitioners. The national associations of different kinds of medicine can recommend qualified practitioners locally. Some allopathic physicians believe in the importance of mind and spirit, even though their interventions are at the bodily level. Some holistic practitioners see their path to the exclusion of others, which is the same narrow focus physicians have been accused of having.

Developing Support

Developing supportive friendships is a crucial ingredient in healing. Knowing someone cared made me care. Since I was hospitalized dramatically, word about my illness spread and prompted responses from my friends. Many autoimmune diseases develop gradually, however, and no one will know unless they are told. Some people will be profoundly compassionate, but most will be awkward discussing illness in a meaningful way. Not only will you have to deal with your own shame, guilt, and denial, but you'll have to hear theirs also. In the beginning, I didn't talk about lupus because it didn't fit in with my upbeat "accent the positive" philosophy, and I was also too vulnerable to handle tactless comments. If you're resilient enough to let insensitive comments roll off your back, sharing can lead to feeling less alone at the very least.

People often ask to help only once, so you must respond then. If you don't know what you need, tell people you'll get back to them when you do or ask them to check with you again. At first, I tried to guess whose giving was motivated by guilt and spare them the effort, but that wasted my energy. Contemplating, "People give what they want to; it is therefore okay to receive," helped.

I learned to let go of the idea that I had to repay people who helped me. Giving to anyone, keeping the chain going, is the essential. Over time, I found ways to give that accommodated my health. When my sister Judi's baby son died, I didn't feel I could fly to Texas for the funeral, but she wanted my support during her grieving so I invited her to call me collect for as long and as often as she needed. For months, that was almost daily, and I scheduled one less client daily so I would have enough energy for her. Creating such personally tailored modes of giving can be richly satisfying.

Collect healing tools. Videos, books, flowers, artwork, and crystals can be quietly nourishing. You can learn stress reduction techniques from television teachers or choose programs that make you laugh. If I were allowed to take only one item with me to the hospital, I'd choose my Walkman. It offered a whole repertoire of support: healing and inspirational music, a yoga teacher or my own recorded voice to lead me through breathing and guided visualization exercises, or inspirational talks by people whose books I couldn't read when my vision was blurred or eyes sore.

Any relationship can be valuable. The young household helpers who responded so generously when I was so needy will live in my heart as much as my close friends and professional helpers, and, in a different way so will the woman who ran the checkout counter at the neighborhood grocery store with whom I rarely spoke.

It is often said that people don't care like they used to. While it does seem that many of us have lost some capacity to reach out, it's more that caring people aren't always found today in the traditional forms of family and neighborhood. Also, forms which were suitable in the past may not be currently relevant. It was inappropriate for me to seek my parents' help when I was immersed in discovering antagonisms I had hidden towards them. Developing friends who were as close as family was the new form I chose.

Building in support for longer than you need it is helpful in an illness with flares and remissions, since support is easy to cancel, exhausting to restimulate. It helped that Rebecca drove without being asked whenever we went somewhere together, and even when I wasn't in dire need.

Let yourself ask for help. Few people see what needs doing and do it without asking. If you can ask, your only limit is your creativity. The line between being demanding and imperious and asking for needed help is so thin many of us shrink from expressing our needs. If you have difficulty asking, this may be the key area in which you need help. As I became able to accept lupus as a reflection of my humanity and not of my personal failure, seeking assistance became a way to acknowledge my interdependence with people, an expression of humility rather than humiliation.

The purpose of all external support is to help you discover, rediscover, and strengthen your own internal support. Theoretically, it is simple: when caring is offered, take it in, convert it to healing energy. Practically, it's usually harder. As your capacity to receive expands, you may go through the same phase I did in which you are so hungry for nurturance, you become anxious about separating from anyone who gives you a dose of unconditional love. The anxiety usually disappears with time. It helps to remember that most people have difficulties with intimacy; illness has forced yours to the foreground.

Touch is a powerful healing force, and sexuality is an important form. Sometimes any touch is too painful, but many times the challenge is to find new ways to give and get affection, comfort, and nurturance. Tender, gentle touch, the intimacy of deeper conversation, and simply holding each other can be very satisfying. If anger at being so dependent doesn't lead to pleasing sex for you, find what ways you can to nourish your self-reliance. Discovering that orgasm was a serious opening of the heart and that the illness was an involuntary closing-down made me want to stand back, understand that more, and create ways to experience the same wonderful feelings independent of another human being. The more autonomous I felt, the more I enjoyed intimacy.

Support groups are useful. Had a local branch of the Massachusetts Lupus Foundation existed when I first became ill, I would have found it helpful in meeting other people with lupus and in gathering medically based information. The Gestalt and bioenergetic training programs were rich with lively body, mind, and spirit discussions and were settings where I could explore myself and different models of healing. Following that, my meditation group became an important support. Even when you are too weak to bowl, you may enjoy having lunch with your bowling group, or just as comrades in battle become fast friends, you may meet someone in the diabetes support group who becomes a trusted confidant.

Today, the listing of support groups in newspapers is expanding. Some support groups are emotionally oriented, but group psychotherapy is the most likely setting in which to look at your life issues in depth.

Psychotherapy offers a special kind of support. No matter how much you see yourself as a well-functioning and rational adult, severe illness usually dramatizes how deeply all interactions are influenced by unresolved feelings and unexamined messages from the past. Therapists can spare you overburdening those closest to you, and paying them means you don't have to listen to them, as you would a friend or family member. Since they aren't quite so invested in results, and are trained to help people look at emotional issues which may surface in illness, they can help you look at your process—*how* you go about decision-making—better than friends and family. Psychotherapy can also be an excellent tool for spiritual growth.

My own therapy helped me sort out my emotional baggage. These interpersonal conflicts were sapping the little energy I had, so

I couldn't concentrate on other healing methods. I concluded that the point of looking at feelings from childhood is less that they cause illness than that examining the past helps you to understand how you relate to your life, and self, and thus illness. Remembering and understanding my birth family's values about time and its use helped me know when I was spending too much time on healing activities and when I was spending too little.

Creating a Prescription for Health

Brainstorming generates new ideas. Head a sheet of paper, "If I could, I'd..." Jot down possible methods without regard to feasibility. Just for the moment, pretend you have no limitations. Ask family and friends to add their ideas. Besides methods you believe in, include new ones which interest or excite you.

Identify and confront your limitations. "Can'ts" are real, although fear makes us say "can't" about many things which turn out to be possible. If chronic weakness is part of your illness, you will need help in carrying out all aspects of your healing remedies. You may be less emotionally stable. If you are in intense or chronic pain, likely you cannot do as much as usual. If you are poor, you have to be twice as clever, especially if you use alternative methods, since most are not covered by health insurance. Students at the local massage school give free massages during their training. Co-counseling is a kind of peer counseling in which you barter each other's time.

Compromising is usually necessary in the selection process, but it should come last. When all else fails, when death looms near, we often find money, time, and abilities we claimed not to have.

A combination of methods is generally best since health and healing involve a constellation of factors and since all healing methods are limited. Yet the specific methods, the number of methods, and the particular combination is less important than making choices intrinsic to you. The laws of good health always apply, but what will promote your health is unique to you.

Putting together your own program at home takes more initiative and costs more if you need teachers to come to you. If you are mobile, you can utilize community resources such as the Y for exercise classes. Basic stress-reduction and nutrition courses are offered by many health-maintenance organization plans, and there are other nonresidential structured programs. Holistic health centers based around Eastern spiritual disciplines such as Kripalu in western Massachusetts or the Himalayan Institute in Pennsylvania have temporary residential programs. The macrobiotic and wheat grass programs offer residential facilities, as well as referrals to local practitioners. The Ayurvedic program I use involves my seeing a specialist who comes to Boston yearly. An advanced student of his follows me in between and could provide referrals if I needed yoga, meditation, massage, or other helpers to carry out the recommended treatment.

Besides money and energy, your choice depends on your answers to a complex of questions. How much do you need to be in charge? How much peer support do you want? How much professional support? Is your home nourishing? How much help do you have?

Since the relationship between change and healing is highly individual, you need to ask: *How important is speed?* How fast can you tolerate change? If you don't know, who has the objectivity to help you answer that? *Is radical change important?* Consider the theory that the crucial ingredient in healing is getting off one track and onto another. A vegetarian switching to a macrobiotic diet is not changing the track. Real revolt is to break away from a pattern, to inquire outside it. What would be radical for you?

Draw up an hourly schedule to help you make the final cuts. Are you spreading yourself too thin? Cut anything for which you cannot build in solid support or do not have a decent chance of executing. I wisely eliminated meditation and visualization from my remedies at first because I realized I needed teachers who would come to my house and I wasn't willing to invest the time and energy to find them. Additional methods can always be added later.

Comitting and Acting

Where you feel unified, commit. Commit to your physicians, to other helpers, to your treatment program. Commit fiercely, without reservation. Make your healing plan an act of faith. Commitment involves entrusting with heart as well as head, and while you cannot will a heart to open, it will bloom with gentle care. When I became aware that I needed a source of motivation besides will, and after gratitude became a stronger force in my life, my **Prescription** became much easier to fulfill.

Concentrate solely on your Prescription. Now is the time to withdraw a bit from the outside world, to talk less about your illness, to surround yourself with people and environments which support your chosen approach.

Expect to feel self-consciously narcissistic, since healing requires that you spend a vast amount of time on yourself. The bottom line, however, is that if you don't take care of yourself, you may never be able to take care of anyone else. On days when I could barely turn over in bed, Dr. Lowen's idea that if I wanted to raise a healthy child, I should heal the child within myself was particularly comforting. For a long time, I couldn't see how time spent healing myself was equally as valuable to the world as time spent in peace marches or on ecological campaigns. Eventually, I came to agree that a culture which creates missiles and bombs, and which fouls its nest, has become out of touch with itself — that change begins on a personal level.

Faith in your decisions is essential. Distinguishing when doubt means you're on an unproductive path and need to change from when doubt reflects lack of faith is difficult. When I became frightened that expressing anger was as harmful as containing it during psychotherapy with Ildri and Dr. Lowen, I had enough faith in them to conclude fairly readily that my doubts reflected my own shaky trust and not that their theory was wrong. One way to gain faith is to practice having it, at first in small decisions. Reading, contemplating, talking with people who share your interest in spiritual topics, and finding teachers and other supports will accelerate your learning.

Adaptation and change in your Prescription may be necessary. A relationship with a physician may deteriorate, like mine did. If you are considering changing professional helpers, make sure you aren't changing because you expect them to perform miracles, to control the uncontrollable aspects of healing. If you are afraid to make a change which seems right, is there someone who can support you through it?

Remember that specific avenues can change: the principles are what count. When I became too weak for tennis, bioenergetic exercises and yoga were fine substitutes. Visualization and chanting were equally as effective as meditation. You've chosen carefully. If contingencies do not force change, reviewing your program a few times yearly should be sufficient.

When you have difficulty sticking with your **Prescription**, you probably need more support, not a different prescription. Try accepting a paradox: there is always more you can do *and* you are doing enough.

Take the view that struggle is necessary, useful, and positive. Since change usually requires struggle, expect to struggle, perhaps as never before. More than once expect to think you have seen the light around the corner and thrown all your energy into getting there, only to arrive and find that not only are you in another dead end, but the old way no longer works and the new is clouded or seems too dangerous. Your insides may be silently screaming: Why should I take these risks? What matters anyway? And this is only the beginning. You may realize lack of results necessitates faith, but that only raises more questions. Is there a force beyond the ego self? What is it? How do you find and keep faith?

Though the thought may comfort you little in the midst of strife, the more you struggle, the more detached you can become. The more detached from results you are, the less fear you will have and the easier your new attitudes will be to integrate. I practiced detachment by going through first minutes, then hours trying not to judge any event. That meant I not only couldn't bemoan a painful day but I also couldn't celebrate a symptomless one. Remaining nonjudgmental for even an hour is quite a feat.

Find new standards to mark your progress. The dilemma is that symptoms have to be noticed and addressed when they are minor to prevent them from becoming major. Yet, focusing on them can reinforce the disease and make it easy to lose yourself in it. After I went through a phase of denial about lupus, I veered toward the opposite extreme and sometimes felt defined by it. Today when someone asks how I am, I occasionally only speak of my spiritual or emotional well-being. Some might think that's denial, but today it's a choice to define myself as I wish.

If you can't resist measuring, note how well you are executing your **Prescription** instead of measuring results. Are you exercising two times a week as you had promised? What would help you reach a deeper state of relaxation more quickly?

Instead of counting how many symptoms you have, could you note how much you've transformed the pain and problems facing you? Could your courage be measured by the amount of fear you've overcome? What would it mean to see your disease as a learning experience, to accept it instead of hating it? Imagine living each day as if you had something to contribute, however weak and misshapen you are.

There is, in the final analysis, no universally accepted definition of health. While most of us agree that health is more than removal of symptoms, what it is beyond that is open for debate. Healing and cure are different. A person may be cured, that is, become physically symptomless, and still not be healthy.

Reducing stress facilitates healing. Deep relaxation is better than the level gained by watching television or reading. Relaxation skills will be easier to use in a crisis if you've learned them beforehand. Stress reduction and meditation courses can help, as can biofeedback therapists. When I used biofeedback devices, I discovered I was more relaxed than I had thought.

Just prior to surgery or other medical procedures, stop debating decisions. Focus your entire attention on relaxing, on entrusting yourself to your chosen treatment and the people who will be facilitating it.

Eliminate stress when you are too weak or disoriented to cope with normal levels. Often your choice will be between getting more assistance or simplifying your life. I was eventually able to enjoy the benefits of getting out of the rat race.

Influence bodily processes as much as you can. Holding a wish or simply thinking about a treatment's success is helpful. Intensive prayer or use of visualization techniques is even better, and the same principles are involved. Visualization directions suggest that being deeply relaxed, believing to your very core in the method, and concentrating so completely on the imagery that nothing else enters your awareness are imperative. Those are staggering prerequisites if you've never used the method. Reserving a time or times of day and a special place, even if it's your bed, and training people not to bother you can demonstrate your intent, and the power of intention is extraordinary. Sitting or lying so that your spine is straight can be your next step in establishing the habit. Ready-made visualizations on audio cassettes can help you develop your own imagery. Practice will eventually lead to success. Some psychotherapists are skilled in teaching visualization.

It is better to be emotionally flowing than blocked. Likely your goal will be to feel the full range of human emotions, whatever is appropriate to a situation, and to change the emotional balance inside you so that joy, hope, peace, and love predominate. When I first became ill, the chronic tension in my body, exaggerated by prednisone, provoked me to consider that buried emotional conflicts stayed alive in my body and mind. Over time, I had little doubt that in the long run, suppression, denial, and repression didn't work.

Feelings, since they are not rational, cannot usually be "legislated" away. For some people, simply *becoming aware* of an undesirable emotion is the key to unlocking the flow. There were many occasions when Ildri and Dr. Lowen reflected, "You sound sad," and I denied the feeling because I didn't want to be or think I should be.

Sometimes, the key is *insight.* It helped me to decide what to do with my feelings when I could distinguish fury at being ill which I took out at Chris from resentment at his inappropriate and uncaring behavior.

At other times, *expression* is important. Talking about feelings with friends has healing effects but is not the same as, or a substitute for, expression. Walking or playing tennis when I was full of anger was beneficial because it kept energy flowing and gave me time and distance to reassess situations, but it often wasn't a substitute for expression either. Hitting the couch reminded me that somewhere in my exhausted, pained body was power. It reminded me in a way words could not that anger was *energy* and was translatable into confidence, assertion, and compassion. Limiting expression of such feelings to a therapy office kept me mindful that their source was within me, not in external situations, and spared me facing the consequences of inappropriate or exaggerated angers.

Creating dialogues, drawing, playing with clay, movement, or music are equally effective, less physically stressful active methods.

The Eastern spiritual disciplines generally advocate deliberately not expressing anger externally and that can be effective, too. Fully experiencing the emotion is far more important than the method you use.

At still other times, *consciously positive affirmations* may be the best choice. Whenever you can, substitute the feeling you desire, the compassion you want, for the anger you feel. I remember Adam sitting on my lap and tenderly saying, "If I had one wish in the world, it would be for you to get well." For many months afterwards, whenever I ran out of patience to the extent of wanting to hit him, I'd invite this memory back, and it dependably calmed me. Use visualization, meditation, yoga, chanting, doing for others, or whatever means rouses your charitable side.

When affirmations aren't working, you often need more support or need to focus more on awareness, insight, or expression. The process seems developmental: you are more likely to be successful replacing feelings after you have a fair amount of awareness and perception and know how to express emotion constructively.

Working with feelings is a lifelong task. A realistic goal is that with practice you will go through the transformative process more quickly.

Face your fear of death. Fear of dying can be so overwhelming as to paralyze you. Expanding your perspective about death and dying helps. Besides reading current Western writers like Stephen Levine and Elizabeth Kubler-Ross, you can learn much from ancient cultures and religions and from the Eastern spiritual disciplines. In Buddhism and Hinduism an experiential knowledge of death is an integral part of life. True fearlessness, they say, comes when you do not value life more than death.

Exploring this sensitive topic when you aren't in the height of a crisis is easier. Once again, read, contemplate, talk with people who share your interest, and seek out workshops about working with fear of death.

Compassion and gratitude melt fear. "To take heart" means to be unafraid. During a terrifying moment, try to focus on what you honestly feel grateful for, whether it's the bed you are in, the nurse holding the vomit dish, or the tree outside your window. This will remind you that you need other humans and elements to flourish and that you are not alone, and those thoughts usually stimulate compassion and gratitude.

Include forgiveness as a goal, not because it may make you well, but because it is a more enjoyable state to live in, whether you live two hours or twenty years. Work to forgive the hospital its inhumanity, your wife her lack of understanding, your friends when they've disappointed you. And remember to forgive yourself. Forgiving people before you've even identified and addressed how they scarred you may be avoidance.

Taking responsibility without self-blame can be learned. Aim for a tender self-concern. In most autoimmune diseases, causality—and therefore, cure—is impossibly complex and so far is beyond anyone's understanding. It helps to look beyond personal causality—your genes, stresses, and health habits. More diseases today seem collectively caused, the result of our society's values on stressful achievement or careless attitudes toward hazardous wastes and pollution.

Try not to blame yourself for what you consider your negative thoughts, or for feeling discouraged or hopeless. Your thoughts do help create your reality, and they are a primary factor you have a choice about. But you can never know the extent to which what happens to you is related to thoughts and the extent to which it's destiny and what some people call karma.

When all else fails, when you lose faith entirely, stick with your Prescription. Do it with venom, do it in abject disgust, but do it. Faith, hope, and commitment often begin to return.

Surrendering and Waiting

Giving in can be a step toward life. The difference between giving up and giving in is very subtle. Surrendering doesn't mean giving up wanting to live; it means letting go of control at a certain level. It's not a passive act. Will is directed, but toward releasing instead of conquering.

Surrendering requires entrusting. You have to believe that there is a larger, positive force you can entrust yourself to, a river that will carry you. It seemed miraculous that when exhaustion pushed me over an invisible barrier which I stopped trying to surmount, the struggle inside me stopped. I felt an amazing sense of peace and a renewed appreciation for life. I was determined to recapture those feelings later when I wasn't at my weakest and by choice instead of chance.

Consciously deciding to let go is tremendously freeing. As a parent, some part of you may argue that no matter how weak or exhausted you are, you should be able to find a deeper strength and interest to be the kind of parent you want to be. Often that can be counterproductive. You have a choice, to keep trying until you are forced into resentful, reluctant defeat, or to acknowledge your frailty and to surrender any need to control, to focus your attention on the river, on trusting the outcome. When you give yourself over to that greater force, however you conceptualize it, you can begin to relax. The energy saved can go into restoring yourself so that you can again contribute as you'd like.

Real surrender entails growth. Turning over Adam's care to David meant adopting an attitude of total confidence in his values and style of parenting, even when I didn't feel that way. It meant abandoning narrow, rigid ideas of what "good mothering" and a "good child" were.

The process seems developmental: you must learn to fight before you can give up the need to win. Nonfighters first need to develop grit, and having a goal helps in this stage. Carrying out any Prescription for Health day after day when you aren't seeing results requires a very tenacious, scrappy, disciplined side. Strong-willed warriors often need to give up the *demand* for success. Continuing to fight, you no longer have to win.

At certain times in an illness, fighting is needed; at others, letting go is more productive; and sometimes a combination is best. Each time your weakness or pain increases you have a signal of an opportunity to decide again when to let go and what level of control to let go of.

In the end, remind yourself that we know as much about healing as we know about the universe. We have drugs which do wonders, but many aspects of the human body still elude us. Remind yourself of your imponderables, the factors over which you have no control. Someone else may have inherited strengths you do not have. A medication which may have saved your life may also have left you with major side effects. And remind yourself that healing takes time. Understanding and acknowledging the complexity of healing and your givens should help you move beyond oversimplified notions, to feel more patient when it seems you're running out of time.

Repeat the cycle, to some extent, daily. Re-invest in your healing plan wholeheartedly. Consciously commit. Do everything you can to romance health. Woo it. Then stand back and let go. Wait. Acknowledge that you cannot make healing happen and that there is an extremely large element of grace.

Eventually, you will feel less struggle. More often and more quickly, your decisions will feel more intrinsic to you, you will compare yourself with others less, you will feel more reverence for yourself, for others, for the world. You will know your strengths and weaknesses, the distance you have gone, the distance still to go. Your accomplishments will nourish you with the hope and confidence that you can meet the next challenge, the next curve thrown your way. Daily, hourly, you will know that the goal worth striving for is beyond the conquest of illness, that the struggle for physical health is secondary. Moments when you will feel at peace will begin to stretch into hours and then days. Your conscience will be clear. Your spirit will flourish.